Ludwig Messel
1847–1915
Founded L. Messel and Co.,
London
m. Annie Cussans
2 sons, 4 daughters

Rudolph Messel
Industrial chemist, London
1848–1920

Simon Messel
1817–59
Took over Aron Messel
Banking House
m. Emilie Lindheim

Lina Messel
1851–1925
m. Isaac Seligman
4 sons, 3 daughters

Alfred Messel
1853–1909
Architect to the Kaiser, Berlin
m. Elsa Altmann
1 son, 2 daughters

Eugenie Messel
1856–1908
m. Eugene de la Penha
2 sons, 1 daughter

FROM REFUGEES TO ROYALTY

FROM REFUGEES TO ROYALTY

The Remarkable Story of the Messel Family of Nymans

JOHN HILARY

PETER OWEN
LONDON AND CHICAGO

Peter Owen Publishers
Conway Hall, 25 Red Lion Square
London WC1R 4RL

Peter Owen books are distributed in the USA
and Canada by Independent Publishers Group/
Trafalgar Square
814 North Franklin Street, Chicago, IL 60610, USA

First published by Peter Owen Publishers 2021
Reprinted 2021

ISBN 978-0-7206-2106-8

A catalogue record for this book is available
from the British Library.

COVER AND BOOK DESIGN
Graphicacy

PRINTED BY
Printworks Global Ltd, London & Hong Kong

For my mother

Contents

The entrance into the
hallway at Nymans

Preface

'I wish you could see Nymans – you would be in ecstasies. The house and park and woods are lovely. The house is huge, about 25 bedrooms and dressing-rooms and all furnished exquisitely with a scrupulous denial of anything verging on display or luxury.' – Nonie Messel writing to her mother on her first visit to Nymans, Christmas 1903

THE WEST SUSSEX estate of Nymans has long been one of the National Trust's most popular properties. Today, Nymans attracts almost 400,000 visitors every year, many returning again and again to catch the changing seasons in what the actress Penelope Keith called its 'beautiful, beautiful garden'.[1] Yet there are a host of reasons to come to Nymans. Sarah Clelland, on her mission to visit every National Trust property in the land, captured it perfectly: 'If a heritage-loving alien arrived on Earth and wanted to be shown one property that sums up the National Trust, I'd take it to Nymans. It has everything: extensive gardens, a picturesque ruin, and a mock-medieval house that you can go inside and see where an Edwardian Englishwoman lived.'[2]

But who was this Edwardian Englishwoman, and what was she doing living in a mock-fifteenth-century manor house? What led the founder of the garden, a successful German-Jewish stockbroker, to buy a rural Sussex estate in the first place, let alone turn it into one of the horticultural wonders of southern England? How did the second generation transform themselves into landed gentry and marry one of their daughters to an earl? And how did the Messels, expelled from their earliest home in Germany by an edict of the British Royal Family, end up marrying into that same Royal Family two hundred years later?

This book is a story of achievement. It tells of a family of outsiders who triumphed over social exclusion across eight generations, during some of the darkest days in modern history. The journey is fascinating in what it reveals about the communities which the Messel family made their own. What was it like to be Jewish in Germany a hundred years before the Nazis? How did 'Court Jews' differ from their less privileged co-religionists? What was life in London like for German Jews in the Edwardian era? Ludwig Messel was reputedly the richest man on the London Stock Exchange, but this did not help him when Germans living in Britain were engulfed in a wave of xenophobic violence in the opening years of the First World War.

The story of the Messel family is a remarkable one, not just for the journey which brought them to England but for the extraordinary contribution they made across so many creative disciplines. Each generation has produced pioneers in their chosen fields, whether architecture or industry, theatre or cinema, fashion or photography, design, horticulture or the decorative arts. The personal collections the Messels built up for their private pleasure now grace the nation's galleries, while the houses in which they lived are open for public education and enjoyment. Several of the specialist plants grown in gardens around Britain were first cultivated at Nymans, and the most famous among them bear the names of individual members of the Messel family as a testament to their success.

Alongside this rich record, there is a more sombre side to the family history. The male members of the family, in particular, suffered from serious bouts of mental illness over at least three generations, at a time when there was limited treatment available to mitigate the impact of the attacks. In its mildest form, this melancholia – as it was then known – manifested itself in appalling outbursts of ill temper. At its most damaging it led to severe depression and at least one suicide. Relations within the family could also be strained to breaking point when personal interests were given precedence over shared needs. Even the royal marriage, the Messel family's breakthrough into the highest stratum of British society, collapsed under the weight of self-indulgence.

Whenever I am at Nymans I pay a special visit to the statuette in the Forecourt Garden dedicated to the memory of my grandmother Phoebe Messel and her brother Rudolph. Both died before I was born, but I was brought up on the stories of their deep devotion to one another and the magical world they created for my mother and her siblings when they were growing up. I was told the basic outlines of the family history, but no one was able to explain to me why the Messels first came to England or what their lives had been like in Germany before they migrated. I read the brief backgrounds in books on the more famous members of the Messel family, but even the best were hazy on the details. The true story was clearly waiting to be uncovered.

My search for answers took me to the German market town of Dieburg, forty minutes' train ride south of Frankfurt. I knew that the earliest Jewish inhabitants of the village of Messel were buried in Dieburg's Jewish cemetery and that my ancestors were among them. The section of the cemetery nearest the entrance contains the last graves of the 1920s and 1930s: severe rows of dark granite obelisks with Hebrew inscriptions above German names. By contrast, the light-grey sandstone of the nineteenth-century graves has been softened with moss and lichen, and the rows are less strictly uniform. The oldest section of the cemetery is gentler still, with red sandstone graves in various stages of erosion scattered haphazardly between the trees. This was where I needed to look, and immediately I was successful. On a beautiful February morning I found myself standing before the last resting place of my five-times great-grandfather Gumpel and his father Aharon, both of whom had died over two centuries before.

Aharon and Gumpel are the earliest-known members of the family that was expelled from its home in north-west Germany and adopted the name of Messel, the village that gave them refuge. Tracing the twists and turns of their journey has been a voyage of constant discovery and deeply enriching in what it has revealed. Most of the individuals in these pages were unknown to me and their life choices far from my own. Yet when I stood before the tombs of my ancestors in Dieburg I did feel strangely moved. Was this because I recognized the challenges they had overcome in their lives and the care they had taken to prepare the way for those who came after them? Or was it because I knew the immensity of what they could not know: that the destiny of our family was to survive and prosper, while so many other German-Jewish families would be extinguished? More than anything, I felt a desire to speak with them as strangers from another world, to tell them the future story of the Messel family in all its wanderings. This book is the story I wanted them to hear.

The graves of Gumpel Löw
Bentheim (left) and his father
Aharon Leib Bentheim in the
Dieburg cemetery that served
the Jewish community of Messel

The Village of Messel 1

THE VILLAGE OF Messel stands in a clearing of the great Odenwald forest that covers much of the southern German state of Hesse. It is surrounded by trees on all sides, so that anyone journeying to the village must pass through miles of dense woodland before catching their first glimpse of its neat houses. This unique situation gives it a magical seclusion that belies its proximity to the busy metropolis of Darmstadt, barely half an hour's bus ride away. It also means that Messel presents essentially the same face to the traveller today as it has done down the centuries – and the same charm.

The name Messel points back to the earliest evidence of social settlement. The Celts who colonized the area set up smelting works owing to the presence of bog iron, and the Latin name for Messel – Masilla – is a reference to the Celtic root *massal*, with its dual meaning of 'bog' and 'bog ore'.[1] Messel grew to be a sizeable community of around two hundred inhabitants by the time it became a protectorate of the Holy Roman Empire at the beginning of the fifteenth century. Under these auspices the village belonged to the Barons of Groschlag for the four hundred years to 1799 and was finally incorporated into the Grand Duchy of Hesse in 1806.[2]

One of the most remarkable aspects of Messel's history was the importance of its Jewish community. The first mention of a Jewish presence comes from as early as 1474, when a 'Jew Meyer from Mössel' was among a group of nineteen Jews accused of failing to abide by the dress code that required them to be instantly distinguishable from Christians. This requirement stemmed from Pope Innocent III's Fourth Lateran Council in 1215, which decreed that all Jews and Muslims must wear distinguishing dress in order to prevent Christians from unknowingly entering into illicit sexual relations with them. In the German states that made up the Holy Roman Empire the distinguishing item was originally the pointed Jewish hat and, subsequently, the yellow ring badge to be worn by all Jews on their outer

clothing. Meyer was warned to abide by the regulations in future but escaped further punishment.

The next mention comes from the year 1600, when a *Schutzjude* – a 'protected Jew' – named Joseph of Messel petitioned the authorities in nearby Hanau for permission to move there and place himself under the protection of its ruler, Count Philipp Ludwig II. For Jews, obtaining this grant of protection from the local sovereign was an essential condition of residency. As a *Schutzjude* already, Joseph was living in Messel under the protection of Baron Heinrich von Groschlag. We have no record of whether his petition to move to Hanau was successful.

There was a major influx of Jewish families to Messel during the eighteenth century, so that by the time of the 1781 census one in every six households in the village was Jewish. In 1813 there were eighty-one Jews registered out of a population of 663 in Messel, or just over 12 per cent.[3] To put these figures in context, the 175,000 Jews who lived in all German states at the beginning of the nineteenth century represented less than 1 per cent of the total population. Confident in its strength, the Jewish community in Messel applied in 1739 to build a synagogue in the centre of the village – one of the very first village synagogues to be constructed in the region. The building served as a place of worship and a Jewish school until 1830 when a new synagogue was built around the corner.

Despite these achievements, life for the Jewish community of Messel was still restricted by fixed boundaries of exclusion and privation. Jews were treated as an alien presence in the village, their community looked upon as a foreign colony living side by side with the Christian majority. Jewish men were excluded from all guild professions and thus could not engage in any form of manufacturing or handicraft production. While some could fall back on money-lending, the vast majority earned a living through petty trade in old clothes, ironware and other second-hand goods. With all Jews forced into the same occupations, competition was intense and margins were thin, so that only the most successful were able to escape poverty. Crucially, most Jews were barred from owning land or property, which made them a welcome source of rent for Christian landlords, just as their exclusion from farming – the main occupation of Messel villagers – left them dependent on buying food from their non-Jewish neighbours.[4]

The family that would eventually carry the name Messel to the wider world settled in the village during the eighteenth century. The first known member of the family is Aharon Leib Bentheim, born in 1723 and sometimes referred to as Aron Löb. His is the older of the two tombstones in the Jewish cemetery of Dieburg. The fact that he and his four sons all went by the surname Bentheim indicates that the family came from the county of that name on the Dutch border in Lower Saxony, where there had been an established Jewish community since at least the seventeenth century. The feudal rulers of Bentheim looked on the Jews as a ready

A typical eighteenth-century building in Messel, today the local museum

source of income for their own coffers, and much of the early documentation concerns the annual tribute that each household was required to pay to the count's personal treasury. As elsewhere, payment of this protection money bought the Jews of Bentheim permission to hold religious services and to bury their dead according to traditional Jewish rites.

The Jewish community was seen in a less positive light by the majority of Bentheim citizens, who regarded them as an unwelcome source of commercial competition. Many Jewish traders had connections across the border in the Netherlands and were thus able to undercut the Christian shopkeepers. Matters came to a head in the mid eighteenth century, when the permanently indebted counts of Bentheim were forced to mortgage the county to the neighbouring Electors of Hanover – who also happened to be the Royal Family of Great Britain. Elector Georg Augustus of Hanover, better known to us as King George II, took over the administration of the county of Bentheim on 22 May 1752 on what was originally envisaged as a thirty-year mortgage, together with responsibility for its debts. In the end, the counts of Bentheim were unable to buy back their sovereignty, and the county remained in Hanoverian hands until its incorporation into the unified German nation over a hundred years later.

The princely rulers of Hanover were not financially dependent on the tribute of Bentheim's Jewish population and had no political reason to stand up for the community's interests. In the face of growing popular intrigue, the Elector of Hanover issued a Jewish Ordinance on 10 March 1763 expelling all Jews from the towns, villages and hamlets of Bentheim, save for a small number granted exceptional leave to remain. 'Mendicant Jews' were banned from entering the county on pain of eight days' imprisonment followed by deportation and a warning that reoffending would meet with 'harsher corporal punishment'. Any Jews allowed to remain in Bentheim were subject to a host of formal restrictions on their personal, religious and business activities that were designed to make their lives increasingly intolerable.[5]

The four sons of Aharon – Gumpel, Abraham, Simon and Ephraim – were born in Bentheim during the ten years leading up to the edict of 1763 and were known throughout their lives by the same surname as their father. It was not uncommon for German Jews to take the name of their home town during the eighteenth century, even though there was as yet no requirement on Jewish families to adopt fixed surnames as there would be in the wake of Napoleon's invasion. Under the terms of the new edict, married Jews were given six weeks to leave Bentheim for ever, so Aharon and his family must have started out almost immediately on their journey to the village of Messel. The 1763 edict was issued in the name of the county's Hanoverian ruler, which by this time meant King George III. The two families would be thrown together again in very different circumstances two hundred years later when Aharon's five-times great-grandson, Tony Armstrong-Jones, married George III's four-times great-granddaughter, Princess Margaret.

Aharon Leib Bentheim soon established himself as a successful tradesman in the Jewish community of Messel. His eldest son Gumpel Löw Bentheim also became a leading figure in the community, and it is with him that we encounter the first written records relating to the family. Gumpel operated as a tradesman with Christian as well as Jewish customers, and the Messel church accounts for the year 1800 contain an order for him to supply eight ells of linen for a new altar cloth, for which he was to receive the sum of five guilders and twenty kreutzer. Yet it is Gumpel's last will and testament, drawn up in Hebrew in the presence of his brothers Ephraim and Abraham on 19 March 1801, that provides a unique insight into his hopes for the family after his death:

TESTAMENT

Which was drawn up by the *Schutzjude* Gumpel Löw of Messel, in full possession of his faculties and according to his wishes, as he lay dangerously ill in bed not long before his death and called for us, the undersigned witnesses, to come to him. He requested us to be witnesses to all the following items recorded hereby for such a time as the Almighty should require of him his soul and through this illness take him away in death.

1 His wife Mündle, daughter of Hirsch, on the basis of her own money as well as that which he now adds to it, should receive 900 guilders in cash, in addition to which she should also retain her clothes and jewellery without these being deducted from the aforementioned 900 guilders.

2 His brother Ephraim Löw of Darmstadt should be designated legal guardian of his children and his estate and should carry out this guardianship in a fair and equitable manner.

3 His home should be sold to best advantage and the money from the sale used for the good of his children.

4 Whatever of his furniture is not needed by his wife and children should also be sold.

5 As regards the division of his estate among his heirs, although under Jewish law daughters are not considered true heirs in the same way that sons are, the aforementioned Gumpel Löw wished herewith to grant that his daughters be treated equally with his sons and that daughters and sons should receive an equal share of his estate.

6 When his eldest daughter Ester comes to be married, the aforementioned Ephraim Löw is authorized as legal guardian to provide her with an extra 200 guilders from the estate in addition to the portion which she has already received.

7 The 300 guilders which his wife's sister has deposited with him should be given to the *Schutzjude* Moses Aron [one of the witnesses], who is to be her guardian and fully responsible for her well-being.[6]

Gumpel's care for his daughters is particularly noteworthy, in that he was prepared to set aside Jewish custom to ensure they received equal shares in his estate with his sons. His eldest daughter Ester, whose dowry is provided for, would remain in Messel and marry Joseph Jakob Brill, who had served as Gumpel's assistant for five years and who would now take over the family business. Gumpel had provided for this in a codicil to his will, the terms of which were brought into effect as of June 1802 once Ester had observed the ritual year of mourning required after her father's death.

Both Gumpel and his father Aharon died in the opening two years of the nineteenth century. Those years saw Messel ravaged by the worst smallpox epidemic in its history, claiming the lives of forty-four of the village's Christian population, thirty-two of them children. Yet Messel's Jewish community was scarcely touched by the epidemic, with only three adults and one child falling victim. The fact that Jewish life was largely self-contained within the village – and that Jewish children were educated separately – may have kept them safe from the disease, just as the sanitary rules within Judaism could have helped

Ludewig I, Grand
Duke of Hesse, from
a portrait by Louis
Ammy Blanc

prevent contagion. From the preamble to his will Gumpel clearly knew that his illness would soon lead to death, which is consistent with smallpox. Perhaps his business dealings brought him into more regular contact with the Christian population and exposed him to the virus.

Gumpel lies buried in the Jewish cemetery of Dieburg next to his father Aharon. His tombstone is well preserved with the top half of the Hebrew inscription clearly legible in the red sandstone below an elaborate pitcher and basin. Both Gumpel and his father bore the Hebrew name Jehuda (Judah, fourth son of Jacob) for use in synagogue, and, in keeping with Jacob's description of Judah as a lion in *Genesis* 49:9, the male members of the family were given the secular nickname of Lion – in Aharon's case the Yiddish versions Leib or Löb; for his sons and grandsons the German version Löw. Yet the presence of a pitcher on the tombstones of both Gumpel and his younger brother Ephraim denotes that they were a Levite family, as it signifies the Levites' ritual duty of purifying the hands of the priests (*cohanim*) before religious services.[7]

As provided for in Gumpel's will, the family passed to the guardianship of his brother Ephraim in Darmstadt. The family home was sold on 9 June 1806 to the innkeeper Johann Michael Wältz for the sum of 700 guilders, and Gumpel's son Aron Löw Messel moved to Darmstadt soon afterwards. Aron was already active as a tradesman in his own right, and his business acumen in this period was to lay the foundations for the Messel family's future prosperity. As with other notable families that built up banking empires in the nineteenth century – both Jewish and non-Jewish – it was war that enabled Aron to accumulate the initial capital he needed.

Ludwig X, Landgrave of Hesse-Darmstadt, had sided with the Holy Roman Empire against Napoleon in the French Revolutionary Wars that raged across Europe until 1801. Yet five years later, with Darmstadt under military occupation by French troops, he signed up as one of the client states in the Confederation of the Rhine created by Napoleon as a buffer against France's principal adversaries on the Continent: Prussia and Austria. By way of reward Ludwig's newly expanded territories were confirmed by Napoleon and his title upgraded to Grand Duke of Hesse, whereupon he enlarged his own name to the grandiose Ludewig I. The village of Messel was incorporated into the Grand Duchy of Hesse and its male inhabitants required to perform several years' military service in order to help make up the three regiments that Hesse had to contribute to the Napoleonic forces. While some fought in Spain or Austria, many were forced to take part in Napoleon's disastrous invasion of Russia during the winter of 1812. Of the

5,250 soldiers who made up the Hessian regiments of the French army, only 316 returned home alive.

Jewish males were not conscripted into the army and were able to turn the war to their advantage. Indeed, the Grand Duke of Hesse is recorded as having relied heavily on the Jews of Messel for military supplies during the Napoleonic Wars.[8] Aron Messel was one of those to establish himself as a military provisioner, providing forage for the Grand Duke's cavalry units as well as uniforms for his men. This in turn laid the foundation for his subsequent business ventures in Darmstadt and the banking house that would bear his name. Under the edict of 15 December 1808 all Jews in the Grand Duchy of Hesse were required to adopt hereditary surnames in place of the traditional Jewish patronymic system. In keeping with the tradition that had inspired his grandfather and father in Bentheim, Aron took the surname Messel from his place of birth.

Darmstadt's fashionable
Ludwigsplatz, in a print by
Ernst Friedrich Grünewald;
the Messel family home is
on the right

Privileged Jews 2

Aron Löw Messel was established as a businessman in Darmstadt by the summer of 1808, when the tax assessment for Jewish residents valued his assets at 1,100 guilders.[1] He was twenty-three years old. From that moment until his death forty years later Aron was to grow into a leading figure in the Jewish community, building on his connections as a military provisioner to the Grand Duke of Hesse in order to establish himself first as a textiles trader and then as head of one of the most important private banks in the city. This remarkable career set the foundations on which future generations of the Messel family would build their lives in Germany, England and the USA.

Darmstadt today bears little resemblance to the city in which Aron Messel made his new home. To begin with, its size was tiny in comparison to its modern footprint, with most of its inhabitants crowded together in the narrow medieval streets of the Old Town that nestled up to the Grand Duke's imposing castle. There were barely six hundred houses in total in the early 1800s, and it would have taken little more than five minutes to stroll from one side of the town to the other. Yet the greater change was to come with the air raid unleashed on Darmstadt by RAF Bomber Command on the night of 11 September 1944. Aerial photographs from after the attack show the total devastation left in its wake; in the Old Town just one solitary house was left standing. Over ten thousand people lost their lives in the firestorm generated by the incendiary bombs dropped on the city that night, half of them women and children. By way of comparison, the Luftwaffe's destruction of Coventry four years earlier had cost 568 lives.[2]

When Aron Messel settled into his new surroundings, Darmstadt was a provincial capital riding high on the fortunes of its newly promoted ruler Grand Duke Ludewig I. The former Landgrave had seen his status and his dominions enhanced by Napoleon as a reward for joining the pro-French Confederation of the Rhine in 1806. The immediate consequence was that his chosen seat of residence, Darmstadt, underwent a population explosion and a building boom that transformed it from a medieval town into a modern city within the space of two decades. The population of Darmstadt had already doubled from 6,700 in 1794 to 13,177 in 1812. It surged again to 21,000 in 1830 and topped 30,000

View of Darmstadt,
by Johann Heinrich
Schilbach, 1816

during the 1850s – a fivefold increase in the space of sixty years. As Darmstadt grew in size, its ruling family grew in stature. Over the course of the nineteenth century the Grand Duchy of Hesse would become one of the most famous royal houses of Europe, closely connected through dynastic marriages to the Russian imperial family and the British monarchy alike.[3]

With new customers pouring into the city, it was a good time to be in business, and Aron Messel was well positioned to take advantage. He had married into the prestigious Stern dynasty from Frankfurt through his union with Caroline Stern on 2 December 1810. The two branches of the Stern family, named after the painted star on the signboard that identified their homes in Frankfurt's Jewish ghetto, had already distinguished themselves as successful merchants during the eighteenth century and would become even more powerful as bankers during the nineteenth. There could scarcely be more auspicious in-laws for an ambitious young man starting a business in the big city.

The first public mention we have of Aron Messel's commercial operations is in the *Darmstadt Advertiser* from January 1814.[4] In the classified advertisements under the heading 'Goods for Sale' the German text translates as 'The undersigned is recommended for all types of woollen cloth: dark blue, grey, green, black and red, at the most reasonable prices. Aron Messel, resident with Master Shoemaker Schaffner in the Langgasse.'

The Langgasse (Long Lane) was the main street that curved through the centre of the medieval Old Town, meaning that Aron had a prime location from which to develop his business. This is also where Caroline must have given birth to their first child, Friedrich Ludwig Messel, on 26 October 1811. Yet Aron clearly had plans to expand his business beyond just trading in textiles, and in 1816 he founded the banking house that would bear his name and make his fortune. His Uncle Ephraim had already established himself as a banker in Darmstadt and had grown rich on the proceeds, amassing a taxable wealth of at least ten thousand guilders by the time his nephew joined him on the register in 1808.[5] Aron was following in his uncle's footsteps, and by 1821 he was successful enough to have moved his family into premises of their own on the Obergasse (Upper Lane) at the top end of the Old Town.

The Aron Messel Banking House quickly grew to become one of the most important financial institutions in Darmstadt, and its founder was rewarded by being granted citizenship on 20 September 1820. The status of citizenship and the rights that went with it were awarded to very few members of Darmstadt's Jewish community in this early part of the nineteenth century. It is a measure of the personal contribution that Aron had made to the Grand Duke's war effort that he was honoured in such a way. Yet this in turn raises two further questions. First, how much did being Jewish matter in early-nineteenth-century Darmstadt? And, second, how closely did Aron and his family identify as Jews?

To answer the questions in reverse order, there is no doubt that Aron and Caroline Messel were fully conscious of their Jewish identity and the responsibilities it entailed. Aron served for many years as one of the five men elected to lead the Jewish community of Darmstadt, a position available only to those in the highest income bracket. He was also a member of the Association for the Moral and Civic Advancement of the Israelites in the Grand Duchy of Hesse and All Germany, a cross-confessional pressure group founded in October 1831 to lobby for full emancipation of the Jews while providing charitable assistance to advance the employment prospects of young Jewish men. Aron Messel was unmistakably Jewish and publicly identified as such.

Whether this was an obstacle to his progress is more complicated. Aron's success as a banker and his presence at the court of the Grand Duke placed him in an entirely different situation to the great majority of his co-religionists, whose lives remained stunted by the restricted opportunities available to them. Court Jews, or *Hofjuden*, were the exception out of a community that typically lived without economic or civic rights. During the seventeenth and eighteenth centuries Court Jews provided the local rulers of the German states with essential services in the financing of their civil and military affairs, extending credit from their own purses and establishing sustainable sources of revenue that would become the basis of a modern system of taxation. Employed directly by the ruling monarch and dependent upon him, they were granted benefits by their patron that were completely unknown to other Jews.[6] As Hannah Arendt described them:

> The *Hofjuden* enjoyed all privileges; they could live wherever they liked, they could travel anywhere within the realm of their sovereigns, they could bear arms and demand the special protection of all local authorities. Their way of life was on a much higher level than that of the middle class of the period. The *Hofjuden* possessed greater privileges than the majority of the population of their homelands, and it would be erroneous to believe that this state of things escaped the attention of their contemporaries.[7]

Aron Messel became one of these 'privileged Jews' as a result of his services to the Grand Duke of Hesse, although the feudal status of *Hofjude* was now replaced by the less loaded title of *Hofbankier* (court banker). Indeed, Aron's independent position as head of the private bank that bore his name meant that he could present himself as a thoroughly modern citizen of Darmstadt, as shown in the twin portraits which he commissioned of himself and his wife Caroline at the height of his success. In these paintings husband and wife are dressed in the elegant Biedermeier style embraced by the German bourgeoisie after the fall of Napoleon. Aron is represented as a wealthy businessman in a sober three-piece costume with cravat and wing collar, the only hint of Jewishness coming from his curly dark hair and the dark eyes that would be a characteristic feature of his Messel descendants. Caroline is shown wearing a full dress with narrow waist and a simple Biedermeier bonnet over her neatly parted hair. Perhaps the most striking feature of the two portraits, in an era when so many individuals were painted with expressionless faces, is that both Aron and Caroline are depicted with a distinct smile playing around their lips and a twinkle of amusement in their eyes. It is as if the artist wanted to convey that the Messel family were not only satisfied with their success in life but at ease with their dual identity as Germans and Jews.

As the privileged Jews of Darmstadt and other parts of Germany savoured their first experience of civil and economic rights, popular resentment against them began to grow. That resentment turned violent in the summer of 1819 with a wave of anti-Jewish rioting that swept across the German states from south to north. Despite the lack of any planning or coordination, roaming mobs united behind the rallying cry of 'Hep Hep' which gave the riots their name.[8] In the Bavarian town of Würzburg, where the violence started, rioters smashed the windows of Jewish houses, tore the signboards off Jewish shops and hurled abuse at any Jews unlucky enough to be found in the streets. Two other Bavarian

Twin portraits
of Caroline and
Aron Messel in
Biedermeier dress

villages saw their synagogues demolished and the Torah scrolls destroyed. Further north there were days of serious rioting in cities such as Frankfurt and Hamburg, while in Danzig a large crowd attacked synagogues and Jewish-owned houses on the Day of Atonement, the highest Jewish holiday. Outbreaks of violence were recorded over a period of two months against Jewish property and people in towns and villages throughout Germany and even into Denmark.

The Hep-Hep Riots flared up in Darmstadt on 12 August 1819, when the mob rampaged through the Old Town, smashing the windows of Jewish businesses. Aron Messel would have looked on helplessly as the violence spread to the synagogue, which had formed the focal point of Darmstadt's Jewish community since its consecration in 1737. There were over four hundred Jews living in Darmstadt at the time of the riots – barely 2 per cent of the population – yet they formed a powerful enough group to attract the enmity of the Christian majority. Grand Duke Ludewig intervened to quell the rioting and was commended by later historians for his prompt action in restoring order. Yet, according to the political commentator Ludwig Börne, himself Jewish, it was precisely the role played by privileged Jews such as Aron Messel in propping up the unpopular monarchy that made them a particular target of any civil unrest.[9]

The Hep-Hep
Riots of 1819, in
a contemporary
image by Johann
Michael Voltz

Aron did not have to live with the physical memory of the Hep-Hep Riots for
long, as he was soon able to move his family out of the medieval Old Town to the
new premises that they would occupy for the rest of his life. To accommodate
the population growth of Darmstadt in the early nineteenth century Grand
Duke Ludewig had commissioned the architect Georg Moller to build an entirely
new city alongside the Old Town. This new development, named Mollerstadt in
honour of its creator, stretched out to the south and west of the medieval centre
and quickly established itself as the most desirable residential district for the
burgeoning middle classes of Darmstadt. The plan included a new commercial
district centred on the fashionable Ludwigsplatz, an enclosed square of handsome
three-storeyed neoclassical buildings that was completed by the early 1820s.

It was here, at No. 9 Ludwigsplatz, that Aron Messel set up his banking house and established the family home.

As the commercial centre of the new city grew wealthier so, too, it became a more attractive place to live. Competition raged to build ever more elegant residential properties and official buildings, with tree-lined avenues and gardens to match. Money was set aside for street cleaning and the upkeep of public places, with over three thousand guilders spent in 1825 alone for the removal of rubble and other debris from Darmstadt's roads. The city's rudimentary street lighting was overhauled, including the purchase of sixty-six new glass cylinders, while those responsible for maintaining the lamps were granted a special allowance to buy winter shoes. By the time of Grand Duke Ludewig's death in 1830 Darmstadt was fêted as 'one of the finest and friendliest cities in Germany'.[10] For a young man like Aron who had grown up in a small rural village it must have seemed like the height of modern living. The Messels had arrived.

Emilie Messel, née Lindheim,
with her mother Philippine

Founding a Dynasty 3

T HE CITY OF Darmstadt embraced the industrial revolution with such dynamism
that it is still known as a hub of science and technology today. Factories began
to spring up in and around the city, manufacturing every possible consumer
item from wallpaper to carriages to shoes. Yet there were no modern banks in
Darmstadt until the second half of the nineteenth century to supply the capital
they needed to grow. In the early years it was private banks such as Aron Messel's
that were on hand to finance – and profit from – the city's industrial expansion.
While the prime loyalty of a court banker may have been to the Grand Duke, the
advent of industrial capitalism created a world of opportunity for those who had
the means and the acumen to take advantage of it.

As Aron saw his business grow, his thoughts turned to the next generation and
the question of who would take it over when he was gone. Under the traditional
Jewish practice of primogeniture, the bank would automatically pass to his
first-born son, Friedrich Ludwig Messel, known (like many other Ludwigs in
French-influenced Darmstadt) as Louis. Yet Aron's succession planning was
thrown into disarray when Louis broke with the family and left Germany to spend
the rest of his life in the USA. His fate has long been shrouded in mystery, with
family tradition suggesting that he may even have died *en route* to America. In
fact, Louis Messel arrived safely on the other side of the Atlantic, settled in Ohio
to pursue a career as a teacher, married a fellow Darmstadt immigrant and left
behind generations of American Messels who stretch out into the neighbouring
state of Indiana and beyond. The marriage holds the key to the mystery, as his
wife Odelia was a Christian and Louis was disowned by the Messel family for
marrying outside the Jewish faith. Louis himself seems to have retained his
Jewish identity regardless: one account of his new life in the USA records that
he could never be prevailed upon to pronounce the name of Jesus Christ or any
combination of the words.[1]

With Louis now cut off in North America, Aron's younger son Simon Messel
was required to take on the family business. Simon had been born on 26 December
1817 and was educated at Darmstadt's oldest Lutheran school, the Pädagog.[2]
While previous generations had been taught separately in traditional Jewish

The Pädagog school in Darmstadt, by Ernst August Schnittspahn

schools, the compulsory education requirements introduced throughout Hesse in 1823 applied to Jewish children just as much as they did to Christians. After his studies Simon was allowed to follow his artistic inclinations and travelled to Paris to be apprenticed to a cabinet-maker, developing a reputation for the particular form of marquetry known as Boulle work. Yet Simon's creative career was cut short by family obligations, and he dutifully took over the Aron Messel Banking House from his father once his elder brother was out of the picture.

Having established Simon as heir to the family business, Aron was able to turn his attention to matters spiritual. In 1842 he bought a plot in the Jewish cemetery of Darmstadt, which has survived to this day thanks to the bravery of its long-serving guardian Oskar Werling, who saved the site from desecration when he stood up to a band of the Nazi paramilitary *Sturmabteilung* (SA) who had come to destroy it. Aron established the Messel family plot on the west wall in the newly expanded section of the cemetery. It was his wife Caroline who died first, however, on 8 December 1844, at the age of sixty-three. Aron followed her to the grave just over three years later, on 13 February 1848; he was also sixty-three. Husband and wife lie buried together in a double tomb looking out across the cemetery to those who would come after them. The red sandstone façade is surmounted by a neo-Romanesque design very different from the traditional Jewish monuments all around them, while the simple legend on its face is one of the very earliest to be written entirely in German with no Hebrew. More clearly even than in life, Aron and Caroline's final resting place provides a tangible statement of their identity as modern German Jews.[3]

Aron was revered as the patriarch of the family, responsible for building up its fortune and establishing its status in the brave new world of the nineteenth century. He lived just long enough to see his son Simon awarded citizenship of Darmstadt on 30 April 1847, twenty-seven years after he had himself been granted that honour. Simon also assumed the position of court banker to the Grand Duke of Hesse, and his position was further secured by his marriage to Emilie Lindheim in May 1846. The Lindheims could boast an equally conspicuous success story to the Messels: Emilie's father, Simon Lindheim, was one of the very first Jews to be employed in the Hessian Civil Service, rising to be a senior diplomat in the Grand Duke's chancellery at a time when other Jews wishing to pursue such a career were required to convert to Christianity. Like Aron Messel, he was one of the leaders of the Jewish community; like Aron also, the inscription on his tomb in the Jewish cemetery of Darmstadt is written only in German.

Simon Messel continued to manage the family business for ten years after his father's death. Yet his health was not as robust as it could have been, and in August 1859 he left Darmstadt with his wife Emilie for a rest cure in Italy. The decision turned out to be a fatal one. Italy was at that time in the throes of the Second War of Independence, in which Italian nationalists under Cavour and Garibaldi had secured the assistance of the French emperor Napoleon III against the imperial Austrian forces. The first stage of the war was effectively ended by the Battle of Solferino, a series of confrontations throughout the day of 24 June 1859 which left over 6,000 dead and 40,000 wounded – a level of carnage which led to the founding of the International Committee of the Red Cross.

War tourism held a special fascination for nineteenth-century travellers, and Simon Messel was one of many to visit the Solferino battlefield in the weeks following the encounter. In his case there was an added incentive in that Prince Alexander of Hesse, brother of Simon's patron Grand Duke Ludwig III, had commanded an Austrian division during the battle. Yet while he was there Simon contracted typhoid fever, a disease much feared in the days before antibiotics and particularly prevalent in military encampments. On doctor's orders he and Emilie travelled into the Swiss Alps in the hope that mountain air might alleviate the symptoms, but to no avail. Simon's health gave

The joint grave of Caroline and Aron Messel in the Jewish cemetery of Darmstadt

Simon Messel

way in Vicosoprano, in the high valley of the Bergell that links Switzerland with Italy. His brother-in-law Ferdinand Sander had been alerted and set out from Darmstadt to bring him home but arrived too late to help. Simon died on 11 September 1859, aged forty-one. His body was repatriated and interred in the Jewish cemetery of Darmstadt five days later.

Simon Messel's marble tomb stands out among the other graves in the cemetery. It is in the form of a broken column, indicating a life cut short in its prime. Still visible through the lichen that covers the column's shaft is a relief carving of a butterfly, classical symbol of the soul and, by extension, the fragility of life. The heavily eroded inscription on the base reveals his epitaph: 'Here lies SIMON MESSEL, born Darmstadt 26 December 1817, died Vicosoprano 11 September 1859. A faithful husband, good father and true friend, he was able to speak his last words with quiet confidence: Lord, into thy hands I commend my spirit.'[4]

The concluding phrase, familiar to readers of Luke's gospel as the last words of Christ on the cross, is from Psalm 31 and forms the traditional ending to the evening prayer recited daily by observant Jews. Simon's own faith comes under the spotlight in one of the most unexpected documents in the Messel family archive: a printed copy of the funeral oration delivered by Rabbi Moses Mannheimer at Simon's burial in Darmstadt on 16 September 1859. Much of the text is what one would expect from such a eulogy, including fulsome praise for the departed as a loyal husband, attentive father and upstanding businessman. Yet there is one surprising section where the Rabbi notes that Simon's 'views on the articles of our faith differed from those of many of his co-religionists', even if he was 'far too noble' to mock those who kept to the old customs and ways. Simon was clearly prepared to question the orthodoxy of his religious heritage, just as many other modern Jews were doing in nineteenth-century Germany. Yet he had served, like his father, on the governing body of the Jewish community of Darmstadt, and he was buried in the Jewish cemetery across from his parents, even if not in a typical grave. It would be only in the next generations that the male members of the Messel family would break with the Jewish faith.

Simon's five children were given the eminently non-Jewish names of Ludwig, Rudolph, Lina (that is, Caroline, after her grandmother), Alfred and Eugenie. They were between twelve and three years old at the time of his death and thus too young to play any part in the running of the family business. Instead, the bank was taken over by their uncle, Ferdinand Sander, who had married their mother's sister, Leonie Lindheim, in 1845.[5] The Messel family continued to live in Darmstadt, where the children seem to have been largely brought up by their maternal grandmother Philippine Lindheim, while their mother Emilie enjoyed the social and cultural life to which she had become accustomed, marrying twice

Simon Messel's grave in
the Jewish cemetery of
Darmstadt

more, both times to musicians. Yet already the plan must have been hatching for
the children to leave home and seek a new life in England. The eldest, Ludwig,
would emigrate within six years of his father's death, followed by both his sisters
and the second son, Rudolph. We cannot leave Germany, however, without
turning our attention to the most famous of the Messels to have remained in his
native land, the youngest brother of the family, who would grow up to be one of
the leading architects of the Wilhelmine period and to design some of the seminal
buildings of early German modernism.

Alfred Messel, by Reinhold Lepsius

Architect to the Kaiser 4

ALFRED PETER FRANZ Wendel Simon Messel was born in Darmstadt on 22 July 1853 and spent his earliest years on the Ludwigsplatz with his siblings. He was just six years old when his father died and eleven when his eldest brother left home for London, and he then saw the rest of his family follow in quick succession. By way of compensation, Alfred forged a life-long friendship with his neighbours, the Hoffmann brothers, and showed early signs of his future creativity by rigging up a miniature cable car between their two houses so as to share news at all hours of day or night. While his direct contemporary Arthur Hoffmann would pursue a medical career, the elder brother Ludwig Hoffmann would remain an inseparable friend to Alfred as they followed the same artistic training and then worked alongside one another as leading architects in Berlin.

Looking back on their years at school together, Ludwig Hoffmann described Alfred as a shy pupil and a dreamer, and his reports do not suggest that he was academically driven. Alfred's best subjects were German, history and geometry, while he derived most pleasure from physical exercise and would in later years become an enthusiastic mountain climber. He was a gifted cellist and a keen actor, particularly noted for a student performance as a young woman in Roderich Benedix's play *The Mossy Head*, for which he had to borrow one of his sister Eugenie's dresses. He took Christian religious education and turned the subject to good use in the presentation he gave for his final school examination on the basilica in the Byzantine era. Alfred's passion for architecture was evident from an early age, and he was always to be found with a sketchbook in his hand. His grandmother encouraged his creative instincts by enrolling him in drawing lessons with the Darmstadt-based engraver Karl Rauch, to which Ludwig Hoffman signed up, too.

After leaving school in 1872 Alfred was required to perform a year's military service in the Hessian infantry, enlisting in the Guards. Hoffmann, who had completed his own military service a year earlier, waited for Alfred so the two could depart together the following summer for a year's practical work experience in Kassel. Such internships were a requirement for all those seeking to enrol at the prestigious Berlin Academy of Architecture, where the two friends began their studies in the autumn of 1874. Overwhelmed at first by the grandeur of their new surroundings, they lived and worked together in Berlin throughout the next four years, and Hoffmann's diary describes their time as enthusiastic students in the capital of the newly united Germany, including regular visits to the opera, music concerts and art exhibitions as well as the circus, the aquarium and the zoo. The bond formed between the two young men was a special relationship. As Hoffmann remarked many years later, 'We used to look back in amazement that two such independent and individual characters managed to live together for four years without any difference of opinion ever causing the slightest disturbance to our peaceful coexistence.'[1]

The two friends graduated in 1878 and found early employment within the Civil Service, in which Hoffmann would remain for the rest of his career. Alfred's first public assignment was to contribute to the enlargement of the Post Office headquarters on Berlin's Spandauer Straße, a vast neoclassical building now known only through old photographs. His career showed early promise when he won the Schinkel competition for architecture in 1881 at the first attempt, which also brought him a bursary for overseas travel. This allowed Alfred to visit Italy in the summer of 1883, a trip which he followed up the next year with a tour of Spain and France, plus a lengthy stay with his Messel siblings in London. He would

Alfred Messel's Werderhaus shopping centre in Berlin

return to visit England at the end of the 1880s together with Hoffmann, who also accompanied Alfred on other trips to experience the art and architecture of Italy, Austria, Belgium and the rest of Germany.

Like many of his contemporaries, Alfred complemented his architectural practice with teaching. He became an assistant lecturer in the architecture faculty of Berlin's Technical College, a position which led to his later appointment as lecturer and then professor at the Royal College of Applied Arts. He began to take on more private commissions alongside his official work, beginning in 1885 with a commercial building on the square Am Werderschen Markt. Completed four years later, the Werderhaus served as an early form of shopping centre for boutiques spread across its four floors. Old photographs give a sense of the *haut bourgeois* spirit of the place, with shops selling women's fashions, boots, shoes

and all forms of haberdashery. The store names Rosenthal, Meyer and Sternberg
are a vivid reminder of the central role played by the Jewish community in the
commercial life of Berlin. The rapid growth of Alfred's private portfolio soon made
it impossible for him to continue his public duties, and he left state employment in
1888. Two years later he established his own practice at Schellingstraße No. 14,
where it remained for the rest of his life.

In his early years as an architect Alfred was actively involved in Berlin's urban
reform movement, which sought to provide housing and other amenities for the
huge numbers of workers that had flocked to the city since its establishment as
capital of the newly unified German state. *Fin-de-siècle* Berlin was in the throes
of a population explosion even more dramatic than Darmstadt had seen at the
beginning of the century, with the number of its inhabitants quadrupling to four
million by 1920. Newcomers found themselves at the mercy of unscrupulous
landlords charging exorbitant rents in Berlin's infamous 'rental barracks', and
many families were forced to divide their tiny living quarters still further in order
to sublet individual beds for the night. Such overcrowding made basic hygiene
impossible, and the tenements became breeding grounds for typhus, dysentery,
cholera, smallpox and diphtheria.

Several of Alfred's earliest projects were to construct decent rental
accommodation for these low-income workers. The principle was to provide
working people with healthy and affordable apartments with proper sanitation,
ventilation and green spaces for families to enjoy. Alfred had first come into
contact with the urban housing movement through the social reformer and jurist
Paul Felix Aschrott – like him the son of a Jewish banker – who had spent years
studying social housing in England and the USA. Alfred himself paid tribute to
the English model of working-class accommodation in his 1891 article for the
German architectural journal *Deutsche Bauzeitung*, in which he profiled the work
of the Society for the Improvement of Small Homes that he and Aschrott had
founded together with the Jewish banker Valentin Weisbach. In the same year
Alfred and three other members of the Association of Berlin Architects initiated a
professional debate on the issue of working-class accommodation and published a
manifesto for how to resolve the housing shortage caused by the influx of workers
to the capital.[2]

Alfred went on to design four housing developments for the Berlin Savings
and Building Society, which still exists as a cooperative providing affordable
accommodation to the residents of the German capital today. As well as being
one of its leading architects, Alfred sat on the board of the society for five years
and as chairman of its building committee actively championed the new discipline
of architectural design for rental accommodation. The international significance
of the initiative was borne out by the gold medal which Alfred won for his

Central garden
in Alfred Messel's
Sickingenstraße
housing development,
Berlin

Proskauer Straße housing development at the Exposition Universelle held in Paris in 1900. The prize recognized the pioneering vision of his design, which provided spacious accommodation for 116 families in an enclosed square made up of twelve apartment blocks. The living quarters were set around a large garden area complete with children's playground and included amenities never before offered to working-class tenants: a library, a bowling alley, communal baths, a washhouse, a bakery and even a free kindergarten for children whose parents were out during the day. The format of an enclosed square looking inwards on to a shared garden would have been familiar to Alfred from visits to his siblings in the more affluent parts of London; his vision recognized that the same principle could be adapted to meet the housing needs of working-class families in Berlin.[3]

A further three of Alfred's earliest designs were created for the Society for People's Cafés and Eating Houses, a social enterprise that provided affordable canteens for working men and women on the ground floor of each new building, subsidized by rents charged at market rates on the apartments above. The society imposed its own moral strictures on customers, including the requirement that women and men should eat in separate parts of the restaurant. The original aim of keeping the establishments entirely alcohol-free proved unfeasible given the cultural expectation of beer with meals. Another progressive venture from this period of Alfred's career is his design for the new technical school of the Lette Association, a proto-feminist organization dedicated to the vocational training and economic independence of women. Both building and organization are still in existence, although now offering professional training to male as well as female students.

Alfred Messel's bright prospects soon brought him into contact with a growing circle of Berlin society and allowed him to think of enlarging his own domestic situation. On 1 February 1893, shortly before his fortieth birthday, Alfred married Elsa Altmann, who had just turned twenty-one. Elsa's father Max Altmann was a successful Jewish banker, as Alfred's had been, but he had married a Christian who brought up their children in the Lutheran faith. Alfred would himself convert to Christianity when he was baptized in Berlin's magnificent New Church on 21 February 1899, but he was still officially Jewish at the time of his wedding, and his marriage to Elsa was a purely civil affair. Just over nine months later, on 25 November 1893, the couple's first child was born – a daughter christened Helene Lina Agnes

Elsa and Alfred Messel,
with children (from
left) Ena, Irene and
Ludwig

Messel but known simply as Ena. Two further children followed at three-year intervals: a son, Ludwig Georg Alfred Messel, on 8 August 1896 and a second daughter, Irene Hedwig Eugenie Messel, on 26 April 1899. All three children were baptized into the Lutheran faith.

The major career breakthrough for Alfred came with the series of department stores he designed for the Wertheim brothers in Berlin. Also from a Jewish family, Georg Wertheim and his brother Hugo had taken on their parents' haberdashery store in the Baltic town of Stralsund and expanded it into one of the most successful businesses of the later nineteenth century, opening their first Berlin outlet in 1885. Within five years they had added a second Berlin store on the Oranienstraße and two years later a third on the Leipziger Straße in the heart of the German capital. Yet the traditional shop form which they had inherited with its myriad crowded rooms proved increasingly unsatisfactory, and Georg Wertheim called on Alfred to devise a new type of building along the lines of the unitary department stores which had already revolutionized the art of shopping in Paris and New York.

Alfred's first foray into this new discipline came in 1893 with the commission to redesign the Oranienstraße premises, which he modelled on the Parisian department store Au Printemps that still towers over the Boulevard Haussmann to this day. His second Wertheim contract three years later required him to rebuild the flagship Leipziger Straße store, and Alfred designed its façade in a more identifiably German style characterized by pointed verticals shooting skywards from pavement to roof. Alfred's conception of the building as a single space unified by verticals rather than a layering of horizontal storeys was recognized as a radically new departure, and such façades were referred to as 'Messelian arrow-type' in the architectural guides of the time.[4]

If the exterior was celebrated for its stylistic innovation, the interior of the store offered the consumer a shopping experience without any parallel in Berlin. The physical expanse of the internal space – twice as big as the Reichstag parliament building – was accentuated by three spectacular atriums with open staircases, lit by exterior windows and complete with their own colossal artworks. There were sixty-five departments including fabrics, fashions, hats, shoes, haberdashery, carpets, furniture, lighting, perfumes, leatherware, stationery, books, glass, china, gold and silver, toys, wines, food, paintings, antiques, watches and musical instruments as well as a travel agent, theatre-booking service, hairdressers, lending library and in-house

Central atrium of the Wertheim department store, Leipziger Straße, Berlin

zoo. For anyone overcome by the experience there was a winter garden of indoor palms and waterfalls in which to relax, plus various refreshment rooms. Six steam engines, ten boilers and over a hundred electric motors generated the power for the store's air-conditioning system, its thirty-two elevators and its twenty thousand lightbulbs.[5] Those unable to make it to the store in person could take advantage of its mail-order service. The 1903 catalogue stretches to over 180 pages of illustrated items, together with a photograph of the fleet of motorized Wertheim vans standing ready to deliver purchases to its customers' homes.

The overall effect of space, luxury and refinement elevated the shopping emporium to the status of secular temple; indeed, Berliners quickly dubbed it 'the Cathedral' for its mystical overtones. The contemporary theologian Paul Göhre likened its effect to the chapel of an Oxford college: 'If you stand at a distance in the evening as the windows shimmer with their subdued, diffused light, you feel as if you must be waiting for the organ to sound out from the high vaults within.'[6] The Wertheim store was such a sensation, recalled the writer Hans Fallada years later, that 'people would regularly make pilgrimage there whether they needed to buy anything or not'.[7] The sheer excitement of this experience made the Leipziger Straße store the most talked-about building in Berlin, if not in all Europe; the contemporary tourist guide *Berlin for Connoisseurs* told its readers to head for Wertheim's before taking in any of the city's other sights.[8]

Yet it was the third and final Wertheim commission – to extend the store front around the corner on to Leipziger Platz – that won Alfred Messel his reputation as a harbinger of twentieth-century modernism. Begun in 1903 and unveiled to great fanfare three years later, the new façade imposed its presence on the iconic square with a radicalism that took Berlin by storm. Uncompromisingly modern in the severity of its line, the unbroken verticals of the building's windows conjured up an allusion to the historical tradition of German Gothic, suggesting a distinctively national response to the globalization of style that threatened to reduce everything to a pastiche of French Baroque. Photographs of the burnt-out roofless Wertheim building at the end of the Second World War could almost be mistaken for a genuine Gothic ruin of centuries past.[9]

The marriage of historicism and innovation had always been at the heart of Alfred Messel's architectural practice. Yet with the Wertheim commission his design solution took on a deeper significance. The phenomenon of the department store had met with serious opposition from cultural commentators and politicians in the new German Reich in that it smacked of an internationalism that ran counter to their patriotic sense of purpose. Instead of upholding traditional German values of hard work and fair reward, department stores were assailed for the supposed loss of quality inherent in the mass-produced goods they sold as well as the potential exploitation of their workforce beyond what would be tolerated

The revolutionary façade of Alfred Messel's Wertheim department store, Leipziger Platz, Berlin

in smaller firms. More sinister was the observation that most department stores were run by Jewish proprietors whose rootless internationalism was seen as the antithesis of a German identity fixed by blood and soil. The twin dangers of vulgar commercialism and Jewish cosmopolitanism were considered a toxic mixture that could eat away at the very foundations of German culture.

The Wertheim brothers were alive to the anti-Semitic undertones of this criticism and took care to ensure not only that the quality of their goods was impeccable but that their employees were treated better than in other establishments. Together with Alfred Messel, they saw to it that the new Wertheim extension on Leipziger Platz would bear no trace of crass commercialism. The consumer paradise within was discreetly hidden behind a deep arcade that carried the weight of the façade, so that the shop windows were effectively invisible from the square itself. Likewise, there were to be no advertising hoardings or signage on the front of the store. This was a sophisticated building confident of its own identity, with a recognizably German design that reclaimed modern architecture from the threat of deracinated internationalism. The historicism embodied in the Wertheim extension enabled the Germans to overcome their fear of modernity, while the cultural phenomenon of the department store was redeemed in the eyes of German nationalists by two men who had both been born Jews.

The success of the Wertheim department store led to another rich seam of commissions that Alfred would enjoy for the rest of his life: the private villas and country houses of wealthy German businessmen, many of them Jewish. His initial commission came from the third of the five Wertheim brothers, Wilhelm, for whom Alfred designed a country house in the newly established villa colony of Grunewald to the west of Berlin. Instead of the Baroque residences that had been the preferred vehicle for successful families to show off their wealth, Alfred created a modest retreat for Wilhelm in the style of the Arts and Crafts movement he had seen while visiting his Messel siblings in England. For the youngest brother, Wolf, he designed a neoclassical villa along more generous lines, while his third and final Wertheim residence, for brother Franz, was a palatial affair to rival the grandest creations. As a result of these and many other such commissions Alfred would come to be remembered as the 'master of bourgeois villa design'.[10]

In addition to residential contracts Alfred was increasingly called upon to design large-scale industrial and commercial buildings for the booming Berlin economy. After winning the competition to rebuild the headquarters of the Berlin Board of Trade in 1897, Alfred received several commissions over the next decade that would leave his mark on the architecture of the German capital

The town hall, Ballenstedt

and beyond. His monumental National Bank of Germany survives only in old photographs, but the building's neoclassical austerity was in architectural terms almost as significant as the Wertheim store. The State Insurance Bureau he designed from 1902 onwards functions today as the offices of Berlin's housing department, its striking two-tone façade in brick and limestone still dominating the street outside. Alfred was also commissioned to design the headquarters of AEG, the electrical company founded by Jewish industrialist Emil Rathenau that would grow into one of the most enduring international brands of the modern age. In civic architecture, the town hall which Alfred created for the town of Ballenstedt was considered by Walter Behrendt, one of his earliest champions, to be the crowning glory of his career.[11]

Despite his successes, Alfred remained frustrated at not receiving a major public commission during his years in Berlin. Anti-Jewish prejudice was still rife within the Prussian administration, linked once again to the fear of modernity as a threat to German national identity. Such insecurity can be seen in the reaction of Kaiser Wilhelm II to the suggestion that Alfred Messel should be appointed to the vacant post of Architect of the Royal Museums; the Kaiser apparently worried

that Alfred was a 'hypermodernist' and thus not appropriate to the task in hand.[12] For official recognition, Alfred was forced to turn to his native Darmstadt, where he embarked on one of his most significant creations, the State Museum of Hesse, under the direct patronage of Grand Duke Ernst Ludwig.

Ernst Ludwig was a great-grandson of the Grand Duke Ludwig II for whom Aron and Simon Messel had served as court bankers in Darmstadt, and he had come to the throne on the sudden death of his father in 1892. On doing so the young man rejected all previous designs that had been submitted for the new Darmstadt museum as inadequate. In their place he chose Alfred Messel to create a building that would be worthy of the Grand Duchy into the twentieth century and beyond. Alfred developed his designs in coordination with the Grand Duke over a period of five years, so that the foundation stone was laid only in 1897.

Construction took a further five years and the installation of the collections four more, so that the people of Darmstadt finally gained access to their new museum in November 1906. A large part of the challenge was that the building needed to house a vast range of different exhibits under one roof, from medieval armour to natural history, geology, archaeology and an exceptional collection of fine art. The restoration project that closed the museum to the public for a full seven years from 2007 has brought the original conception to life in the most spectacular way. The exterior

One of the two bronze lions outside the State Museum of Hesse donated by Ludwig and Rudolph Messel

has also been renovated, including the two monumental bronze lions that were given as a donation by Alfred's brothers Ludwig and Rudolph Messel to the city of their birth.[13]

The success of the Darmstadt project paved the way for Alfred Messel's last great commission: the Pergamon Museum in Berlin. This was to be the final piece in the grand imperial design conceived by Kaiser Wilhelm II for the Berlin museum island that would allow the young German capital to rival the cultural glories of Paris and London. For Alfred it was quite simply 'the realization of a long-cherished dream', as the Kaiser had now agreed to his appointment as Architect of the Royal Museums, with responsibility for one of the most important cultural building projects of the time. Berlin already boasted four museums holding world-class collections of Egyptian, Islamic, Byzantine and Renaissance art. The challenge for the Pergamon Museum was that it had to display three distinct collections within the one building: Greek and Hellenistic antiquities, the treasures of Mesopotamia and post-medieval German art. Alfred resolved this conundrum by designing a three-winged building around a central courtyard, allowing each collection to exist independently while indulging the programmatic vision of a dialogue between three great civilizations of the ancient and modern worlds.

Yet Alfred would never see his last great work completed – or even begun. He had been diagnosed with a degenerative heart condition in 1902, and this required him to take more and more time off work as his health declined. He suffered a serious heart attack in early 1908 which forced him to spend the summer in complete rest at the health resort of Baden-Baden. From there he travelled to the Italian spa town of Levico Terme, where he spent several weeks putting his professional and personal affairs in order. His architectural practice had by this time expanded to employ sixteen members of staff, and he clearly felt the need to secure the future of his unfinished commissions beyond the time that he could no longer oversee them personally. Although his letters reveal his mounting frustration at not being able to begin work on the Pergamon Museum, his health remained dangerously frail. He returned to Berlin at the end of 1908 but suffered another heart attack in February 1909 from which he never recovered.

Alfred Messel died on 24 March 1909, aged fifty-five. His life-long friend Ludwig Hoffmann had promised him that he would see the Pergamon Museum through to completion, although neither man can have imagined that it would take a further twenty years before he would be able to fulfil that promise. A shortage of funds, the intervention of the First World War and subsequent doubts as to whether such a grandiose imperial design was appropriate for the Germany of the Weimar Republic delayed the construction of the museum dramatically, so that it eventually opened to the public only in 1930, just two years before Hoffmann's own death. Alfred Messel's original conception of a colonnade on the fourth side of the courtyard was left unrealized, but a modern variation on that theme is at last under construction.

Alfred was buried in Berlin, where his last resting place is a handsome neoclassical grave shared with his Altmann in-laws in St Matthew's cemetery. His presence there is a final indication of his passage away from the faith of his fathers and a reminder that German Jews were still under intense pressure to renounce their Judaism if they wished to succeed in any public profession. Alfred had designed the tomb himself in a style close to that which he used for the mausoleum commissioned by the Rathenau family in 1903.

Courtyard entrance to Alfred Messel's Pergamon Museum, Berlin

Nor is the grandeur misplaced: by the end of his life Alfred had overcome all earlier suspicions to become one of the Kaiser's most trusted arbiters of taste. There is an indication of just how completely he had made the journey to court insider in a letter from November 1907, when Alfred was asked not to sit on the judging panel for a Berlin architectural competition precisely because his influence on Kaiser Wilhelm II was felt to be so great. As Ludwig Hoffmann recounted proudly to his friend: 'You must not be allowed to be one of the judges under any circumstances, I was told. His Majesty would be called upon to make the final decision, and if you were there he would simply follow your opinion and make his decision under your influence so that no one else would have a say in the matter. Alfred, how times have changed!'[14]

Alfred Messel had risen to the pinnacle of his profession and succeeded in becoming the ultimate insider, serving as architect to the Kaiser within the imperial court of the unified German Reich. In addition to the buildings designed by Alfred that survive in Berlin, the German capital boasts a Messelstraße and a Messel Park named in his honour. His native Darmstadt also acted to keep his memory alive, bestowing the title of Alfred-Messel-Weg on one of the streets that leads out of Darmstadt in the direction of the village of Messel. During the Nazi era, the ethnic cleansing of Jewish names from public places saw Alfred-Messel-Weg dissolved into Richard-Wagner-Weg. Twenty years after the end of the Second World War the injury was redressed. On 6 January 1965 Alfred-Messel-Weg was officially reinstated by the Darmstadt municipal authorities, and you can walk down it to this day.

Ludwig Messel at the time
of his marriage

New Life in London 5

LUDWIG ERNST WILHELM Leonhardt Messel arrived in England on 21 May 1865. He was just eighteen years old. As the eldest son of Simon and Emilie Messel, Ludwig would normally have expected to take on responsibility for the family banking house in Darmstadt, but his father's premature death saw the business go to his uncle Ferdinand Sander instead. Ludwig's decision to emigrate set an example that would be followed by each of his siblings except Alfred, who stayed in Germany to follow his architectural career. Family tradition tells that Ludwig made the journey from Darmstadt to London with gold coins sewn into the hem of his shirt.[1]

Ludwig Messel was one of five million Germans to leave their homeland in the nineteenth century in search of a better life abroad. While the vast majority crossed the Atlantic and settled in the USA, as Ludwig's Uncle Louis had done, tens of thousands came to Britain, where the German community constituted the single largest foreign presence for most of the century. The industrial revolution in Britain had been one cause of this mass migration, in that its factories had undercut the traditional cottage industries of western Germany and driven the redundant workforce to emigrate in search of employment. Yet most of the German migrants who chose Britain as their destination were not jobless paupers but middle-class merchants, entrepreneurs, tradesmen, governesses and waiters. The German population of England and Wales peaked at 53,324 in 1911, with around half of the total in London.

Jewish Germans had an added incentive to emigrate. Gradual emancipation had brought them legal rights across the various states of what would eventually become Germany. Yet for all their theoretical entitlements Jews continued to face institutional discrimination and popular prejudice, with varying degrees of hostility depending on where they lived. Access to the top professions was still heavily restricted for Jews in the 1860s – not just the military, diplomatic and civil services but also university positions and the judiciary – and the process of emancipation unleashed its own wave of anti-Semitism, with local petitions opposing the extension of civic rights to the Jews.[2] For all their integration into the dominant German culture, the Messel family lived with the realization that their

Lina Seligman,
née Messel

Eugenie de la Penha,
née Messel

Jewish heritage made them a potential target of popular aggression, not least in Hesse. Otto Böckel, founder of the Anti-Semitic People's Party, would become the first representative of an expressly anti-Jewish party to take his seat in the German Reichstag when he was elected to a constituency in north Hesse in 1887.[3]

There were specific attractions for the ten thousand or so Jewish Germans who chose to settle in Britain during the Victorian era. Britain was still the leading power in trade and industrial production, while London was universally recognized as the finance capital of the world. But, to many, the relative lack of social prejudice in Britain was attraction enough after the daily indignities they suffered back home. To be sure, there were strains of anti-Semitism in Britain, and negative stereotypes of 'the Jew' abounded in English literature and the press. Yet even 'low-key' prejudice was not allowed to go unchallenged, so that the leading scholar of anti-Semitism during this period could conclude that 'the predominant ideology in Britain between 1876 and 1914 presented a favourable image of Jews'.[4] The difference was palpable to Jews coming to Britain from the Germanic states. Sigmund Freud visited his half-brothers in Manchester in 1875 and was profoundly moved by the freedom of their lives compared with his own in Vienna. He recalled the experience in a letter to his fiancée later, asking, 'Must we stay here, Martha? If we possibly can, let us seek a home where human worth is more respected.'[5]

Ludwig Messel was taken on as a clerk by Isaac Seligman, a German-born Jew who had founded the London branch of the Seligman banking empire in 1864. The Seligman story is a remarkable one in its own right.[6] Originally from the Bavarian village of Baiersdorf, all eleven children emigrated to the USA, where the men of the family made their way as peddlers selling household goods from town to town. Their big break came with the American Civil War, when Isaac – the youngest of the brothers – made the acquaintance of Abraham Lincoln and secured over a million dollars' worth of contracts to provide uniforms to the Union Army. Lincoln was unable to pay for the uniforms in cash, however, so the Seligmans were forced to accept much of the debt in government bonds, which they then had to sell on. Thus was born the Seligman banking empire, as each brother was sent out to establish a presence in the key financial centres of London, Frankfurt, Paris, San Francisco and New York. The London branch would grow into one of the most prestigious merchant banks over the next century, before being bought by S.G. Warburg and Co. in 1957.

Ludwig worked at Seligman Brothers from the time of his arrival in England, and the family connection would soon be cemented through the marriage of his sister Lina Messel to Isaac Seligman in January 1869. Their daughter Louise tells the story of their first meeting in the memorial tribute *Mother and Memories*, published privately after Lina's death:

> To return to Mother's biography, when she was seventeen years old she was invited by her brother, Ludwig, then clerk in the newly opened London branch of the American firm of Seligman Bros, to visit him in London. She accepted, and, when calling for her brother at the office one morning, the head of the firm, Isaac Seligman, then thirty-four years old, saw her and fell in love with the beautiful girl at first sight. A few months later, in January 1869, they were married, and at the early age of seventeen she left her first home for her new home in England.[7]

The new home to which Lina moved was at 100 Lower Tulse Hill in south London, but in spring 1873 the Seligman family, enlarged by the arrival of their first two children, moved to a substantial mansion in nearby Clapham Park. The house had belonged to the master builder Thomas Cubitt, and Isaac renamed it Lincoln House after the US President whose friendship had been so crucial to Seligman family fortunes. Visitors approached the villa down a substantial carriage drive of elm and oak trees, with lawns on one side and meadows on the other. The house had fourteen bedrooms on the upper floors plus a nursery, school room and billiard room, with a suite of reception rooms on the ground floor sixty feet long. Twenty-four acres of grounds contained a kitchen garden, a coach house, a cow house and an aviary.[8]

Lincoln House, home of Lina and Isaac Seligman

Lincoln House was to be the setting for the marriage in 1879 of Ludwig and Lina's younger sister Eugenie Messel, who had made the journey over from Darmstadt to join her siblings in England. Like Lina, Eugenie married within the Jewish faith – in her case to a German-born stockbroker, Eugene de la Penha. The couple settled at Grove House in Clapham Park, a stone's throw from Lina and Isaac Seligman, and brought up their two sons and daughter there before moving to the even grander address of Stoke Lodge in Hyde Park Gate, now the official residence of the Australian High Commissioner.

On 19 April 1871 Ludwig Messel himself got married, to Annie Cussans. The ceremony took place at the Brixton Unitarian Chapel near the Tulse Hill address where Ludwig was living at the time. The choice of a Christian venue for the wedding represents a further stage in Ludwig's journey away from Judaism

Annie and Ludwig
Messel at the time
of their wedding

towards the dominant religion of his adopted nation, although there is no evidence that he ever became a believer. It is noteworthy that Ludwig chose a Unitarian rather than an Anglican service: many German Jews favoured Unitarianism as the most appealing form of Christianity, not least because its rejection of the doctrine of the Trinity accorded more easily with the monotheism of their own upbringing.[9] A Unitarian marriage service would have required the least personal commitment from Ludwig in terms of his own profession of faith. It would be the next generation of Messels that made the decisive move into the Church of England under the influence of their mother Annie.

Annie herself came from a fractured family background which made her an unlikely match for the upwardly mobile Ludwig. The original Cussans family had been plantation owners in Jamaica, with substantial holdings centred on the Amity Hall sugar estate in the south-east of the island. The estate received the considerable sum of £3,831 12s. 9d. in the act of mass compensation to slave owners undertaken by the British government after the abolition of slavery in 1833.[10] Yet Annie's father, Thomas Cussans, had been born out of wedlock and as an illegitimate son seems to have inherited none of the family money. Instead, he was sent overseas at the age of eighteen to serve in the Madras Army of the East India Company for the next fifteen years of his life.[11] On his return to England Thomas married and had eleven children but moved around the country unable to hold down a steady job. He was initially in receipt of an income of up to £60 a year, but, according to his wife Matilda, when this income ceased in 1849 he 'never earned anything afterwards towards the maintenance of himself and his family except a few small sums which he gained by teaching drawing and Hindoo dance'.[12] Thomas abandoned his family altogether in 1857, and Matilda was forced to petition the Divorce Court for a protection order so that neither he nor his creditors could touch the money she had saved after he left her. Thomas did not even answer the summons requiring him to testify in the case.

Ludwig and Annie Messel made their first home at 34 Wiltshire Road in the Angell Town development of Brixton. Angell Town was a new suburban development for the wealthier residents of south London, with Wiltshire Road as its main axis. While No. 34 no longer exists, the remaining original buildings show that they were handsome houses set in extensive greenery – an eminently desirable residence for a young professional wishing to start a family. Annie was soon pregnant with their first child, a son, who came into the world on 19 February 1872 and was named Leonard Charles Rudolph Messel – good German names but in anglicized form. Just over a year later the family was expanded further with the birth of the first of their four daughters, Ottilie Maude Messel, on 24 March 1873.

With the prospect of a growing family, Ludwig's natural ambition saw to it that he would not remain a clerk at Seligman Brothers for long. He had already gained admission to the London Stock Exchange in 1871, and two years later he founded his own company, L. Messel and Co., which would develop over the next century into one of the City's most successful stockbroking firms. Ludwig had applied for naturalization as a British subject – a requirement for foreigners seeking membership of the Stock Exchange – while he was working at Seligman Brothers, and the application was duly granted on 30 October 1869. He was now able to establish the family firm in his name, with offices first in Throgmorton Street and then in Angel Court, where they remained until 1894.

Ludwig's partners in his new venture offer an insight into the people who made up his circle during his early years in London. His first business partner was Alfred Hyam de Pass, a young stockbroker who had been born and brought up in London, the de Pass family having originally come to England as Sephardi Jewish immigrants in the seventeenth century. At the end of June 1877 de Pass left L. Messel and Co. to set up his own family firm and was replaced by Daniel Marks, who remained a partner with Ludwig until 1892. Marks had also been born and brought up in London, the second son of a Polish-born Jew who served as *shomer* or beadle of the Great Synagogue in Duke's Place. In 1881 Messel and Marks were joined by a third partner, Maurice Wetzlar, from the German-Jewish family of that name, and the three men remained sole partners in the firm until its expansion in 1889. For the first fifteen years of its existence L. Messel and Co. was a business run by individuals who shared a Jewish heritage, whatever their personal adherence to the faith.

David Kynaston remarks in his history of the City of London that Ludwig Messel 'epitomized' the influx of foreign talent into the Stock Exchange during the 1870s.[13] Germans accounted for 70 per cent of Stock Exchange members of foreign birth in 1914 and the same proportion of clerks; when Austrians are added to their number the figure nears 80 per cent. While this was still a tiny fraction of the overall total, it was a distinct enough minority to attract attention. One member recalled later that it was 'very derogatory to us as a British institution the amount of German we have heard in the Stock Exchange'.[14]

Like other German brokers, Ludwig's business focused on serving German clients and trading in foreign securities. The latter was an especially lucrative market: more than 150 foreign government loans were issued in London between 1860 and 1876 alone, with a value of over £720 million.[15] The number of equity issues in foreign firms also rose dramatically in the latter part of the nineteenth century, with returns a great deal higher than from British investments.[16] In particular, L. Messel and Co. prospered from the explosion of trading that accompanied the gold rush in South Africa, so that by 1896 the partnership was identified as one of the two largest stockbroking firms of foreign origin dealing on orders on the London Stock Exchange.[17] In 1907, when the investment bank Morgan was asked to provide information for a French client on potential London brokers, it singled out L. Messel and Co. as one of a handful of 'first-rate' firms.[18]

Although it was a partnership, L. Messel and Co. was clearly understood to be Ludwig's firm. The goodwill of the company – its intangible assets – remained his exclusive property, and early partnership deeds stipulate that the other partners could not continue trading under the name Messel if Ludwig should die early unless one of his sons be admitted into the partnership. By 1897, when his eldest son Leonard was made a partner, Ludwig owned £100,000 of the firm's total £150,000 capital and was entitled to 53.5 per cent of its profits. By this time

The 'El Greco' features of Ludwig Messel, drawn by his grandson Oliver Messel

there were six partners, but Ludwig kept the company under his close control, as the articles of partnership demonstrate. Not only did he have absolute authority over the hiring and firing of staff but in any difference of opinion Ludwig's decision was final.

The control that Ludwig exercised over his business gives a clue as to his character as a man. Throughout his life he was a taciturn figure who observed social niceties but kept his thoughts to himself. Such reserve stemmed from his awareness of being an outsider in British society. He spoke English with a pronounced German accent and was cautious as to how much he expressed himself in public. Surviving photographs of Ludwig tell the same story: a neatly dressed man with a stern demeanour, the trademark dark Messel eyes staring out above a bushy but well-kempt beard. Yet beneath his forbidding exterior he clearly harboured deep feelings, particularly when it came to family relationships. A letter he wrote in later years on the death of his sister Eugenie betrays a reservoir of understated emotion. 'We have just laid our poor sister to rest. She was our youngest and the first break in the family. Alas.'[19]

Ludwig's grandson, the theatre designer Oliver Messel, remembered him as a benign but remote figure with 'fine features and a head like an El Greco portrait'; he was equally conscious of his grandfather's reputation as 'a martinet in the office, with a brilliant business mind'.[20] Those who did not get to see beneath the veneer could be left with a wholly unflattering impression of Ludwig. Alan 'Tommy' Lascelles, the future private secretary to George VI and Elizabeth II, memorably described him as 'the melancholy Messel, who has never been known to smile except once when he had the luck to see a child run over by a motor-bus in Threadneedle Street'.[21]

The early success of Ludwig's business enabled the Messel family to move from Angell Town in 1874 to a new family home at 5 Pembridge Villas in Bayswater, a significant step into the world of the upper-middle class. The opening of London's first underground railway between Bishop's Road (Paddington) and Farringdon Street in 1863 had brought this pleasant suburban district into easy contact with the City, cutting out the traffic jams that even in those days meant the five-mile journey could take up to an hour and a half. The villas themselves were substantial double-fronted stuccoed houses with libraries, conservatories and such unheard-of luxuries as fully fitted bathrooms with hot and cold running water.

Ludwig and Annie moved in next door to William Powell Frith, the celebrated Victorian painter who had settled in Pembridge Villas twenty years earlier and whose works provide a visual record of just how opulent the houses were.[22] A few streets to the north and west, the metropolis still gave way to open fields and farms, so the prevailing wind would have brought in fresh air from the countryside – no small matter given the high levels of air pollution in nineteenth-century London. The environment clearly agreed with them, and the family would soon be enlarged further with the birth of a second daughter, Ruth Margaret Messel, on 3 August 1874, a second son, Harold George Messel, on 9 February 1877 and a third girl, Hilda Louise Messel, on 18 April 1878. This growth led to a search for more living space than Pembridge Villas had to offer. Before long Ludwig and Annie took their five children off to the even grander address that would become their permanent London home.

Mrs Ludwig Messel, by
Solomon J. Solomon, 1885

Tyburnia 6

I N 1880 LUDWIG and Annie Messel moved to 8 Westbourne Terrace, the family's London home for the next thirty years. The house stood at the fashionable end of what was once described as the finest street in the capital, leading into Hyde Park to the south and what was still open countryside to the north.[1] The development's grandeur can be appreciated from a splendid lithograph by George Hawkins dating from 1843, soon after it was first built. The generous carriageway is flanked on both sides by an avenue of plane trees that screen the tall neoclassical houses from the road, forming a secluded driveway in front of each terrace. The houses themselves are stuccoed to each of their four storeys, with pillared porches shading the entrances and balustraded balconies on the first floor.

This was Tyburnia, the highly desirable residential development designed to rival Cubitt's Belgravia on the other side of Hyde Park. While the area was more closely identified with the *nouveaux riches* than the aristocratic families who lived around Belgrave Square, Westbourne Terrace had already boasted such eminent residents as the statesman Richard Cobden and the colonial administrator Sir Charles Trevelyan. When the Messel family moved in, their next-door neighbour was the Consul-General of France. Ludwig and Annie established Tyburnia as their home territory, and both Messel sons would later buy their own London properties in adjacent streets.

Tyburnia was not just a desirable destination for the aspiring upper-middle class; it held a particular attraction for successful Jewish families as they migrated westwards across London, and Westbourne Terrace had already established itself in the area as 'the main axis along which Jews lived'.[2] This is the cultural milieu so memorably captured in Amy Levy's novel *Reuben Sachs*, written at precisely the time the Messels settled there. While her descriptions expose the snobbery of those families who congratulated themselves on their superiority over their less exalted neighbours in Maida Vale, Levy paints a vivid picture of a confident community which had cemented its place in the upper echelons of British society while proudly upholding its Jewish heritage.[3]

Despite settling in an area with such a strong Jewish presence, Ludwig Messel does not appear to have identified strongly as Jewish himself. Born to a Jewish

Westbourne Terrace,
in an 1843 lithograph
by George Hawkins

mother and father from two of Darmstadt's foremost Jewish families, Ludwig
was undeniably a Jew. Yet he and his brothers had been educated at Lutheran
schools and brought up in a secularized environment. He had married Annie in
a Christian ceremony – albeit in a Unitarian chapel whose relaxed approach to
doctrine did not require him to be formally admitted into the Christian faith – and
his own children were baptized into the Church of England, marking the decisive
break with the family's Jewish heritage. Even this was not a straightforward
matter: the children were not christened in infancy, as customary in the Anglican
communion, but only once the family had moved to Westbourne Terrace. All
were then baptized at St James's, Sussex Gardens: Leonard on 20 January 1886,
when he was thirteen years old, and Ottilie, Ruth, Harold and Hilda a year later,
on 25 January 1887. Only the youngest child, Muriel, would be presented for
baptism in the traditional manner on 24 June 1889, at the age of just two and
a half weeks.

Leonard Messel's baptism coincided with his starting at Eton – still very much
an Anglican school at the end of the nineteenth century, where full participation
was easier for those who were members of the established Church. Harold Messel
followed his brother to the same school in 1890, so his baptism would have

equipped him equally. The expenditure incurred in sending both sons to Eton was considerable. While fees were around a hundred guineas a year, the full cost of sending a boy to the school was anything up to three times as much, including pocket money and travel expenses.[4] Average annual earnings in the mid-1880s were under £45, so the cost of an Eton education for both Messel boys would have been well over ten times this. Yet, for Ludwig, the decision to send his sons to the most prestigious public school was an essential part of his quest to integrate the Messel family into English society within a single generation.

The high importance given to assimilation was a defining feature for German Jews coming to England in the Victorian era. In their native Germany most Jews accepted that their life chances would be enhanced according to how much they abandoned their Jewish identity in favour of the dominant German culture. Those who migrated to England carried that same instinct with them to their new home environment, so that by the second generation many families had shed all vestiges of their former identity. The trend was so noticeable that their English co-religionists regularly complained at the refusal of German-Jewish immigrants to join local synagogues or to be in any way identified as Jews.[5]

This drift away from Judaism applies equally to Ludwig Messel, even if he was never baptized into the Christian faith as his brother Alfred had been in Berlin. Yet this does not mean Ludwig was oblivious of his Jewish roots or the connections which they offered him as a first-generation immigrant. When he wished to commission a portrait of his wife Annie, Ludwig chose the young Solomon J. Solomon as his preferred painter, on his way to becoming only the second Jewish artist to be elected a full member of the Royal Academy. *Mrs Ludwig Messel* was exhibited at the Royal Academy in 1885, the first of many portraits from the Anglo-Jewish community that Solomon would show there over the course of his career.[6] That same year Solomon was also commissioned to paint portraits of Ludwig's sister Lina and her husband Isaac Seligman in what seems to have been a concerted act of family patronage. The large portrait of Annie Messel is a *tour de force*, her natural beauty and good humour evident over the dazzling display of turquoise silks and floral underskirts.

The most visible way in which Ludwig embraced his Jewish heritage was through his charitable giving, not least through his membership of the Anglo-Jewish Association from its earliest beginnings in 1871. The association was a philanthropic organization run for the purpose of supporting Jewish communities around the world. Membership of its council reads as a roll call of the most powerful scions of Anglo-Jewry, including representatives of the Rothschild, Goldsmid, Montefiore, Samuel, Sassoon, Jessel, Lousada and Mocatta clans. This was the Cousinhood: the interrelated body of established Anglo-Jewish families who had been instrumental in winning emancipation earlier in the nineteenth century and who had set themselves up as *de facto* leaders of the Jewish community. More than any other body, the Anglo-Jewish Association was the institution that symbolized the assumed right of the Cousinhood to speak on behalf of all British Jews, even when their views clashed with those of their poorer co-religionists. Their power was challenged only when the influx of refugees from the Russian pogroms transformed the demographic profile of British Jewry after 1881.

Although he was also a newcomer to Britain, Ludwig's brother-in-law Isaac Seligman was an important enough figure to be a council member of the Anglo-Jewish Association. Ludwig himself is registered in the earliest reports of the association as paying an annual subscription of two guineas, well above the minimum membership fee of five shillings. There must have been an element of enlightened self-interest on Ludwig's part in rubbing shoulders with the families who ran the association: not only were these among the very richest people in the land but most had made their fortunes in the world of finance, where Ludwig wished to further his own career. The results were not inconsiderable: among other triumphs, L. Messel and Co. was to become stockbroker to the Rothschilds. Yet there is no sense that Ludwig's philanthropy was motivated by commercial calculations alone. Even when he had discontinued his membership of the Anglo-Jewish Association he continued to give generously to Jewish causes for the rest of his life, as well as to mainstream British ones. The £200 donation made by L. Messel and Co. in February 1882 to the Mansion House fund for the relief of Russian Jews stands out as just one of his larger gifts.[7]

Whatever their own sense of identity, the Messel family would still be identified as Jewish by others. This comes out nicely in the eulogy to Ludwig's younger brother Rudolph given by the English chemist Henry Armstrong when delivering the first Messel Memorial Lecture in 1922. In a touching encomium to 'one of the most lovable men we have met', Armstrong dwells on Rudolph Messel's appealing and open personality, 'his vigorous frame, his black hair and sparkling eyes, his smiling face, his hearty bass staccato laugh, his peculiar guttural accent', concluding, 'Honest and sincere himself, he hated insincerity and all meanness of spirit. He combined in his person all the best of German good qualities, fired and softened by Jewish imagination.'[8]

Dr Rudolph Messel, FRS

Armstrong's lecture provides an overview of Rudolph's career as an industrial chemist, and we can fill in the missing biographical details from other sources. Born on 14 January 1848 and brought up in Darmstadt along with Ludwig and his other Messel siblings, Rudolph was eleven years old when his father died. He was sent to a Huguenot school at

Friedrichsdorf, just north of Frankfurt, where he was identified as a gifted pupil and encouraged to become a scientist. It was a rarefied atmosphere, as Rudolph recalled years later:

> In 1861, when I was at school at Friedrichsdorf, in Germany, my master, Philip Reis, invented the first telephone. I was present at its birth and assisted Reis in making the mechanical parts of some of his instruments and also repeatedly in his experiments, Reis being at one end of the circuit, speaking or singing, I listening at the other, or vice versa.[9]

Rudolph's chosen career took him first to Frankfurt, where he worked as an apprentice in the chemical works of Eugen Lucius, and then to further studies in Zurich and Heidelberg, where he worked under Robert Bunsen, the chemistry professor known to generations of schoolchildren for the laboratory burner that bears his name. After gaining his doctorate from Tübingen in 1870, Rudolph travelled to England to be the private assistant to Professor Henry Roscoe at Manchester University but was recalled to Germany almost immediately to serve as an ambulance orderly in the Franco-Prussian War. Wounded in action, he was awarded the Military Medical Cross, a medal introduced by the Grand Duke of Hesse for men and women who had distinguished themselves in the care of injured soldiers.[10]

Rudolph was well enough to return to England in 1871 to take up a position with Dr William Squire at the east London chemical works of Dunn, Squire and Co., and he remained with Squire in the new partnership formed with Spencer Chapman in Silvertown soon after. Rudolph took over management of the firm in 1877, and it was renamed Spencer Chapman and Messel; his devotion to the business is shown by the fact that he lived almost all his life in a small house attached to the works. The scientific achievement for which Rudolph Messel is remembered was his perfection of a new method for producing oleum, a substance in high demand from the dyestuffs industry. He demonstrated the process with Squire in April 1876 at the Chemical Society in London and was granted a provisional patent for its invention on 5 April 1878. By the time of the First World War it was discovered that oleum could also be used in the production of explosives, so that Spencer Chapman and Messel was eventually producing a thousand tons of the substance a week.

Rudolph was a founder member in 1881 of the Society of Chemical Industry. Its Belgrave Square headquarters remember him today with a display of the platinum still which he used in developing the oleum production process. He served as the society's foreign secretary for many years and became its president twice in the period leading up to the First World War. In 1912 Rudolph was elected a fellow of the Royal Society, the highest accolade for any scientist working in Britain. His career made him a wealthy man, allowing him to make any number of donations during his lifetime, such as the £500 he gave in 1915 for the completion of the joint physics and chemistry workshops at University College London. His will bears testament to his sense of being first and foremost a scientist:

> I am a German by birth, but have been for many years naturalized in this country, the country of my adoption. I have devoted my life to scientific pursuits, and such fortune as I may leave has been acquired by me in this country, and consequently (my immediate relatives being already provided for) I am enabled to devote the bulk of my fortune to other uses.[11]

The greatest portion of Rudolph's estate was bequeathed to the Royal Society and a smaller sum to the Royal Institution, of which he was also a member. To the Society of Chemical Industry Rudolph left a £20,000 endowment, which was used to fund the award of a Messel Medal every two years for 'eminence in applied chemistry', together with a Messel Memorial Lecture. Today the Messel Trust Fund still provides travel bursaries to support postgraduate students in attending meetings or visiting laboratories overseas.

While his work clearly took up most of his waking hours, Rudolph was a sociable person of cheerful disposition. He remained a bachelor all his life but was closely involved with the rest of the Messel family, often travelling across London to dine with his brother and sisters or spend time with his growing army of nephews and nieces. He was active in the community around his works, playing the piano at concerts given by the Silvertown Choral Society and even financing the production of local theatrical performances.[12] Rudolph was also a regular visitor to the Savage Club, a Bohemian institution that brought together members of the scientific, artistic and literary communities including such notables as Edward Elgar, W. Somerset Maugham and founder of the Proms Henry Wood. The focus was on conviviality, as remarked by one of its more famous foreign visitors, Mark Twain, who recalled 'lively speeches, lively anecdotes, late hours, and a very hospitable and friendly and contenting and delightful good time'.[13] One of the Savage Club celebrities to become a particular friend of Rudolph's was the librettist W.S. Gilbert. Gilbert became a lasting friend of the wider Messel family, as did the composer Arthur Sullivan, his partner in success.

A Savage Club
celebration menu,
January 1913

Ottilie Loring, née Messel,
by Keturah Collings

Cultural Integration 7

FRIENDSHIPS WITH LITERARY and artistic figures were an important feature of life in the Messel household, such connections being more readily accessible to first-generation immigrants of Jewish origin than any entry to the aristocracy. Sometimes the initial contact was made through business links: the family's enduring connection with the Shakespearian actor Sir John Gielgud came through his father Frank, a fellow stockbroker who was made a partner in L. Messel and Co. in 1912. Similarly, the original introduction to Linley Sambourne and his wife Marion that was to prove so important for the next generation of Messels came through Marion's father Spencer Herapath, another stockbroker. Yet from 1895 onwards Ludwig was a member of the Arts Club, at which he rubbed shoulders with leading Royal Academicians such as Sir Luke Fildes, Sir Ernest Waterlow and Sir Lawrence Alma-Tadema, all of whom became family friends. Other members of the Arts Club would play important roles in the life of the Messels over subsequent years, including the architects Sir Ernest George, Harold Peto and Norman Evill as well as the painters Robert Brough, Alfred Parsons and Marcus Stone.

Soon after joining the club Ludwig commissioned Stone to paint his eldest daughter Ottilie. The portrait was shown at the Royal Academy in 1896, where it was praised for being 'strongly painted and well posed'.[1] It was also reproduced in the monograph on Stone published by the *Art Journal* for Christmas 1896, which remarked that the portrait showed 'a young brunette with features of a somewhat foreign type of beauty'.[2] Ottilie retained her beauty into married life, as shown by the striking portrait of her painted years later by the society artist Keturah Collings. Ludwig had earlier arranged for Ottilie's younger sister Hilda to be the subject of a portrait in pastels by the Austrian-born artist Marianne Stokes, one of the leading women painters in London at that time. The portrait was shown at the Grosvenor Gallery's dedicated pastels exhibition in the autumn of 1888, when Hilda was ten years old.[3]

Ludwig also entered the market for Old Masters, purchasing five major works put up for auction from the celebrated Angerstein and Burghley House collections in the latter years of the nineteenth century. The collection of the financier John Julius Angerstein is most famous for having formed the nucleus of the National Gallery in London; yet many works were passed down through the family to his grandson William Angerstein, from whom several were sold by Christie's in a series of auctions between 1874 and 1897. The most significant painting acquired by Ludwig from the Angerstein collection was a large *Holy Family with the Infant St John* by Sir Joshua Reynolds, sold by Christie's in the sale of 6 April 1895. Also listed as a purchase from the Angerstein collection was a seventeenth-century Flemish painting of a young St Agnes, her right hand resting on the head of a lamb.

The Burghley House art collection had been put together by successive generations of the Earls and Marquesses of Exeter from the seventeenth century on. Thirty-nine paintings from the collection were sold at auction by Christie's on 9 June 1888 as part of a three-day sale to pay off the debts of the profligate Third Marquess, and of these Ludwig acquired three significant works. The most spectacular was a large *Repose of the Holy Family* by Bonifazio Veronese, one of the highlights of the auction. Equally impressive was Angelica Kauffman's *Portrait of Sarah Harrop (Mrs Bates) as a Muse*, a life-sized work described by its present owner, Princeton University Art Museum, as 'arguably the artist's masterpiece in portraiture'.[4] Yet the most intriguing painting bought by Ludwig was a portrait of an advocate, catalogued as an autograph work by no less an artist than Diego Velázquez.[5] Owning Old Masters was as much a sign of learning as it was of material success, and Ludwig was clearly keen for his art collection to project an image of cultured sophistication to counter any suggestion that he might be just another wealthy *parvenu*.

Portrait of Sarah Harrop (Mrs Bates) as a Muse, by Angelica Kauffman

In addition to his artistic pursuits, Ludwig was one of the early members of the Royal Historical Society, most probably in support of his brother-in-law John Edwin Cussans, the antiquary and historian of Hertfordshire, who had been a fellow from its inception. Family loyalty may also have been the impetus behind Ludwig's membership of the Devonshire Club, which provides us with our only insight into his political affiliations, such as they were. The Devonshire was established in 1874 as a spillover for the Reform Club, the bastion of Liberal politics which had become such a success that it now had a long waiting list. The Liberal Party had traditionally been seen as the natural political home for Anglo-Jewry, given its support for Jewish emancipation in the face of dogged Tory resistance, and almost all of the first wave of Jewish MPs to take their seats in the House of Commons were Liberals. The immediate attraction for Ludwig was that his brother-in-law Isaac Seligman had been one of the Devonshire Club's original members, but it is striking that such an affluent member of the upper-middle class should not have been a Conservative supporter at this date.

For the Messels were assuredly members of the upper-middle class, if we follow the rule of the contemporary social reformer Charles Booth, who ascribed to that class any family with at least three servants. There were seven domestic servants at 8 Westbourne Terrace at the time of the 1881 census: an indoor manservant, a nurse, a nursemaid, a cook, a kitchen maid and two housemaids. Ten years later, with most of the Messel children in their teens and nursery care needed only for the 'afterthought' baby Muriel, there were eight servants: a butler, a footman, a cook, a kitchen maid, a lady's maid, a nurse and two housemaids. There is no suggestion that such an establishment was out of the ordinary for families of the same status at the end of the Victorian era: the Messels' neighbours at 10 Westbourne Terrace, where the head of the household was also a stockbroker, had nine domestic servants in 1891.

Ludwig Messel was intent on integrating his family into English society. Yet for all their determination to become English, in certain respects the Messels remained resolutely German. The 1881 census shows that the family employed a German cook, Louise Muhle, to prepare their meals, while the butler in the 1891 census was from Germany, as was the live-in nurse employed for Muriel.[6] Most of the books in the library were in German, and German was certainly spoken within the Messel family home, even if they kept to English in the presence of their mother Annie. Leonard Messel's future wife Maud wrote to her mother from her first visit to the family's country home of Nymans in summer 1893: 'The German which goes on all round is awfully amusing', and we know that care was taken to ensure the Messel children could speak it properly.[7]

Perhaps the most compelling sign that the Messels did not wish to jettison their German identity was the fact that they kept their name. Many German families, Jewish and non-Jewish, had anglicized their surnames during the nineteenth century or abandoned them completely, and many more would do so in the face of rising anti-German feeling at the time of the First World War. 'Messel' may not have been such an obviously German marker as Saxe-Coburg-Gotha or Battenberg, but it was recognizably not home-grown. The decision to keep the name when so many others were changing theirs represents a conscious choice to retain a vestige of their original identity even while the family was becoming ever more English.

Leonard Messel finished his time at Eton and went up to Merton College, Oxford, in 1890. There he was a member of the coterie of dandies that sprang up around Max Beerbohm, the renowned wit and caricaturist whose initial friendship with Leonard was founded on an interest in their shared German ancestry. The two used to go canoeing on the Cherwell together, and Leonard made up a four when Beerbohm invited Lord Alfred Douglas and Oscar Wilde to visit him in his Merton rooms in May 1893.[8] This was just two years before the latter's trial and incarceration for 'gross indecency', and any mention of Wilde in the Messel household in later years used to lead to a hushed silence. Beerbohm celebrated his friendship with Leonard by giving him a portfolio of his own youthful caricatures, including a recognizable sketch of Leonard himself.

While he belonged more to the artistic than the sporting fraternity at Oxford, Leonard was an accomplished oarsman: his leadership as stroke of the Merton eight saw it rise four places in the 1892 Torpids. He was also a sociable student, being a member of the university Gridiron Club and Merton's own Myrmidon Club. Leonard's future brother-in-law Eric Parker, a contemporary at Merton, remembered years afterwards how Leonard used to entertain the Myrmidon with 'wit and merriment in song and recitation'.[9] Yet it was his early contact with the leading lights of the Aesthetic Movement that would leave the most lasting influence on Leonard's future life, actively encouraged by his even more artistic wife-to-be, Maud.

Maud Frances Sambourne was born into a solidly English family which combined financial and artistic influences, much as the Messels did. Her maternal grandfather Spencer Herapath was a successful stockbroker with his own firm, while her father Edward Linley Sambourne was for over forty years one of the principal cartoonists for *Punch*. Maud was brought up at 18 Stafford Terrace, a Kensington household filled to bursting with pictures and *objets d'art*. She was taught to sketch from an early age and inherited her father's artistic talent: her drawing of a girl dancing won first prize (and ten shillings) in June 1891 in a children's competition run by *The Gentlewoman*, while later illustrations by her were published in *Punch*, *The Minster* and the *Pall Mall Magazine*.[10]

The Sambournes had known the Messels from the time that Maud was a young girl, and she loved her first visit to Nymans, writing to her mother, 'I don't think I ever stayed in such a jolly house.'[11] Maud celebrated her eighteenth birthday there with Leonard, Ruth, Hilda, Harold and Muriel and was made to feel one of the family. While she wrote approvingly of Leonard's kindness to her and the devotion he showed his mother, there was no hint of romantic interest. A spirited young woman, Maud's early adulthood was a constant round of parties, trips to the theatre and visits to the country, and she had numerous young men who kept her feeling desirable without requiring her to choose between them.

Leonard had spent much of his time in Germany since coming down from Oxford, working in the banking sector and building up contacts that would be useful for his future career. He continued to see Maud when he was back in London, and his affection for her grew more purposeful. He duly proposed to her on 24 February 1897, with the hope of settling everything within a matter of weeks. This sent Maud crying to her mother, who noted that the 'poor child' was unhappy at having to give up her charmed life as the object of five suitors' affections in favour of marriage to just one. Maud wrote to Leonard turning down his proposal, just as she had rejected an offer of marriage from a Scottish suitor, Mr Blair, and promptly went off to stay with friends in the country.

The young Leonard Messel

Leonard persisted, visiting Maud's Stafford Terrace home on 16 May and declaring to her mother Marion that he would leave England altogether if he could not have her. Marion wrote in her diary, 'Poor boy feel v. sorry for him but it cannot be thought of for many reasons & M. does not seem to care for any of her lovers at present.'[12] What these 'many reasons' might have been was left unspoken; Marion had confided to her diary the previous year that she thought Leonard looked 'v. handsome' now that he was older, and she could hardly have wished for anyone wealthier to marry her daughter.[13] Leonard followed up the visit with a letter to Linley Sambourne himself, declaring his love for Maud and asking for a meeting to press his case. Yet Linley wrote back on 21 May saying he would not hear of Maud being engaged to Leonard; again it is not clear why.

Were Maud's parents simply protecting their daughter from being married against her will, or was there something more significant in their oblique references to Leonard's unsuitability? For an aristocratic family, marrying into 'new money' like the Messels carried a social stigma that provided nineteenth-century novelists with endless amusement, as epitomized by Miss Georgiana Longestaffe in Anthony Trollope's *The Way We Live Now*, who despairs of ever meeting anyone suitable and warns her parents that they 'must not be surprised if I take some horrid creature from the Stock Exchange'.[14] Yet the Sambournes were very far from being aristocrats: Maud's maternal grandfather had been a stockbroker himself, while her father was a cartoonist of distinctly middle-class origins. Might it have been the Messel family's Jewish roots that counted against Leonard? The same Georgiana Longestaffe appals her family when she becomes secretly engaged to Ezekiel Brehgert, a Jewish financier over twenty years her senior, and her father intervenes to prevent the marriage from going ahead. Yet, once again, it is hard to ascribe such prejudice to Maud's parents. The Sambournes enjoyed a wide circle of Jewish friends and often dined with the Levy, Cohen, Mocatta and Montefiore families, to name just the most celebrated – and if Leonard's Jewish ancestry were really such a problem it is highly unlikely that Maud's parents would have welcomed the union so readily just a few weeks later.

The Messel family's German background might have proved a greater obstacle, at a time when relations with that country had become strained as a result of German support for the Boers in South Africa. Kaiser Wilhelm II had become a hate figure in the British press when he sent a telegram to the Boer President Paul Kruger congratulating him on the successful repulse of the Jameson Raid by British irregulars at the beginning of 1896. The Kruger Telegram inflamed popular anger against Germany – hundreds of British patriots sent abusive letters to the Kaiser in person – but worse was to come in April 1897 when the British media reported that a shipment of German arms had been sent to assist the Boers. Linley Sambourne contributed a full-page cartoon of 'Germania Arming Kruger' to *Punch* for 24 April 1897, just days before Leonard visited Stafford Terrace to ask for his daughter's hand in marriage.[15] Yet, once again, it seems unlikely that this should be the cause of any serious breakdown in relations between the Sambournes and the Messels. Ludwig Messel, who had made a significant part of his fortune as a result of the British presence in South Africa, can have had little sympathy with the Kaiser's position, and two years later he donated one hundred guineas to the Mansion House fund for refugees seeking sanctuary in British South Africa from persecution at the hands of the Boers.[16]

The true reason behind Leonard's rejection at this point seems to have been a more personal matter, and the Messels rather than the Sambournes may have been to blame. Linley Sambourne's letter of 21 May 1897 telling Leonard that he could not be thought of as Maud's husband hints at some disrespect shown towards Maud and her social standing, perhaps by other members of the Messel family:

> For yourself personally I would have no reasonable objections, so far as I have knowledge of you, provided my daughter was also of the same mind. But I could allow my daughter to enter no family where there would not be even *more* than the ordinary cordial reception due to a marriage into it. This is warranted by her qualifications to say nothing of my own position in Society and the World.[17]

As Leonee Ormond has commented, this was an 'uncharacteristically pompous' reaction on Linley's part.[18] Yet the otherwise friendly tone of his letter to Leonard suggests that the disagreement was not an insuperable obstacle. His wife Marion's diary entries also reveal that there had been bad blood between the two families; yet she, too, remained sympathetic to Leonard throughout the

Christmas party at Nymans – back row (from left): Ludwig Messel, Marion and Linley Sambourne; middle row: Maud Sambourne, Annie Messel, Frank and Kate Gielgud; bottom row: Roy Sambourne, Muriel and Leonard Messel

crisis and was pleased to report that the Messels 'had all been most kind' when Maud dined with them on 23 June.[19] Five days later Leonard wrote again to Linley Sambourne seeking his permission to marry Maud, arguing that, in the weeks since he last wrote, Sambourne had 'received abundant proof that your daughter will be welcomed in the manner she deserves'. To enhance his prospects, Leonard added that he had recently been made a partner in L. Messel and Co. and was therefore earning 'a sufficient income to enable me to support a wife in a suitable way'.[20]

Whatever the upset had been, Maud was soon having a happy time staying with the Messels in the country once more. By now both sets of parents had been won over and only the practical arrangements remained to be settled, including the delicate issue of Maud's dowry. Linley Sambourne had what he called a 'disagreeable interview' with Ludwig Messel at the Devonshire Club on 13 July which lasted twenty minutes and ended with a 'sort of settlement'.[21] It must have been deeply uncomfortable for Linley to discuss Maud's future in this context, in that the Sambournes were at such a disadvantage over and against the financial power of the Messels. In a letter written six months later, when all had been settled, Linley Sambourne took pleasure in telling his wife Marion that Ludwig was 'known by everyone as the richest member of the London Stock Exchange', but this must have made the earlier discussion hopelessly one-sided.[22]

Any awkwardness seems to have been forgotten when the whole Sambourne family was invited to spend Christmas 1897 with the Messels and their friends the Gielguds at Nymans. Linley played golf and billiards with Ludwig, while Maud's brother Roy Sambourne went off cycling and shooting rabbits with Leonard. All went for long walks together, and Marion enjoyed herself immensely, writing in her diary that it was 'a very charming visit'. The only reference to any financial consideration is Marion's statement that she had never seen so many Christmas presents as were given to the servants at Nymans, but this was a positive comment on Annie Messel's generosity. The two families had become friends again, and the engagement of their two eldest children was a source of lasting joy.

Leonard and Maud's wedding finally took place at the Kensington parish church of St Mary Abbots on 28 April 1898. The bride, who was given away by her father, 'wore a charming gown of white satin with a tulle veil'. The church was filled with over two hundred guests and the reception held in the Empress Rooms of the nearby Kensington Palace Hotel, where their five hundred wedding presents were laid out on display. The happy couple then departed to Dover *en route* for Paris and a further five weeks' honeymoon in Italy.

Maud wrote to her mother from every stage of the trip, declaring herself 'so happy that there are no words fit to describe my feelings in the English language'.[23] She was aware that this marked a considerable change in her attitude to marriage from the previous year – 'I am now only too thankful that I was not a little fool in the summer and autumn' – but most of her letters are full of the fun that she and Leonard are having together, with Leonard determined to add Italian to his stock of foreign languages. The time away clearly agreed with them, as Marion made clear in her diary when they came back to London: 'Darling Maud & Lennie return fr. their wedding trip . . . both looking so well. Lennie much fatter.' The couple then travelled down to Nymans, where they were welcomed with flags, bunting and a musical tribute from the Handcross Brass Band. It was the start of a loving marriage that was to last over fifty years.

Maud's parents grew fond of Leonard, and the bond was strengthened further when Maud gave birth to the couple's first child – named Linley after her father – on 31 August 1899. By way of congratulations Linley senior put his son-in-law forward for membership of the Garrick Club and was highly offended when Leonard was blackballed. The Garrick was famously protective of its membership, often citing the founding principle of its original committee 'that it would be better that ten unobjectionable men should be excluded than one terrible bore should be admitted'. Yet most candidates put forward to be members were successfully elected, and Leonard's rejection was keenly felt.[24]

Linley Messel flanked by
his cousins Charlotte
(left) and Dulcie Loring

DAILY SKETCH, THURSDAY, MAY 13, 1915.

GAOL IS THE HOME FOR THE HUN IN WAR TIME.

DAILY SKETCH.

GUARANTEED DAILY NETT SALE MORE THAN 1,000,000 COPIES.

No. 1,927.   LONDON, THURSDAY, MAY 13, 1915.   [Registered as a Newspaper.] ONE HALFPENNY.

Clear Out The Germans, Say The People.

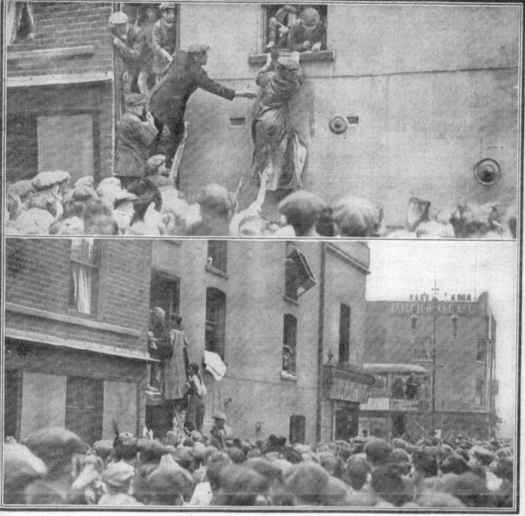

For the anti-German scenes which took place in London and all over England yesterday the German Government alone is responsible. In the words of Mr. Asquith, in the House of Commons, " No one could be surprised that after the progressive violation by the enemy of the usages of civilised war and the rules of humanity—culminating *for the moment* in the sinking of the Lusitania—there had arisen a feeling of righteous indignation among all classes in this country for which it would be difficult to find a parallel." The above pictures were taken during attacks on shops in Poplar, which was the scene of fierce anti-Teuton outbursts.—(*Daily Sketch* Photographs.)

Front page of the *Daily Sketch*, 13 May 1915

72

'Clear Out the Germans' 8

EONARD MESSEL HAD married into an artistic but solidly middle-class English family. It is striking that the Messel daughters also found spouses from established English backgrounds. Ottilie, the eldest, was first to wed. Her husband was a naval officer, Ernest Kindersley Loring, whose father had served as vicar of St Andrew's, Cobham, and whose grandfather had been the first Archdeacon of Calcutta. They were married at the Messel family church of St James's, Sussex Gardens, on 7 April 1897, at which time Ernest held the rank of lieutenant in the Royal Navy; he would later serve as captain at the Battle of Gallipoli and rise to become vice-admiral by the end of his career.[1]

The second of the Messel girls to marry was Ruth. She had fallen in love with one of Leonard's Oxford friends, Eric Parker, the son of a London solicitor. Eric had first tried his hand as a schoolmaster and was at one point even engaged as a tutor for Leonard's younger brother, Harold, but he was determined to make a career as a writer, contributing articles to *The Spectator* while working as assistant editor on the *St James's Gazette*. Ludwig Messel was concerned at the prospect of his daughter marrying into such an uncertain future but relented when Eric was appointed editor of the *Country Gentleman* in 1902. He went on to become a renowned naturalist, editing *The Field* and writing numerous books on gardening, dogs, birds, cricket and country sports. Ruth and Eric were married on 12 June 1902, again at the family church of St James's. 'The bride, who was given away by her father, wore a gown of soft white satin, beautifully trimmed with lace and chiffon, and having a train from the shoulders.'[2] The honeymoon consisted of just three days in Boulogne, after which Eric had to return to work.[3]

The third Messel daughter, Hilda, married into an equally English family, originally from Wiltshire but long established in London. Her husband-to-be was Arthur Montagu Gibbes, a professional soldier in the Northumberland Fusiliers whose father had been a fellow stockbroker with Ludwig. The Gibbes family had previously lived up the road from the Messels at 111 Westbourne Terrace, making it a simple matter for Arthur's brothers and sisters to find their way to the church of St James's, where the marriage was solemnized on 20 June 1903. After

Ruth Parker,
née Messel

their wedding Hilda and Arthur Gibbes lived in an apartment in the newly built mansion block of Washington House on Basil Street, behind Knightsbridge, but in 1914 they bought the estate of Wickenden Farm at Sharpthorne, ten miles from Nymans, and built the delightful Wickenden Manor as their country home.

Each of the girls' weddings was followed by a reception at 8 Westbourne Terrace, which was often used for entertaining. Ludwig and Annie held regular afternoon and dinner parties there, as well as summer parties and New Year's dances for the children. In keeping with other Victorian ladies, Annie held weekly 'at homes' when she would be present to receive callers from among her friends and acquaintances (her day was Monday). The tall house was laid out with the entrance hall and the dining-room on the ground floor and a double drawing-room plus a boudoir on the first floor; the upper three floors were given over to bedrooms for Ludwig and Annie, their children and, on the top floor, for the domestic servants, while the basement contained the butler's pantry, the kitchen, the housekeeper's parlour and the footman's room.

The sumptuous décor of the drawing-room is described in an early inventory of 1881: a suite of flowered amber satin curtains at the windows, echoed by a pair of crimson velvet portières lined with blue silk over the doors; five Persian carpets, with a pair of cabriole Louis XVI couches and numerous other settees, lounging and mahogany-framed chairs covered variously with brocaded silk, damask or Utrecht velvet; a rosewood grand piano accompanied by a pair of music stands in the same material with panelled doors; and several inlaid satinwood Pembroke tables, card tables or other tables for occasional use. The Messels were not immune to the Victorian craze for blue and white porcelain, and the drawing-room contained four satinwood cabinets displaying their collection, together with a Florentine satinwood and marquetry enclosed cabinet and two satinwood escritoires. The room was lit by a pair of twelve-light chandeliers, front and back, as well as two further five-light girandoles. The whole effect was lovely, according to Marion Sambourne, and the parties given in the house could certainly be jolly: one dinner hosted by the Messels extended to fourteen courses, with wines.[4]

The most vivid indication we have of private life at 8 Westbourne Terrace comes from the pen of Ludwig and Annie's second daughter-in-law. While their elder son Leonard had married into the Sambourne family, the younger Harold had fallen in love with a penniless American, Leonora Putnam Gibson, whom he had met while visiting his sister Ruth when she was studying German in Hamburg. The object of Harold's affection, known to all as Nonie, could trace her pedigree back to the earliest English settlers of the Massachusetts Bay Colony. Her more immediate family had suffered financially in the Panic of 1893, leading to the collapse of her father's skate business and his death from pneumonia shortly afterwards. Nonie's mother was forced to run a boarding-house in Manhattan to make ends meet and clearly had a hard time of it. Yet through their German neighbours she arranged for the talented Nonie to continue her musical studies in Hamburg from the age of thirteen, and it is there that she met her future husband.

Harold first proposed marriage when Nonie was barely eighteen years old. He had followed his brother Leonard to Eton and to Merton College, Oxford, but had yet to embark on a career, so Nonie insisted he should establish himself before they could think of married life together. Neither of the two families approved of the union in any case, and Harold was packed off to spend a year in Australia in the hope that the young lovers might forget one another. He left Southampton on the German ocean liner SS *Barbarossa* on 10 January 1900, passed through the Suez Canal a fortnight later and arrived in Sydney on 26 February, having spent almost seven weeks at sea. Yet the bond between him and Nonie was strong enough to survive the year's separation, and their families were won round. The couple were married in the grand surroundings of St Agnes Chapel on New York's Upper West Side on 18 November 1903.

Hilda Gibbes, née Messel

Nonie was remembered as a 'very serene personality' as well as 'a brilliant pianist and a witty, amusing companion with a quiet, gentle charm'.[5] She continued to write to her mother in New York during the early years of her marriage, just as she had done while studying in Hamburg, and it is thanks to her letters that we have a contemporary description of the life led by the Messels at the family home in Westbourne Terrace. It is worth quoting at length Nonie's first impressions of meeting her in-laws, especially her father-in-law Ludwig

Above
Harold Messel

Right
Nonie Messel,
née Gibson

Messel, when she and Harold arrived in England the month after their wedding. Here is her account from the moment they were met at the station in London by Harold's mother and his sister Hilda to be taken to their temporary lodgings in Sussex Gardens:

> I liked them all from the start and there was nothing strained or awkward. Hilda is charming, very pretty, exquisitely dressed with perfect manners and general breeding and the sweetest quietest kindest little thing in the world, not a butterfly at all in the American sense.
>
> Harold's mother is a very dear old lady with a sense of humour. They none of them speak above a whisper and laugh like a faint little ripple. They are unconsciously and innately lady-like.
>
> We were asked to dinner directly and 'Mama-in-law' sent over her maid 'Mould' to unpack for me which she did beautifully stowing everything away in tissue paper to guard against the fog and enthusing all the time over the perfect

way all the things had been packed. It was a masterpiece, dear, not a ruffle was crumpled of all the evening dresses.

I wore my blue and ruby over to dinner as it was *en famille*. As yet I had not encountered his Imperial Majesty, you must remember. But he was on the staircase when we entered and Harold brought me forward solemnly. After having each distinguished ourselves by saying 'How do you do' conversation flagged when the old man remarked 'I suppose we ought to kiss' but made no move. I forthwith up and kissed him without any more ado and then we were interrupted by someone coming in. Harold had been called to the telephone and missed the choice scene but he declares that he would willingly have given £5 to have been a witness.

The old gentleman conducted me in state to the drawing room where 'Ma' was standing with Hilda in magnificent evening dress, very quiet though, black with lots of handsome lace and exquisite pearls and diamonds. A footman announced dinner and we trooped down. A butler with the aid of a second butler served us the meagre repast of nine courses, conversation flourished, there was quite a cross-fire of repartee and I had quite a 'heart-to-heart' with 'Pa'. I like him best of all. Under several layers of his formality there is a genuine personality. I played for them in the evening on rather a 'rattly' piano. At 10 o'clock the ordeal was over. It *was* an ordeal but not appalling.

Nonie's first experience of Ludwig Messel echoes that of others who found him taciturn and forbidding to begin with. The fact that she was fluent in German as a result of her many years' living in Hamburg must have given her an advantage in penetrating his outer shell. The other striking feature of life in the Messel household which Nonie remarks on is the number of domestic servants employed in the household; as she writes playfully in her first report to her mother: 'I was taken back to tea which was handed round by two butlers – it being too hard for one.' Within a few years Nonie and Harold would find themselves employing just as many servants in their own household.

The Messel family had found success in their adopted country, but it was to prove a fragile security. This time it was not their Jewish heritage that marked them out as targets but the fact that they were German. Anti-German feeling had been building steadily over the decades prior to the First World War as a result of competition from cheap German goods and labour; German support for the Boers against the British in South Africa soured relations further, while the Tirpitz Plan under which Germany resolved to create a maritime fleet to challenge Britain's Royal Navy raised the stakes to a new level. The publication of Erskine Childers's 1903 novel *The Riddle of the Sands* caused a sensation with its uncovering of a German plot to invade England and spawned a new generation of 'invasion literature' that left no doubt as to the threat posed by German militarism.[6]

As the spectre of war drew closer, Germans living in Britain were viewed as potential imperial agents, feeding back strategic information to their headquarters in Berlin. William Le Queux's best-selling novel *Spies of the Kaiser* claimed that 'a vast army of German spies' existed in England and was already engaged in preparing for a German invasion. Spy mania spread rapidly among the British populace, with Le Queux's readers sending in so many reports of Germans acting suspiciously that the government set up a committee of inquiry to ascertain the true level of threat. The arrest and conviction of several genuine spies working for German naval espionage in the years after 1911 stoked the flames of suspicion, so that by August 1914 feelings were at fever pitch.[7] Ludwig Messel was himself caught up in the popular paranoia, with locals in Sussex spreading rumours about his role as a German agent keeping tabs on his neighbours from the new tower he had built at Nymans.

The outbreak of the First World War heightened the tension still further. There were scattered attacks on German businesses in east London and the Yorkshire town of Keighley during August 1914, followed by more disturbances in south London two months later. Yet the trigger for serious violence came with the sinking of the passenger liner *Lusitania* by a German U-boat off the coast of Ireland on Friday 7 May 1915. Holed by a single torpedo, the *Lusitania* went down within eighteen minutes with the loss of 1,198 lives, many of them women and children.

The killing of so many hundreds of non-combatants provoked revulsion and outrage worldwide. Reaction was swiftest in Liverpool, home to the *Lusitania* and to almost all the crew members who lost their lives in the attack. By the end of the weekend a crowd of 2,000–3,000 people was roaming the streets of the city attacking German shops and throwing their contents into the street. The rioting quickly spread to nearby Birkenhead, Bootle, Wallasey and Seacombe, where a fountain-pen factory believed to be German-run was attacked. Once all the German shops had been ransacked, the mob's attention turned to houses where Germans were known to live. Manchester and Salford were soon experiencing their own riots, with German butchers, jewellers, hotels and private homes coming under concerted attack from a crowd that numbered 5,000. The *Manchester Courier* described the unrest as 'without parallel in the history of the city', adding ominously, 'The windows of scores of shops were broken, and the occupants in many cases had to be smuggled away secretly by the police lest they should be subjected to personal violence.'[8]

By Tuesday the rioting had reached London. The East End witnessed the most intense violence as angry crowds descended on German shops and homes, but disturbances sprang up in so many parts of the capital that London was turned into 'one vast riot area', according to the *Daily Mail*. 'Great crowds, in some

Anti-German rioting in
Poplar, May 1915

cases numbering 3,000 to 4,000 people, hunted their districts for shops owned
by Germans and wrecked them. The result is that today there is hardly a shop
with a German name on the fascia board which has a whole window pane.'[9] The
press did little to disguise its support for the rioters: the front page of the *Daily
Sketch* for 13 May carried the headline 'Clear Out the Germans, Say the People'.
As the leading historian of the German experience at this time concluded, 'No
national or racial minority in twentieth-century Britain has endured hostility as
destructive and widespread as that faced by Germans during the Great War.'[10]

At the height of the rioting, the celebrated playwright Sir Arthur Pinero sent a
letter to *The Times* calling on all naturalized German-born subjects in prominent
positions to make a public declaration of loyalty to the King, together with 'an
expression of their detestation of Germany's methods of warfare'. The letter left
it up to the individuals concerned how best to declare their commitment to their
adopted nation but concluded with a thinly veiled threat to any who failed to do so.

What I would emphasize, however, is that continued silence on their part lays
them open to the supposition that, thinking that the fate of England is hanging in
the balance, they are – to use the common phrase – sitting on the gate. A word of
warning, therefore, is neither gratuitous nor unfriendly. The temper of this country,
slow to rouse, is becoming an ugly one. The gate may fall from its hinges.[11]

The response was immediate, with several prominent figures of German
extraction penning 'loyalty letters' that were published in *The Times* over the
following week. Within ten days 1,800 people of German or Austrian origin
had 'signed a memorial to the King protesting their loyalty to the British Throne
and their abhorrence of the barbarous acts of the German Government in the
conduct of the war'.[12] There is no record of either Ludwig or Rudolph Messel
sending in loyalty letters, even though both men were severely affected by the
hostility directed towards German-born individuals during these years. Ludwig
suffered a heart attack in 1913 and withdrew to his country home of Nymans
with depression, his health in such decline that he now had to be pushed round
the garden in a bath chair.[13]

The new wave of xenophobia hit even closer to home for Ludwig when the
Stock Exchange turned against its German-born members following the sinking
of the *Lusitania* and barred them from entry for the duration of the war. Ludwig
had worked at the Stock Exchange for forty years and had made England his home
for fifty. His sons had gone to the most quintessentially English public school and
were both enlisted in the British Army, even though neither would see active
service overseas. His daughters had married into respectable English families,
and he was grandfather to sixteen English grandchildren. Yet he had retained
his German identity alongside British nationality, and the conflict between his
native and adopted countries caused him immeasurable personal distress. Ludwig
Messel died on 21 July 1915 at Nymans, the country estate he had built up as proof
of his family's Englishness. He was sixty-eight. The coroner's report ascribes his
death to atheroma with cardiac dilatation and degeneration. The family version
is that he died of a broken heart.

Ludwig's brother Rudolph was similarly affected. He had lived and worked
at his firm in Silvertown for forty years, but now 'his health gave way under
the excessive strain of the times' and he was forced to go into retirement.[14] The
method he pioneered for producing oleum had been turned to military ends in the
manufacture of explosives for use against his native Germany, and this intensified
the stress he already experienced as a first-generation German immigrant in
Britain. Worse was to come before the end of the war with the news that their
brother Alfred's only son, Ludwig Georg Alfred Messel, had been killed in
action on 30 May 1918 fighting in the German army on the Western Front.[15] The

young Ludwig had visited his English cousins at Nymans in the summer of 1910 and now lost his life fighting against the very forces in which they were enlisted. Dr Rudolph Messel, fellow of the Royal Society, died on 18 April 1920 in his chambers at 147 Victoria Street, aged seventy-two.

In his classic study of the industrial revolution, *Industry and Empire*, Eric Hobsbawm highlighted the role played by immigrant entrepreneurs in bringing dynamism to a British economy that was showing unmistakable signs of decline by the beginning of the twentieth century. Among the types he identified as responsible for this injection of new energy were German-Jewish financiers and German scientists working in the chemicals industry.[16] Ludwig Messel was a representative of the former category, Dr Rudolph Messel of the latter. Yet even in death there would be one last reminder that the first generation of Messel migrants remained outsiders. The vicar of St Mark's, Staplefield, felt unable to allow Ludwig a final resting place in the consecrated ground of his churchyard on the grounds that he was a 'Lutheran Jew'. Instead, Ludwig was buried alongside his sister Eugenie and her husband Eugene de la Penha in the multi-faith All Souls Cemetery at Kensal Green in north-west London. His brother Rudolph was buried next to him. Ludwig's wife Annie, who died on 7 December 1920, shares her husband's grave.

Ludwig Messel in later years

Summer border in the
Wall Garden at Nymans

Nymans 9

THE COUNTRY ESTATE of Nymans lies to the south of the Sussex village of Handcross, just up the hill from Staplefield on the edge of the High Weald. Originally known as Nynians after its fourteenth-century owner Philip Nynian, the estate belonged to the old Sussex family of Gatland from the fifteenth to seventeenth centuries, but it does not appear to have been rich agricultural land. Prior to the introduction of modern farming practices, the poor quality of the soil meant that this part of the Weald was mostly associated with timber production and the breeding of rabbits. Indeed, the owner of Nymans in the 1720s is recorded as being involved in rabbit husbandry, and it was the son of another warrener who eventually sold the estate for £665 to Thomas Poynton Cooper of Brighton in 1823.[1]

This sale marks the moment when Nymans first became the rural estate of a wealthy townsman rather than an agricultural holding, as Thomas Cooper had already made his money as proprietor of a sugar factory in Whitechapel. The estate was sold to the Brighton solicitor Thomas Hill in 1836 for £1,200 and then again three years later to his brother-in-law George Harrington, owner of the Preston brewery in Brighton. Harrington enlarged the estate in the eighteen years up to his death in 1857; witness the far higher price of £18,500 paid for it the following year by William Carr of Bayswater. Carr lived at Nymans with his second wife and two sons from his previous marriage, a son and daughter from his second marriage and a teenage nephew. The 1861 census lists thirteen servants in the household, not counting gardeners.

Nymans passed to Carr's trustees on his death in July 1863, and they saw to it that a full prospectus was compiled prior to its sale by auction on 19 October. This prospectus describes Nymans as a 'choice residential estate, comprising a most substantially built moderate-sized family mansion, in thorough repair, commanding extensive and beautiful views over the South Downs, from Chanctonbury Ring nearly to Hastings, and surrounded by lawns and pleasure grounds, all in perfect order, with excellent kitchen garden, stabling, coach houses, riding house, and other usual outbuildings'. The interior of the house is described in detail. The ground floor consists of large dining- and drawing-rooms, each with

The Regency house at
Nymans as shown in
the 1863 prospectus

bay windows looking out on to the lawn, as well as a boudoir and a library; the
upper floor comprises nine bedrooms, three dressing-rooms, a school room, three
nursery rooms, a bathroom 'completely fitted for Hot, Cold, and Shower Baths,
with Water Closet attached' plus two further lavatories; the extensive servants'
quarters are listed separately. A fine lithograph included with the prospectus
shows the ivy-clad Regency villa situated at the end of a broad carriage drive and
framed by two semi-mature trees: a monkey puzzle and a Morinda spruce. To
underline that this was a property designed for the enjoyment of the gentry, the
lady of the house is depicted strolling across the lawn in bonnet and parasol, while
a gardener tends the grass.[2]

The freehold estate of Nymans was transferred to Captain John Dearden on 25
June 1864 for the sum of £19,000. In May 1860 he had married Henrietta Maria
Edwards, the eldest daughter of Colonel Sir Henry Edwards, in the society church
of St George's, Hanover Square, and the rapid arrival of three children meant that
the couple were soon searching for a larger home. Dearden had enlarged the estate
to just over 400 acres by the time he sold it to Ludwig Messel on 23 December
1890. Yet for all the work which Dearden put into the property, the sum Ludwig
paid for Nymans was £20,000, only a thousand pounds more than it had cost in
1864. This reflects the dramatic decline in the value of land across Britain during
the final quarter of the nineteenth century, as prices for agricultural produce
tumbled and the face of the countryside began to change for ever.[3]

What led the German-Jewish immigrant Ludwig Messel to buy a 400-acre
estate in the heart of rural West Sussex? On one level, having a country retreat
outside London was a natural ambition for those who could afford it. Most

middle-class Londoners tried to escape the smog and smells of the capital for at least part of the year, and the Messels were no exception, regularly taking holidays at Ramsgate or Eastbourne. It should also be remembered that Nymans in the 1890s was in a much more rural setting than it is today. Turnpike roads connecting the metropolis to the fashionable resort of Brighton had made the trip to the coast far more practicable, and the advent of the railway in the 1840s cut the journey time in half again. Yet most Londoners were heading straight for the seaside, not stopping off at sleepy Sussex stations such as Balcombe, Crawley or Three Bridges. Until the advent of the motor car in the twentieth century, the roads around Nymans lay quiet for much of the day, with just the occasional horse-drawn wagon or dog cart to break the silence. 'This will surely always be a remote, unspoiled, unbuilt-over part of Sussex,' was Ludwig's assumption. 'How could it be otherwise, so far from the railway as it is?'[4]

In addition to the attractions of peace and quiet, Ludwig was a devoted family man and prized the idea of having a property big enough to accommodate not only his children but the grandchildren he soon hoped to have. This devotion to family was a tangible aspect of his German-Jewish heritage, felt all the more keenly as a result of losing his own father when still a boy. Ludwig cherished the time he was able to spend with his children, as shown by photographs of him boating with them on the lake at Nymans or otherwise joining in the fun. Posed *carte de visite* portraits in family albums show Ludwig, Annie and their two eldest children dressed up in costumes from early Renaissance Germany – a reference to the Messel family history and an indication that the gruff and reserved Ludwig was not above indulging in the Victorian passion for fancy dress. The English country house had been conceived afresh in the late nineteenth century as a private space in which to retreat from public and commercial pressures. Ludwig's devotion to his wife and children inspired him to seek out a property in which he could enjoy the warmth of family life to its fullest.

On top of his family aspirations, the acquisition of Nymans was the clearest possible statement that Ludwig had succeeded as a first-generation immigrant in his adopted country. Nothing could be more English than becoming a member of the landed gentry, and few individuals who made their fortunes in the Victorian era were able to resist the 'aura of territorial dominion' that came with purchasing a rural estate.[5] For anyone of German-Jewish heritage, owning a country house held a deeper significance, in that it spoke of that security of tenure which had for so long been elusive in a German context, where most Jews had been forbidden to own property at all. Purchasing the country estate of Nymans was a statement that the Messels were here to stay.

Yet there was no automatic route to being socially accepted as a foreigner in the English countryside, as the city-born Ludwig would have found in rural West

Sussex. His strong German accent marked him out as an alien presence as soon as he opened his mouth, while his artistic inclinations set him apart from many of his neighbours. Ludwig cared little for the traditional country pursuits of hunting, shooting and fishing that bound the landed classes together and defined them as a social group over and against the landless. Yet an active interest in such activities was expected of any landowner, as underlined by the prospectus for Nymans when Ludwig bought it in 1890.

> A special feature of the estate are the splendidly matured woodlands, which, being well watered, afford every facility for the breeding, rearing, and preservation of game . . . Some of the best trout fishing in the county is to be had in a large lake teeming with fine trout and in a stream intersecting the estate. The woods are traversed by beautifully kept rides, making them particularly easy for shooting, an idea of the quality of which is afforded by the fact that the annual bag averages upwards of 1,000 head.[6]

Ludwig's son Leonard was a member of the Flyfishers' Club and used to hire holiday cottages in Ireland and Scotland so that he could try the local rivers; he would often head down to the lake at Nymans to spend a couple of hours in solitary sport as soon as he returned from a day's work in London. Leonard's son Linley favoured shooting, keeping annual records of the number of pheasant, partridge, woodcock, hare and rabbit he killed during each season at Nymans and elsewhere. Blood sports did not hold the same attraction for Ludwig as they would to future generations of the Messel family brought up in the English traditions. His passport into rural society would come through the more refined activity of gardening.

Ludwig Messel made his first public appearance in Handcross society on Monday 20 July 1891 at the annual gala of the local lodge of the Independent Order of Oddfellows, the mutual welfare society founded at the start of the nineteenth century.[7] The gala began with a meeting at the Red Lion public house before moving in procession to the principal residences of the area, led by the Cuckfield Town Band. Over a hundred people then sat down to dinner in a marquee next to the inn, after which they relaxed into their business with a series of toasts led by the local Justice of the Peace, Captain Lister, and the rector of Slaugham, the Reverend R.A. Watson. Ludwig, who 'met with a hearty reception on his first appearance at a public gathering at Handcross', proposed the toast to the Army, Navy and Auxiliary Forces with a joke at the expense of his own non-military background. He further expressed his admiration for the volunteers who gave up so much of their free time to training – a discipline that his own sons would soon embrace in the following years.

The Messels quickly established themselves in the area around Handcross, making Nymans available to the local community for functions, including regular dinners for the Royal Sussex Volunteers. The Staplefield village school held its annual treat at Nymans on 19 August 1891, with games and prizes for racing: 'After the little ones had partaken of a hearty meal they again returned to the park, when some very useful presents were distributed by Mr and Mrs Messel and family, not one child having to go without.'[8] Just what a 'useful' present might consist of is made clear in the report of the children's treat at Nymans the following summer.

> On Saturday last the children attending Miss Ruth Messel's Sunday School class, together with the children on the estate, were entertained by that lady in the Park, where all sorts of amusements were provided, not least amongst them being the donkey riding. About 5 p.m. a capital tea was laid on the lawn, which all seemed to do justice to. Returning to the park after tea, a series of athletic sports were then engaged in, prizes being given to the winners. About 7 p.m. all were collected on the lawn, each one receiving some useful present, such as needle cases, work baskets, &c. After giving cheers for Miss Messel and Mr and Mrs Messel the happy party separated, all having thoroughly enjoyed their afternoon's treat.[9]

It is interesting to note that Ruth Messel was already teaching her own Sunday school class, although she had only just celebrated her eighteenth birthday at the beginning of August 1892. Sunday schools were no longer as important a source of education in the late Victorian era as they had once been, but teaching in them was still considered a suitable activity for unmarried daughters from the landed classes. Indeed, the Messels adopted the traditional behaviour of the landed gentry so successfully that by the time the local children were back at Nymans for their annual jamboree in 1901 Ludwig was referred to in the local press as 'the Squire of Staplefield'.[10] Yet he was essentially a private man who felt more comfortable in family surroundings than in public life, and he never took any part in the formal running of local affairs. It was primarily the women of the Messel family – not hampered by Ludwig's German accent – who were involved locally in charitable works, as also in the life of the church. Ludwig and Annie's two younger daughters Hilda and Muriel were complimented on their decoration of the lectern

Annie and Ludwig Messel at Nymans in later years

at St Mark's, Staplefield, for Harvest Festival in October 1902; their father was thanked for sending flowers, fruit and vegetables, although there is no suggestion that he attended any of the services.[11]

The Messel girls were spirited young women, active in more than just religious pursuits. Ruth and Hilda played the parts of two schoolgirls in the amateur performance of Maurice Johnston's operetta *Agatha* at the Cuckfield Drill Hall in January 1895. According to the local press report of the performance, the singing of the two sisters – 'irresistible in sun bonnets and bye-play' – won them loud applause.[12] Ruth took part in the annual women's cricket matches organized by the Sturdy family at the nearby estate of Paxhill Park, even if the record suggests that she did not share the natural aptitude of her brother Harold, who had been a keen cricketer from an early age.[13] Ludwig himself provided the Handcross Cricket Club with free use of a large field at Nymans on the club's revival in 1901, for which he was accorded a vote of thanks at its end-of-season dinner; in time there was even an annual cricket match instituted between Handcross and the Nymans estate.[14] Village cricket was an egalitarian sport when compared to the aristocratic pursuits of hunting, shooting and fishing, in that it pitched the social classes against one another on the same terrain. Ludwig also provided a field for the Handcross Stoolball Club inaugurated in June 1910, stoolball being the ancient form of air cricket still played in Sussex today.[15]

Yet it was Ludwig's eldest son Leonard who made the greatest name for himself in Sussex society, as a performer of comic songs in the concerts that peppered the social round. The brio with which he threw himself into these theatrical renditions is a surprise to those who know of his tight-lipped character in later years, but local press reports leave no doubt that he was a popular sensation. His repertoire extended to musical-hall numbers and sketches from contemporary songwriters such as Richard Corney Grain and Albert Chevalier. One of Leonard's favourites, the 'Four-Oss Sharrybang', serves as a fine example of the type of song involved, and readers are encouraged to seek out the modern recording made by Brian Cant and Toni Arthur to get a sense of its comedic value.[16] Harold Messel also played his part in the local talent shows, as when he recited Robert Ganthony's comic poem 'The Single Hair' at a concert in aid of the Handcross Band on 29 December 1896.[17] But it was Leonard who stole the show when it came to lighting up the local evening entertainments.

These activities, together with the society balls and dances attended by the Messel children, reflect only those times of the year when the family was in Sussex and not at their London residence or abroad. Nor was it all fun and games in the country. Ludwig was an active participant in the inquiry held at the Red Lion by the Cuckfield Rural District Council in May 1905 into the vexed issue of sewage disposal. Forty years after Joseph Bazalgette's monumental sewerage system had conquered the problem in London, the residents of Handcross were still pumping the contents of their cesspools into buckets which were then emptied into an open cart and dumped on to a field at the edge of the village, far too close for comfort for the nearest residents. Ludwig's intervention shows just how exercised he was over the failure of the local authorities to keep up with the latest sanitary practices.

> Mr Messel said it was an easy matter for those living ten miles away to talk philosophically about the matter, but those who were on the spot and experienced the disagreeable state of things which prevailed found it difficult to do so. The other day he started out for a walk accompanied by his daughter, and he was literally driven back by the smell from the pumping at a cottage opposite his drive. He did not suggest that they should have an expensive drainage scheme. It was not necessary in a small village like Handcross. What they might do was to purchase a better cart – one that was hermetically sealed. Such carts were used on the Continent, and it was impossible to detect any smell from them.[18]

This practical solution was approved at a meeting of the two parish councils responsible for Handcross, doubtless encouraged by Ludwig's offer to contribute £50 of his own money towards the cost of the new cart.[19] In a parallel case he gave evidence in support of the application made in October 1907 to reduce the speed limit on the main road as it passed through Handcross from 20 miles per hour to 10 miles per hour – an early attempt to introduce traffic calming in the face of concerted opposition from the motoring clubs. To cries of 'hear-hear' from other local residents, Ludwig argued before the inquiry that 'there was not a more dangerous corner in Sussex than that where the main road branched in two directions before going down Handcross Hill', adding that he 'often found it dangerous to go out of his front gates, and he dared not take a dog on the road at all'.[20] He was not against motoring itself, as shown by the fact that he had recently bought a luxury CGV 20-horsepower double phaeton to go alongside his two existing Daimlers.[21] His plea for road safety was inspired by the tragedy that had taken place on the morning of 12 July the previous year, when a bus carrying a party of thirty-six day-trippers from Orpington veered out of control and crashed at the bottom of Handcross Hill, killing ten of its occupants and seriously injuring many more. Ludwig was one of the first on the scene to witness the carnage of what still remains the worst road traffic accident in Sussex history, and he later donated £20 in sympathy to the relief fund set up for the relatives of those killed.[22] The application to introduce a speed limit of 10 miles per hour to Handcross was successful, and it came into effect on 14 December 1907.[23]

Anbau zum Landhaus Nymanns bei Crawley (England); erbaut von Professor A. Messel in Berlin.

1. Vorderseite.

(Siehe auch Tafel 18.)

Architektonische Rundschau 1896. 3.   Verlag von J. Engelhorn in Stuttgart.

Alfred Messel's design for
the extension at Nymans

House and Garden 10

LUDWIG AND ANNIE made Nymans their home, and they would spend more and more of their time there over the years. Yet soon after their arrival in 1890 the house was deemed too small for the prospects of an expanding Messel family, and Ludwig looked to extend it. The initial choice for the commission was the architect Leonard Stokes, in his early thirties when he was approached by Ludwig but already president of the Architectural Association. Stokes produced a design which recast the Regency villa of Nymans in neo-Jacobean style with a modest tower and three gabled bays on the south front, as well as a new east wing with a billiard room on its ground floor. The design was exhibited at the Royal Academy and published in the *Architectural Review* for 1891, but Stokes never realized the project. The architect was known for his violent temper and for falling out with clients. Equally, Ludwig may not have wished to remodel his country seat as an Old English manor house; that transformation would have to await the next generation of Messel owners in the years following the First World War.

Ludwig instead turned to his architect brother Alfred in Germany with a request that he design an extension to the house at Nymans in the continental European style. The two preparatory drawings that survive show how literally Alfred interpreted his brief.[1] Echoing the fashion set by family villas on the Wannsee outside Berlin, Alfred added a four-storey tower with lantern and viewing platform on the south side of the house, providing a central architectural focus and a visual link between the original building and the new wing. It was this structure that Ludwig was accused of using as a spy tower when anti-German feeling reached new heights at the start of the First World War. The upper floor of the extension was given over to a large billiard room in which Ludwig installed an electric organ with self-playing pianola attachment. Such organs would become 'the ultimate status symbol of the Edwardian country house', according to Clive Aslet, and Ludwig's grandchildren would listen to the one at Nymans for hours on end.[2]

Several more bedrooms were added and the conservatories on the west side of the house enlarged so that they resembled full-sized orangeries. The extension itself protruded into the garden, while the wooden balconies on the first floor and the peculiar sloping roof gave it the impression of a displaced Alpine chalet. The bizarre ensemble this created with the Renaissance tower and the original Regency villa left the house something of an 'architectural freak', as Ludwig's grandson Rudolph Putnam Messel remembered later. His cousin Oliver Messel was more forthright, calling it 'exceptionally hideous'.[3] The overall mish-mash goes some way towards explaining why Maud Messel demanded a full redesign when she went to live at Nymans twenty-five years later.

While the newly extended house was undeniably large enough, it does not appear to have been fitted out with all the modern conveniences expected at the beginning of the twentieth century. Harold Messel's American-born wife Nonie, writing to her mother after spending Christmas at Nymans in 1903, was perplexed at the absence of basic amenities: 'Only one bathroom in the house! and no gas or electric light. I have twelve candles to light my bedroom, and the bath is brought in in the morning with huge jugs of hot water.' These were not the only privations. While the 1863 prospectus for Nymans had boasted of an 'excellent apparatus' for warming the entrance hall, staircase and other communal areas, the Messel family gave no quarter as far as heating was concerned. Nonie started up a lament over the penetrating cold of English homes: 'England is charming, but they don't heat the houses. Now I have chilblains, which are horrid.' Those brought up on cold interiors did not necessarily share Nonie's bleak assessment: Leonard's wife-to-be Maud wrote to her mother that she loved being at Nymans because 'it is one of the few houses in which I really feel snug and comfortable'.[4]

Whatever its creature comforts, Nymans was often used for entertaining family and close friends. Recalling his boyhood visits, Oliver Messel pictured his kindly grandmother Annie at Nymans as she 'presided at a tea table of splendour, with additional tiered stands laden with almond macaroons, a vast array of sandwiches, rich cakes & innumerable goodies, for innumerable grandchildren'.[5] Ludwig and Annie particularly valued Christmas at Nymans as a time for bringing the Messel clan together. By way of an example, they were joined for dinner on Christmas Day 1908 by Ludwig's brother Rudolph; the three adult de la Penha children of Ludwig's sister Eugenie; Leonard, Maud and her parents Linley and Marion Sambourne; Harold and Nonie Messel; Ottilie and Ernest Loring, together with a Fräulein Kordt from Dresden; Hilda and Arthur Gibbes, plus Arthur's sister Beatrice; and Ludwig's youngest daughter Muriel.[6] With charades following dinner, Marion Sambourne pronounced the whole evening 'very amusing'; her husband Linley recorded in his diary that Nonie Messel had acted out the charade for 'Winchester' by climbing into a chest.

If the house was for fun and family, the garden at Nymans was a serious undertaking from the start. The High Weald was fast becoming known for its specialist gardens as new owners set about populating their estates with exotic trees and shrubs brought back from the latest plant-hunting expeditions to Japan, China and the Himalayas. The influential horticulturalist William Robinson had bought nearby Gravetye Manor in 1885 and was already turning it into an example of the naturalistic planting that he had espoused in his book *The Wild Garden*. Robinson would become a close friend of the Messels and a regular visitor to Nymans. The botanist and big-game hunter Sir Edmund Loder had taken over the estate of Leonardslee just four miles to the west of Nymans and established a pinetum there along with a rockery, a rose garden, a rhododendron park, an orchid house, a sub-tropical garden and even a wildlife park with wallaby, emu, beaver and Sika deer. He, too, became a close friend of Ludwig's, encouraging him in his own horticultural adventures. Sir Edmund's younger brother Wilfred inherited the family home of High Beeches, the neighbouring estate to Nymans, and developed a woodland garden along similar lines to those at Leonardslee. The naturalist Frederick Du Cane Godman created his own garden at South Lodge in Horsham; the *Rhododendron* 'Old Cornish Red' he planted with his wife reputedly has the largest spread of any rhododendron tree in the country today.[7]

Ludwig was deeply attracted by the prospect of joining this society, and Nymans offered the perfect opportunity. Perched on a hilltop 500 feet above sea level, the garden enjoys a microclimate that protects it from the frosts experienced by other estates just a couple of miles away. With the additional shelter of the trees that Ludwig would plant for protection against the north-east wind, Nymans provided exceptional conditions in which to raise plants normally considered too tender to survive an English winter. The garden's soil, a sandy loam with good drainage, may not have been suitable for traditional agriculture, but it was perfect for modern horticulture: fertile and acidic, it was particularly conducive to the cultivation of the new varieties of magnolia, camellia and rhododendron that were being brought back to Britain by plant hunters and which formed such a feature of the colourful gardens of the Weald.

Conditions at Nymans were ideal for horticultural experiments, but Ludwig still needed a professional plantsman to take the lead on design, propagation and cultivation. He was to find the perfect partner in James Comber, who started as head gardener in September 1895, six months before his thirtieth birthday, and who would remain at Nymans for the rest of his long life. Comber was thirteen when he got his first job as a garden boy at Wakehurst Place, the large estate to the east of Nymans, and was taken on by the London nursery of James Veitch and Sons in 1888. The Veitch business specialized in rare plants brought back to Britain by expeditions to Asia and the Americas, and Comber was exposed to some of the most exotic introductions of the day. After jobs at country gardens in Northamptonshire, Suffolk and Wiltshire, Comber returned to Sussex as head

James Comber, head
gardener at Nymans,
with his team

gardener of Bignor Park at Pulborough on the South Downs. Two years later he
took up the post of head gardener at Nymans.[8]

Comber's first responsibility in his new position was to ensure that the kitchen
garden was functioning properly to keep the estate supplied with fresh fruit and
vegetables. He was interviewed by the magazine *Garden Life* in June 1905, and
the resulting article opens with a tour of the fruit trees grown next to Comber's
house.[9] After a brief discussion of the latest varieties of blackcurrants, redcurrants
and strawberries grown at Nymans, the interview continues with a list of the
various glasshouses used to grow melons, tomatoes, figs, strawberries, nectarines,
greengages and grapes. There is a brief visit to the peach house, in which Comber
had planted a selection of new trees in his first year after coming to Nymans,
whose fruit, he proclaims, 'is well up to exhibition standard'. The head gardener
remained proud of his peaches throughout his life: Ludwig's great-granddaughter
Victoria Messel remembers being warned by Comber not to help herself to any, as
he had counted every one.

With Comber in post, Ludwig could embark on the development of the garden
in earnest. The two men began by planting a pinetum on the slope to the north of
the house, adding shelter by means of an outer ring of quick-growing spruce and

populating the inner field with many other conifers, including fourteen varieties of *Thuja orientalis*, eleven varieties of *Tsuga* (hemlock), numerous sequoia, cedar, juniper and cypress and at least fifteen different species of pine. A summer house was constructed for the pinetum; now resituated next to the entrance of the garden and known as the Messel Temple, it contains a plaque in memory of Ludwig's brother Alfred, although the suggestion that the Berlin-based architect designed the building is unsubstantiated.[10]

To the east, Ludwig planned a fuller arboretum which would feature a wide range of specialist trees including tupelo, sweet gum, American lime and nine different species of eucalyptus. A lime avenue swept round to the house from the bottom of the arboretum, with a laurel walk running in parallel on which successive generations of Messel children would learn to ride their bicycles in years to come. Below the Prospect, a balustraded terrace that looks out over the park, the ground falls away past the Lily Pond to wildflower meadows, woodland and the lake – a favourite spot for Messel family picnics in the summer and ice-skating in the harsh winters.

Ludwig next turned his attention to the garden around the house itself. To the south of the main lawn he designed a heath garden with fifty species of heather. This was an innovation: save for a small area near King William's Temple at Kew, which gave Ludwig the inspiration, Nymans was the first heath garden to be planted anywhere in England. Next to it the landscape gardeners Pulham and Sons (who had worked at Sandringham for the Prince of Wales) created a sandstone rockery on the slope leading down to the croquet lawn, which allowed for the planting of numerous rare alpines. The croquet lawn itself was bordered along its far side by a pergola of larch and oak lattice supported on sandstone piers; the wisteria to cover the pergola was specially imported from Japan, the theme taken up by Japanese stone lanterns positioned at each corner of the lawn.

To the east of the heath garden, Ludwig planted a rose garden around a central feature of five Istrian carved stone vases; the Italian loggia on its far side is a later addition from the 1920s, when it served as a store for tennis equipment to be used on the adjacent Tennis Lawn. The Wall Garden to the north of the house was laid out as a functioning orchard, although herbaceous borders had already been installed along the main paths by the time of the *Garden Life* interview with Comber in 1905. Between the different sections of the garden were the massed banks of flowering shrubs that still form a central attraction of Nymans today: rhododendrons, camellias, magnolias and azaleas in springtime; hydrangeas, buddleias and potentillas in later summer; plus a vast number of lesser-known trees and shrubs to delight the specialist.[11]

Nymans was a gardener's garden from the outset, and early visits by leading horticulturalists such as Gertrude Jekyll, William Robinson and Ellen Willmott spurred Ludwig on. He soon began to contribute plants to local displays put on by the Cuckfield Horticultural Society and offered prizes for the best cottage gardens and allotments in the Handcross area.[12] He opened the garden at Nymans to enthusiasts from the Crawley and District Gardeners' Association but shrank from displaying the garden's plants outside the immediate locality.[13] Even though Ludwig had been elected a fellow of the Royal Horticultural Society in May 1898 he chose not to exhibit at the society's fortnightly plant shows in London.[14] Once again, this reticence betrays the diffidence of a first-generation immigrant not wholly at ease in society. It would be Ludwig's son Leonard who would regularly send specimens from Nymans to be shown at the Royal Horticultural Society and win acclaim for the garden's achievements.

While Ludwig may not have wished to exhibit at London shows, he was keen to use Nymans for the propagation of new and exotic plants – both those grown from seeds brought back from the plant-hunting expeditions of the late Victorian and early Edwardian eras and also new hybrids cultivated by his own head gardener. James Comber's connections with his former employers at Veitch's nursery meant that Nymans was able to obtain many rare introductions from the Chinese expeditions of pioneers such as Ernest Wilson and George Forrest, as well as discoveries from the South American expeditions financed by Veitch in the mid nineteenth century. Nymans acquired an early seedling of Wilson's most famous discovery, the handkerchief tree (*Davidia involucrata*), which was planted out in the Wall Garden from 1908; today there is a whole glade of handkerchief trees at Nymans in its honour.

Comber was equally keen to create his own hybrids and began to experiment with the specimen truss of the new *Rhododendron* 'Loderi' which he was given in 1913, so that before long Nymans boasted no fewer than eighty species and fifty named hybrids of rhododendron. Yet the most famous of the early plants raised at Nymans, the award-winning *Eucryphia x nymansensis*, was the result of a natural hybridization between the free-flowering, evergreen and spreading tree *E. cordifolia* and the fastigiate, deciduous but not free-flowering *E. glutinosa*. The hybrid's potential was quickly appreciated, and seedlings were raised in the hope that they might represent an important addition to the genus. Writing many decades later as 'the last survivor who can remember the origin and timing of this *Eucryphia*', Ludwig's grandson Godfrey Messel Loring recalled how 'privileged' he was to have helped his Aunt Muriel with the planting out of the new tree.[15]

Muriel Messel had been brought up to share her father's passion for gardening. Born eleven years after her nearest sibling, she was Ludwig's favourite from an early age and spent more time with him in the garden at Nymans than any other member of the Messel family. She accompanied her parents on holidays abroad and lived with them in the opening months of the First World War, when she

The Messel Temple
in its current position
at Nymans

served as Secretary of the Girl Guides for Sussex.[16] Muriel was an independent Edwardian woman with a lust for life and a penchant for hats, which, family tradition records, she used to buy six at a time. Inherited wealth allowed her to live comfortably on her own means after her father's death, first at Coldharbour Manor in West Hoathly and then at nearby Mayes House; both places were close to Gravetye, the home of her friend and mentor William Robinson, who helped her design the borders in the Wall Garden at Nymans. Yet Muriel's life was cut tragically short when she contracted influenza in the global pandemic at the end of the First World War that claimed the lives of 228,000 people in Britain alone. She died on 1 December 1918, aged twenty-nine, leaving most of her £96,849 estate to her sister Ruth.[17]

Muriel not only managed the garden in the immediate period after Ludwig's death; she also saw through to completion the project of cataloguing the more than two thousand plant species that had been grown at Nymans. Muriel had originally encouraged her father to embark on the catalogue in 1913 as an antidote to the depression he felt at the looming threat of war with Germany. Once war broke out Ludwig could no longer face the task of completing the project, and it remained unfinished at his death. Muriel took on the work and expanded it to include personal notes on the cultivation and habits of the more unusual plants

Muriel Messel

'in the hope that the knowledge gained in making this collection may not be entirely lost'. She dedicated the final publication, *A Garden Flora*, to the memory of her father; its subtitle, *Trees and Flowers Grown in the Gardens at Nymans by L. Messel, 1890–1915*, pays tribute to him as the inspiration for all that had been achieved. William Robinson wrote a generous foreword in which he described Ludwig as 'a kindly thoughtful man with a genius for finding new ways in our garden trials and pleasures'. The artist Alfred Parsons, a longstanding friend of the family, contributed ten botanical drawings to accompany the text.

Looking back on the publication of *A Garden Flora* from the latter part of the twentieth century, the *Daily Telegraph*'s gardening correspondent Fred Whitsey remarked, 'It still reads like a horticultural Debrett: embothrium, erythrina and eucryphia, davidia, dacrydium and a dozen different daphnes, nothofagus and nyssa, 100 rhododendron species and nearly as many roses with forgotten names.'[18] The book was equally well received at the time, as much for its artistic qualities as for its content; the *Country Life* review dwelt on the physical enjoyment of handling its 'strong, pure linen-rag paper' and called it a 'thoroughly well done volume'.[19] As the contemporary reviewer for the *Kew Bulletin* put it:

Had Miss Messel lived to see the publication of her work, she could have been congratulated on producing a very pleasant and attractive, as well as useful, volume; unhappily she succumbed to an attack of influenza last December. The book is inscribed to her father's memory, but it is pleasant to feel also that it will keep in long remembrance a young and charming personality cut off in the flower of her age.[20]

Leonard Messel in the uniform
of the East Kent Regiment

For King and Country 11

While Ludwig Messel was busy developing the garden at Nymans, his eldest son Leonard was thinking of a country home for his own growing family. Maud had given birth to their first child, Linley Francis Messel, on 31 August 1899. Named after her father, Maud was insistent that he should be just as much a Sambourne as a Messel; as she wrote to her mother, 'If he dares to have dark hair, well – I shall dye it golden!!'[1] Infant Linley would be joined by a sister, Anne, on 8 February 1902 and a younger brother, Oliver Messel, on 13 January 1904.

While they still had just the one baby, Maud and Leonard took on the country house of Glovers in Charlwood, on the border between Sussex and Surrey. With Anne's arrival the family moved to their new country home of Balcombe House, four miles east of Nymans. To help him with the purchase Leonard was given an advance of £8,500 on his inheritance by Ludwig, who wished to have all his children and grandchildren near enough that they could come over for family lunch on Sundays. In time every one of his children would acquire a country property within striking distance of Nymans.[2]

Balcombe House is a delicate eighteenth-century mansion with shuttered windows that give its façade the appearance of a doll's house. Maud and Leonard's three children grew up there until their teens, and they adored it. In his later reminiscences Oliver described the balcony that ran around three sides of the house as 'covered with jessamine, honeysuckle & roses, giving almost the effect of a welcoming bird's nest'. The interior was equally magical:

> From a wide Hall where the Georgian panelling was painted white, doors opened, left into my Father's study & right into the Morning Room. This as I remember was a room of great atmosphere being filled with favourite objects that my Mother had collected. High-backed William & Mary chairs were beside the fireplace which sparkled with an array of polished brass . . . The Dining Room was further down the Hall beyond the Study on the left, a congenial room with 3 long windows opening on to the trellised gallery, & the vines which made an arboured foreground, as a frame to the views over the garden. On the right opposite the door

to the dining room was a sturdy carved Georgian staircase, where we as children used to sit in dressing gowns & overhear what seemed an overwhelming noise of chatter & laughter like a Parrot House, from the dinner parties. We would snatch some of the goodies before they disappeared.[3]

Maud Messel with her first two children, Linley and Anne

Leonard and Maud quickly made Balcombe their country home and became well known in the neighbourhood. Like Ludwig and Annie, they took on the responsibilities expected of the local gentry, hosting the Balcombe Association's annual flower show in the grounds of their house, with sports in the afternoon and dancing in the evening.[4] Leonard continued to perform in the occasional concert during their early days at Balcombe, such as the fundraising event for the Sussex County Hospital on 5 October 1904, in which he 'proved himself a first-rate interpreter of comic songs'.[5] Yet he soon matured into a respected figure of society whose duties were of a more serious nature. He served as vice-president of the Balcombe Association and of the Balcombe Conservative Association from 1907 onwards and was elected vice-president of the Balcombe Cricket Club as well.[6] He also supported the Balcombe Boy Scouts both financially and practically, offering them use of the premises at Balcombe House.

Much of Leonard's time in the country was devoted to his role as commander of the local volunteer company of the Royal Sussex Regiment, which meant he was regularly engaged in military exercises and other drills.[7] In 1906 he was promoted to honorary major, the rank he held when awarded the Territorial Decoration for twenty years' continuous service in the Volunteers on 15 March 1912.[8] Leonard relinquished his commission the following July, little suspecting that the First World War was just a year away. Almost as soon as hostilities commenced he was selected by the War Office to be recruiting officer for the Balcombe district, and on 14 October 1914 he was appointed captain with the honorary rank of major in the 4th (Reserve) Battalion of the East Kent Regiment, commonly known as the Buffs. Cleared for home service only, Leonard never saw action overseas; instead, his role throughout the war was to raise and train the fighting men of the Buffs on their way to the front.

Leonard took on responsibility for raising the 3/4th Battalion of the Buffs at Canterbury in July 1915 and was promoted to the rank of lieutenant-colonel the following June. His time as commanding officer in charge of the battalion was to have an enduring impact on him, and the depth of feeling he elicited in the troops is shown by the hundreds of personal letters which he received from soldiers of all ranks once they had arrived in France. Others wrote to him from India, Egypt, Mesopotamia, South Africa and the Balkans. Leonard kept their letters and wrote back in return; he also sent personal condolences to the families of those who had lost their lives on active service. On several occasions he provided money to pay off debts that individual soldiers had run up during their time in the army and was thanked for that in turn.

The importance Leonard attached to the letters is shown by the fact that he had them transcribed into typed copies and compiled in leather-bound volumes after the war.[9] They remain a unique testament to the reality of life in the trenches and the capacity of the human spirit to rise above the most unspeakable horrors. The opening of one letter, written to Leonard on 11 August 1917 from No. 8 General Hospital at Rouen by Second Lieutenant A. Stanley Peters, illustrates the wry tone of many reports from the front.

> Dear Col. Messel,
>
> Many thanks for your recent letter. You will guess from the address that I have been hit again but it's not very much. The same night poor Sherren was killed instantaneously. We all miss him – he was splendid in the line. Far worse than the shelling, the machine guns and this new gas (which leaves big blisters) was the *mud*. It was indescribable. Several of my chaps went in up to their armpits and I am afraid quite a number never got out. Still – the stunt went splendidly.

The 'stunt' in question was the Third Battle of Ypres, otherwise known as Passchendaele, where Captain Arthur Oswald Sherren of the Buffs was killed on 3 August 1917. The letters from the families of those who lost their lives in the fighting are predictably among the most moving. One of Leonard's most faithful correspondents was a Private Alfred Henry Scillitoe, who was killed in action on 9 August 1918, aged twenty-one. His mother Harriet received the news two weeks later and wrote to tell Leonard the same day, saying that her son had 'spoken to us so many times about your goodness to him when under your command'. Leonard wrote back asking for a photograph to remember him by.

Leonard's military career was a defining part of his identity. He was always referred to locally as 'The Colonel', he wore his regimental uniform at formal occasions and the companies of the 4th Battalion of the Royal Sussex Regiment competed each year for the Messel Cup, donated by Leonard to encourage excellence in platoon inspection, drill and attack.[10] The militant imperialism of the period from 1870 onwards had encouraged public schoolboys to develop a rugged, self-sufficient masculinity that would willingly embrace the opportunity to fight and die in the service of their country, a glorification of martyrdom whose consequences were brutally laid bare in the charnel house of the First World

War.[11] Leonard's long service record exemplifies this martial ideology, and in the speech he gave on his retirement from the Volunteers he expressed his profound distaste for those 'hang backs' who would not come forward to serve King and Country.[12] Yet in his thirty years in the army Leonard never saw active service himself. Nor did he live up to the late-Victorian ideal of physically imposing manhood. Like other Messel men, Leonard was short – five foot seven, according to his military records – and fastidious in his appearance, a far cry from the epitome of the rugged male.

Was it these internal contradictions that made Leonard such a difficult man to get along with in adult life? Or was it simply that, as the eldest boy child, he had been spoilt to distraction from his earliest years? Certainly the newly married Maud wrote to her mother from her first Christmas at Nymans in horrified disapproval of how the Messel girls had been brought up to wait hand and foot on their two brothers.[13] Yet the evidence from Leonard's closest male relatives shows that there were mental-health issues in the family, which could explain why his youthful sense of fun gradually gave way to the less personable side of his character. Leonard's daughter Anne acknowledged that her father had an explosive temper which made him 'immensely intolerant', and his elder son Linley lived in such terror of him that the headmaster of his preparatory school wrote a letter to Maud and Leonard pleading with them to be kinder to the boy.[14] As the baby of the family Oliver Messel was treated more leniently, but he, too, acknowledged that his father was 'something of a pocket Napoleon' with 'a peppery temper which exploded on the slightest provocation'.[15]

Maud's mother Marion provides further evidence of Leonard's unstable mental state in her diaries, regularly referring to him as 'nervy' when he lost control of himself. In the face of his constant irritability while she was staying with Leonard and Maud at Balcombe in summer 1911 Marion confided to her diary that 'these tempers make me dislike coming here'.[16] Yet it is in the diaries of Maud's brother Roy Sambourne that the strongest evidence of Leonard's mental instability presents itself. Roy knew Leonard at close quarters for much of his life and bore the brunt of Leonard's most violent outbursts. 'Lennie in a passion – his manner to me is unbearable. I ought to remember that insanity runs in the family. For Maud's sake I bear with an impossible spoilt rude uncharitable selfish & God forgive me – detestable character.'[17]

Maud carried out her own duties at Balcombe before the war, running needlework classes for local girls and distributing prizes at the annual exhibition held by the Balcombe Association. She was joined at the February 1908 show by her daughter Miss Anne Messel, aged six, 'whose exhibit was a handkerchief worked by herself'.[18] Maud sat on the governing body of the Church of England school in Balcombe, and in 1905 she agreed to serve as local representative of the National Society for the Prevention of Cruelty to Children. Four years later she was appointed vice-president for the East Grinstead Division of the British Red Cross Society, a connection she would maintain for many years after the family had left Balcombe.[19] Maud also became commandant of the hospital for the wounded established in Balcombe at the beginning of the First World War, as well as serving on the committee of the Voluntary War Work Scheme and leading the fundraising effort for the armed forces on flag days. In recognition of her service as hospital commandant she was awarded the MBE in March 1920.[20]

Maud Messel in the Morning Room at Balcombe House

Ludwig Messel's death in 1915 brought great change to the lives of Leonard and Maud. To begin with, Leonard became senior partner in the family stockbroking firm, assuming overall responsibility for a business whose fortunes rose and fell with the times. The First World War was particularly hard on companies such as L. Messel and Co., which had based much of its business on trading in foreign bonds. During the war it was forbidden to deal in securities held outside the country. Even when the general restriction was lifted in August 1919 it remained in place for a further four years in the case of bonds held by enemy nationals, so that L. Messel and Co. was unable to collect any of the outstanding money owing to it from its many German clients. The firm's exposure to Russian securities proved to be equally ill-fated after the Bolshevik revolution of 1917, and only by developing new links with the French bond market in the 1920s was Leonard able to set the business back on its feet.[21] Yet the net worth of the company contracted again in the turbulent 1930s as the overseas market declined even further. The weight of responsibility on Leonard as senior partner must go some way towards explaining why the fun-loving gaiety of his youth was less evident during his later life.[22]

Ludwig's death was not the only shock to hit the Messel family during the dark years of the First World War. The other major blow fell on Leonard's younger brother Harold, who had joined the family firm just prior to his marriage in 1903 and who quickly made a name for himself as a gifted stockbroker. Harold's wife Nonie soon became pregnant, and their first child Rudolph Putnam Messel – affectionately known within the family as Put – was born on 28 November 1904. Within three years the marriage was further blessed by the arrival of a daughter, Phoebe Messel, on 6 July 1907. The young family lived first at 10 Talbot Square and then from 1910 onwards at the even grander residence of 8 Gloucester Square, both properties in the fashionable Tyburnia area of London that the Messel family had made their own. Harold and Nonie were given the additional privilege of a

country home in July 1914 when Ludwig Messel helped them buy the imposing
mansion of Danehurst outside the Sussex village of Danehill.[23]

Like his elder brother, Harold had served as a volunteer in the Royal Sussex
Regiment from 1901 to 1905, and he joined up again as a lieutenant in October
1914. He was seconded to the Censor's Department in June 1915, but the
secondment was abruptly cancelled in the wake of his father's death the following
month. Harold, who had long suffered from bouts of depression, was present at
Nymans when Ludwig died, and the loss affected him deeply. He had a nervous
breakdown and was compelled to resign his commission in the Royal Sussex
Regiment on grounds of ill health later in the year.[24]

The family was soon shattered by even greater tragedy. Ten years after
Phoebe Messel's birth Nonie became pregnant with a third child, but there were
complications with the pregnancy and the doctors advised that they needed to
begin proceedings early. Nonie wrote in advance to Harold's eldest sister Ottilie
thanking her for taking care of little Phoebe 'over the event' but asked her not to
tell the rest of the family exactly when it was due to begin. 'The doctors never quite
know how long these affairs will take after they have started things – sometimes
it is a matter of hours, sometimes two days.' In all events she said she looked
forward to taking Phoebe back from Ottilie within a short time.

It was not to be. Nonie died in childbirth on 19 May 1918, aged thirty-six. The coroner's certificate records the cause of death as premature labour with *placenta praevia*, leading to haemorrhage and shock. The story passed down in the family tells that Nonie's gynaecologist had been called away for active service in the war and that her death was due to there not being sufficient medical expertise available to cope with the complications of the birth.

Harold was devastated. In a letter to his mother the day after Nonie's burial he wrote of 'such sorrow as I hope few can ever know'. A long diary note written two years later by Maud's brother Roy Sambourne, who was close to Harold, describes how Nonie's death had 'completely unhinged his mind'. His brother Leonard even talked of having him certified insane to keep him from harming himself, but he was overruled by his sisters. Harold became increasingly unreasonable and difficult to live with, with the brunt of his mental illness falling on Nonie's mother, Jennie Gibson, who had moved to Danehurst to help with the children after her daughter's death. Roy Sambourne's diary for early 1920 contains numerous references to Harold's increasingly unpredictable behaviour, not least when he learnt that he had become engaged to be married again, to a 'not bad-looking Welsh girl' called Nesta Lloyd. Yet his mental health was still an issue, and on the morning of Sunday 21 March 1920 Harold walked out of his house and vanished completely, to the immense concern of his family. He turned up again at Danehurst six days later with no recollection of where he had been.[25]

In the end it was too much for him. At his London home on the morning of 25 August 1920 Harold shot himself through the heart with his revolver. The coroner recorded that he 'did kill himself during a state of temporary insanity', the standard verdict used to allow the deceased a Christian burial, which was traditionally denied to suicides in full possession of their mental faculties at the time they took their own life.[26] The funeral was a discreet affair, and Harold was reunited with Nonie in a joint tomb within the burial ground of All Saints, Danehill.[27] Her epitaph, a variant of John Ruskin's celebrated dictum, reads, 'The path of a good woman is strewn with roses; but they rise up behind her steps not before them.' Harold's is the text of *Ecclesiastes* 41:13: 'A good life hath but few days, but a good name endureth forever.'

Despite the relief that accompanied the ending of the First World War these were years that brought the Messel family immense grief. In addition to the premature deaths of Nonie and Muriel and of his German cousins Ludwig and Ena Messel (the latter died of a burst appendix in August 1919), Leonard had lost his Uncle Rudolph in April 1920. Harold's suicide four months later came at a time when their mother Annie was entering the last phase of her life. Now in her seventies, Annie had been in failing health for some time. A moving document written by Leonard as she lay dying reveals how much he drew on his Christian faith for support and comfort during this difficult time. Sitting with his mother and recording her last words of farewell as she slipped in and out of consciousness, Leonard consoled himself with the thought that 'In his or her last illness there often comes a time when pain and suffering are over, when the beloved personality still lingers on earth, but in an altered condition far removed from the trivialities and emotions of normal existence.' The document provides an insight into the trauma which the Messel family suffered during this period and the struggle they faced in moving forward with their lives.

Despite this image of the Messels as a group of individuals tormented by mental illness and personal loss, there is also touching evidence of a deeper joy and affection within the family, and it comes from the most surprising of sources. Hilda Messel's sister-in-law Beatrice Gibbes was a devotee of psychic research and had formed a lasting friendship with the Irish medium Geraldine Cummins, who specialized in contacting the spirit world through automatic writing, whereby the spirits of the departed take possession of the medium to write messages back to the living. Bea, as she was known, had been close to the Messel family for many years, visiting them at Nymans even before her brother Arthur married Hilda. Through Cummins she established contact with Muriel, Nonie and Harold Messel in the years after they died and with Ludwig and Annie Messel as well. Bea recorded the long and detailed correspondence she enjoyed with them in an extraordinary book called *Travellers in Eternity* published in 1948. When Hilda died suddenly in July 1941 she, too, became one of Bea's correspondents in the spirit world.[28]

Most readers will discount such evidence as being outside the realm of acceptable historiographical source material. Yet the first-hand details of the Messel family which Bea provides alongside the spirit writings are useful data from someone who knew them intimately in life. The book's broader contents have a claim on our attention by virtue of the foreword written by Eric Parker, husband of Ruth Messel, who affirms that the characters portrayed in the book's pages are 'exactly as I knew them in the life on earth'.

> They are as alive to me in these pages as they were in the years before they passed, gay or grave, serene, critical, difficult, loving – each and all the same men and women, boys and girls whom I knew. It has been, it always will be, a happiness to meet them again.

By now a leading British naturalist, Eric Parker was himself interested in psychic research and had consulted mediums following the sudden death of his wife Ruth, so he is not an unbiased witness.[29] Yet the fact that he, Bea and others were prepared to verify that the picture painted in *Travellers in Eternity* was an accurate reflection of the Messel family in life justifies including a little of the book's content as a counterweight to the sad image which comes from other sources at this time.

Most of all, the book paints a benign picture of the Messel family in the afterlife as a group bound together by tender concern for each of its members, alive or dead. Much time is spent describing the new Nymans that Ludwig and his daughter Muriel have lovingly created together in the spirit world and the parallel garden which Muriel is preparing for her sister Hilda when she comes to join them. Mention is made of the depression experienced by Ludwig and Harold while they were alive; a communication purporting to be from Ludwig himself notes that he is 'no longer aloof and stern' as a father, while Harold is described by Muriel as having 'kept the bright, gay side and lost all the queer moods and melancholies'. The manner of Harold's death is also touched on obliquely, as he is required to work with other suicides in the afterlife, helping them to break out of the darkness which afflicts them. Yet the ultimate purpose of the communication from those Messels who have passed over is to provide reassurance to those still living of the love and happiness they will encounter in the world to come. As Bea Gibbes describes it in her preface, the unique and unexpected effect of *Travellers in Eternity* is that it offers 'a connected, coherent biography of certain members of a family joyfully re-united after death'.

Back on earth, the other major change brought about by Ludwig's death was that Leonard now inherited Nymans, the Messel country home. Ludwig had bequeathed the freehold on Nymans to Leonard and the leasehold on his last London residence of 3 Hyde Park Gardens to Harold, with the proviso that his widow Annie should be able to live in either property rent-free for as long as she wished. In an adaptation of the Jewish tradition whereby the first-born son receives a double share in his father's inheritance, Ludwig's will gave both Leonard and Harold a double portion of his residuary estate with the instruction that each should use it 'so as to be a source of strength and support to his sisters or his sisters' children in their endeavours to make their way in the world'.[30]

To Leonard, inheriting Nymans completed his rite of passage to becoming head of the Messel family. Yet neither Maud nor the children wished to leave their pretty home at Balcombe. Not only had they built a happy life for themselves there but Maud was appalled at the architectural hotchpotch that Ludwig had made of the house at Nymans when he called on his brother Alfred to design its extension in the 1890s. It would take a grand bargain on Leonard's part to persuade Maud to agree to the move – one that would change the face of Nymans for ever.

The west front and
dovecote at Nymans

Making History 12

LEONARD AND MAUD Messel moved to Nymans with their three children in autumn 1916, a period when Leonard was at home on leave from war duties following a breakdown in his health.[1] The price for Maud's acquiescence was that Leonard would agree to a radical redesign of the house which Ludwig had left them, and by the beginning of the 1920s the couple were able to turn their thoughts towards the rebuilding project that would keep them occupied for much of the decade.

Maud was the driving force behind the project to turn Nymans into a medieval manor house. Drawing on the artistic talent she had inherited from her father Linley Sambourne, she produced numerous sketches of how she wanted each aspect of the finished house to look. In their previous home she and Leonard had lived a mile away from Balcombe Place, the imposing 'Tudor Gothic' mansion that was built for the businessman John Alexander Hankey in 1856 and further enlarged in 1899 – a perfect example of how an ancient building could be created from scratch in the modern age. For her purposes Maud looked to the fifteenth century and drew her inspiration from West Country houses such as Great Chalfield Manor in Wiltshire, as well as nearer models such as Brede Place in East Sussex. Yet the point of the Old English style that Maud favoured was not to attempt the slavish reconstruction of any single moment in architectural time but, rather, to suggest the organic development of a manor house over centuries of accretion. In this way the new Nymans would stand as a realistic monument to a history that never existed.

The first architect whom the Messels contracted to create their dream house was Norman Evill, the celebrated pupil of Sir Edwin Lutyens and, like Leonard, a member of the Arts Club. Beginning with the designs he drew up in 1922 Evill created the western part of the building, including the dovecote, and several photographs survive showing construction work in progress as the new house emerges from the old. Yet Evill fell out with Maud and withdrew from the project in 1924. In his place Leonard and Maud employed the equally distinguished church architect Sir Walter Tapper, who would be responsible for rebuilding the major parts of the south and east of the house, including the long drawing-room, the oak-panelled library and the adjoining book room. The upstairs rooms were designed in seventeenth-century style, with Maud's bedroom and the Bristol Room both boasting fine ceilings of Jacobean derivation. The central piece in the grand composition was the Great Hall, completed in time for Christmas 1927, with a cavernous billiard room beneath it. The rebuilding continued almost to the end of the decade, with the new oak staircase and front door finished only in early 1929.

The result of so many years' planning and construction was a masterpiece of its kind. Unlike the mock-Tudor timber-framed homes being built in Sussex during the 1920s such as Crowhurst Place and Old Surrey Hall, Nymans looked back to the stone manor houses of an earlier age. Original masonry had to be sourced for the purpose, just as Lord and Lady Moyne were scouring the country for stone to construct their own medieval manor house at Bailliffscourt on the Sussex coast. Inside, too, the Messels' extensive collection of old English furniture was to be complemented by doors, fireplaces and ceiling beams salvaged from genuine medieval manor houses around Britain. This could have led to design chaos, but the handling of the materials was sensitive enough to remove any inconsistencies.

The artist E.H. Shepard, best known for his illustrations of *Winnie-the-Pooh* and *The Wind in the Willows*, visited Nymans in summer 1929 and produced sketches of the newly finished house. Yet the fullest documentary evidence we have of the remodelled building comes from the series of three articles on Nymans published in *Country Life* in September 1932. The architectural historian Christopher Hussey wrote the first two pieces on the house and its contents, while George Taylor added a third on the garden. Hussey began by concocting what he called 'an imaginary history' of the estate, in which he playfully traced the origins of its name to a Norseman by the name of Gruff Nyman, a later tenant called Cedric Anyman and a thirteenth-century knight named Robert le Nyuweman.[2] His suggestion that medieval walls were discovered during the rebuilding of the house should likewise be taken with a pinch of salt. Hussey defended the Messels against the charge that reproduction of ancient styles was 'in all cases reprehensible' by pointing out that Nymans was not intended to be a copy of any existing building. 'Rather, it is an exquisite example of pastiche – a form of invention that in literature holds an honourable place and is capable of producing works of art in their own right. Such a work of art this building must generally be held to be. Pastiche as a form of building has an aesthetic of its own.'

Whether or not one accepts this line of argument, the recreated manor house was so convincing that, in Hussey's words, 'some future antiquary may well be deceived by it'. Nikolaus Pevsner agreed that the result was 'amazingly deceptive', while the architect Percy Newton remembered it as 'the most marvellous fake': 'Having tea in the banqueting hall seated on a dais looking towards a minstrels'

The completed south front of Nymans in 1932

gallery with traceried clerestory windows filled with stained glass one could not believe one was not in some medieval College Hall.'[3]

The rebuilding of Nymans created a *faux* dynastic pedigree for the Messel family, distinct from their identity as German-Jewish immigrants. Nor was this an end to the refashioning, as Leonard had obtained the official grant of a Messel coat of arms from the College of Arms in 1911. The design is based on a simple fir tree – an appropriate symbol for a family increasingly identified with the garden at Nymans – and the arms were carved in stone at various points around the walls of the new manor, sometimes in combination with those of the Cussans or Sambourne families as well.[4] With the main entrance to Nymans relocated by Maud and Leonard to the north-east of the house, guests would pass under a simple carving of the Messel escutcheon as they entered through the Postern Gate. On the right just inside this main entrance is a Star of David fitted into the wall in stone relief – one of the few indications that Leonard Messel, a practising member of the Church of England, did not forget his Jewish roots.

On taking over Nymans, Leonard became just as dedicated to the garden project as his father Ludwig had been. He subscribed to all the main plant-hunting expeditions of the day and paid £10 for seeds collected during the 1921 British reconnaissance expedition to Mount Everest.[5] Leonard was himself instrumental in organizing a joint expedition to south-west China in collaboration with the eminent Chinese botanist Professor Hu Hsen-Hsu, which led to the discovery of numerous new plants. James Comber remained head gardener to Leonard as he had been under Ludwig Messel, and his own son Harold travelled to collect seeds in the Andes and in Tasmania during the 1920s, from which Nymans derived a great many varieties. In 2016 the garden's Harold Comber Collection of Chilean

Leonard Messel
escorting Queen Mary

and Tasmanian plants was awarded National Collection status, and two years later Nymans participated in the joint British-Irish botanical expedition to Tasmania with the aim of reintroducing some of the 147 species collected by Harold on his original visit to the island.

Leonard was keen to exhibit plants from Nymans at the shows held by the Royal Horticultural Society at its headquarters in London, and a large nursery was established on a plot of land across the road from the main garden where thousands of new specimens could be raised. One early success came in 1924 when the famous *Eucryphia x nymansensis* 'Nymansay' won the Cory Cup for best hardy plant of garden origin; it was also given the Award of Merit that same year, upgraded to First Class Certificate in 1926.[6] Leonard was awarded a gold medal at the society's 1926 annual show for his exhibition of flowering plants and shrubs, including several new specimens collected from Tibet. Of the many plants from Nymans recognized by the Royal Horticultural Society in the early years, *Rhododendron decorum* 'Mrs Messel' was given the Award of Merit in 1923, while *Rhododendron* 'Muriel Messel' received the same honour at the 1929 Chelsea Flower Show.[7]

By now head gardener James Comber was on his way to becoming a celebrated horticulturalist. He had started contributing articles to gardening journals before taking up employment at Nymans and continued to do so throughout his career. He was also in demand as an expert plantsman, regularly adjudicating at plant shows and lecturing to garden societies across Sussex, Surrey and Hampshire. In 1936 Comber was awarded the Victoria Medal of Honour in recognition of 'his long service to horticulture'. The medal is the Royal Horticultural Society's highest accolade, awarded to no more than sixty-three individuals at any one time in commemoration of the sixty-three years of Queen Victoria's reign. The society's president, Lord Aberconway, presenting the Nymans head gardener with the award in February 1937, congratulated him on successfully raising so many exotic plants that other horticultural experts had failed to germinate.

Seeing Nymans publicly recognized through Comber's success meant a great deal to Leonard and spurred him on to become increasingly involved in horticulture himself. He was elected a fellow of the Linnean Society in May 1931 and served on the council of the Royal Horticultural Society from 1936 to 1941. He sat on the executive committee of the Garden Club and was also elected to the Garden Society, the élite dining club of (male-only) garden owners who came together three times a year with the aim of sharing information on new and exotic plants in the company of fellow enthusiasts.[8] As with Comber, Leonard's crowning achievement came in 1945 when he, too, was awarded the Victoria Medal of Honour for his contributions as 'a keen amateur gardener and grower of rare plants'.

Maud was similarly enthused by the horticultural opportunities afforded by Nymans, keeping a detailed garden diary over the years 1922 to 1947 and sketching out her own designs for the planting of the Forecourt Garden and Knot Garden closest to the house. A keen plantswoman in her own right, she built up a significant collection of early historic roses, working with the horticulturalists Ellen Willmott and Edward Bunyard to preserve many fragrant varieties that had been supplanted in modern gardens by the more showy hybrid teas. In recognition of her contribution to garden history the botanist Eleanour Sinclair Rohde dedicated her most celebrated book, *The Scented Garden*, to Maud.

Maud used her position as chatelaine of Nymans to express her creative spirit beyond the garden alone. In the summer after the end of the First World War she inaugurated a new celebration of the traditional May Day festival on Staplefield Common, with local residents joined by hundreds of people from nearby towns and villages of West Sussex. A vast amount of organization went into the undertaking, for which Maud enlisted the support of the Handcross Women's Institute as well as countless others. The central attraction was the garlanded maypole which James Comber supplied from Nymans, around which most of the proceedings took place.

The afternoon commenced at 2.30 p.m. with a pageant of rural characters including the May Queen attended by fairies and a page (Hilda Messel's young son, Nigel Gibbes); Flora, scattering flowers; Robin Hood, Little John, Maid Marian, Friar Tuck and Much, the miller's son; the King and Queen of the revels, on hand to crown the May Queen; a Jack-in-the-Green; six woodmen in brown jerkins with their axes; six young maidens in blue kirtles leading a cow with horns tipped with gold; and many others following on. Stalls were set up in marquees around the common, including the gingerbread stall run by seventeen-year-old Anne Messel with her cousins Charlotte and Dulcie Loring; the 'oranges and lemons' stall run by Hilda Gibbes and Nigel; and the stall of the Nymans Needlework Guild, overseen by Maud and other members of the group. Teams of schoolgirls from Handcross, Staplefield and Warninglid provided the Morris-dancing; various musical performances and folk plays followed, along with

Dancing at the 1919 May Day festival on Staplefield Common

refreshments throughout. A final procession brought the festival to a close at 7 p.m., 'everything having gone well from first to last'.[9]

The May Day celebrations were repeated in each of the subsequent three years, and photographs survive in the Slaugham archives of the dancing, processions and costumes. The programme (priced threepence) also survives from the 1920 celebrations. With a nod to the teachings of the Arts and Crafts movement, Maud ensured that it was printed on traditionally made paper and bound together by thread.[10] The revival of rural traditions was a central part of Maud's self-appointed mission as lady of the manor, and she later donated a cup for folk-dancing to the annual competition of the East Sussex Federation of Women's Institutes.[11] Nostalgia for the innocence of a bygone era was a common reaction to the horrors of industrial-scale slaughter seen in the First World War, and Maud took up the theme with passion, even arranging tutors for her own children in skills such as 'the early art of weaving', as her daughter Anne recalled. 'Our teacher was an eccentric old woman dressed as a shepherd, smock and leggings and all, and speaking as a man in brogue. How vividly these escapades linger in my mind: the collecting of dirty sheep's wool from the hedges under her crook, the washing, the carding, the spinning and finally the weaving.'[12]

In similar vein Maud was a leading light in the Shakespeare Society formed by the Handcross Women's Institute, and the completed buildings at Nymans formed the backdrop for its all-female productions. In August 1933 the society gave two performances of *The Tempest* in the Great Hall at Nymans, with Maud ably supported by her faithful secretary Daphne Dengate. Good weather the following August allowed for open-air performances of *The Merchant of Venice* in the garden at Nymans, in which Daphne played Portia. Maud was in charge of casting and the creation of authentic Elizabethan costumes, the latter being made at Nymans out of coloured hessian bought especially for the purpose from Barnet and Co. in Covent Garden.

Leonard and Maud also participated in local celebrations to mark the return of peace after the dark days of the First World War. Leonard still held the rank of honorary lieutenant-colonel in the Territorial Force Reserve and had been awarded the OBE for his war service, so he spoke on behalf of all servicemen at the local supper held in July 1919 to honour those who had served. Thanking the people of Staplefield, Leonard noted that all 'had done fine work during the war, but no other work could compare to that done by those who had lived through the actual horrors of warfare'. He spoke movingly of his own experience in training the men of the East Kent Regiment: 'All went off to face the most terrible experiences, often knowing well what these were, with a never-failing cheerfulness and bravery which no words could describe, intent only on one thing – to do their duty.' Leonard, Maud and the three Messel children also attended the

Peace Day celebrations held later that month on the cricket
pitch at Staplefield, with sports, fireworks and the burning
in effigy of the German Kaiser.[13]

As peace returned to rural Sussex, Leonard and Maud
took up their duties in the community around Handcross.
They opened up the grounds of Nymans in summer 1919
for the annual show run by the Slaugham Association, with
the usual athletics, Morris-dancing and glee-singing that
accompanied the exhibition of vegetables, fruit and flowers.
Among the dancers were the teenagers Anne and Oliver
Messel, together with their cousins Charlotte and Dulcie
Loring.[14] Leonard also opened up the garden to groups such
as the Brighton, Hove and Sussex Horticultural Society
and the Sussex Beekeepers' Association. He even raised a
cricket team to represent Handcross against Staplefield – and
it won.[15]

Leonard Messel as
High Sheriff of Sussex
in 1936

Leonard was also active in civic duties in the district
around Nymans. Soon after the First World War he paid for the construction of
six new cottages in Handcross at the cost of £1,000 each, with a view to easing
the shortage of housing locally. As one press report commented, 'Other wealthy
persons might well imitate this example.'[16] He served as president of the British
Legion's Handcross and District Branch, the Handcross Orchestral Society and
the Staplefield Musical and Dramatic Society. In recognition of his services to the
community Leonard was appointed High Sheriff of Sussex for the year 1936, in
which role he proclaimed the accession of George VI at County Hall in Lewes.
His official portrait for the position shows him in full dress uniform, as permitted
for senior members of the armed forces. There can be no more eloquent statement
that he had made it as an English gentleman.

Nor was it just in Sussex that Leonard kept up this busy schedule. The
family's weekdays were usually spent at their London home in Lancaster Gate,
while Leonard and Maud took regular holidays of up to six weeks at a time in
Scotland, Ireland or continental Europe. Leonard also became actively interested
in Freemasonry during the inter-war years. He was initiated into the Doneraile
Lodge in London on 13 December 1921, a few weeks before his fiftieth birthday,
and joined several other lodges and chapters in order to expand his network of
contacts still further. The importance of Freemasonry to Leonard comes alive
most vividly in the contents of a large black tin box still in the family's possession
and marked on the outside 'Lt. Col. L.C.R. Messel. O.B.E., P.G.D.' The latter
initials identify Leonard by the senior rank of Past Grand Deacon, and the box
contains an impressive collection of Masonic jewels and regalia, including several

The Muriel Messel
Memorial Window in
St Mark's, Staplefield

embroidered collars and aprons, all beautifully preserved in
tissue paper.

With Leonard's time taken up with social activities, Maud
was left with the responsibility of running the household at
Nymans. This was no small matter, as the memoirs of her
secretary Daphne Dengate make clear.[17] Daughter of the
vicar of Staplefield, Daphne started helping Maud in January
1931 at the age of twenty-three, cycling up the hill to Nymans
each morning and freewheeling home in the evenings. Like
Maud's equally dedicated lady's maid Barbara Adamson,
known as 'Addy', she would remain with the Messel family
for sixty years. According to Daphne's account, the Great
Depression and general shortage of domestic servants in
Britain after the First World War had little effect on Nymans,
where the household staff still numbered sixteen in the 1930s,
including a butler, two footmen, a head housemaid with two
or three housemaids under her, a cook, a kitchen maid and
a scullery maid, a lady to look after the linen, a batman for
Leonard, an odd-job man and a head chauffeur. This last was
responsible for Leonard's seven motor cars, including his two
Rolls-Royces, but he had assistance in the form of a French
chauffeur who was expected to mend the Renault whenever
that was *en panne*. The Frenchman had originally been
meant to deliver the Renault to the Messels and return home
to his own country, but he fell in love with the housemaid
who opened the door to him and stayed.[18]

Maud formed the Nymans Needlework Guild to
continue the classes she had started at Balcombe, with the
aim of providing country girls with a skill that might offer
them an independent income in later years. As at Balcombe
the classes were taken by Miss Warren, a strict teacher whom Maud paid to attend
the Royal School of Needlework in London so that she might learn the finer points
of her craft to pass on to her pupils. A number of girls were selected each week to
go up to Nymans from Staplefield village school in order to take part in the classes,
although the excursions were most valued for the sticky buns that the girls were
given with their tea.[19] In addition to her continuing work with the Red Cross and
British Legion, Maud was president of the Servers of the Blind League, which
opened a new home at Bolney Court, four miles from Nymans, in 1947.

Throughout their time at Nymans Leonard and Maud enjoyed a strong
connection with the local parish church of St Mark's, Staplefield. Even before

they moved from Balcombe Leonard donated a chalice, paten and ciborium to St Mark's, the chalice being singled out for attention as 'a beautiful specimen of Messina work of about 1810'.[20] During the war they gave a pair of candlesticks to the church, which were felt to 'add greatly to the dignity of the sanctuary'.[21] Leonard joined the parochial church council in 1919, serving as churchwarden until his death thirty-four years later. Over those years he and Maud donated the stained glass in the church's east window in memory of his youngest sister Muriel; the oak screen, altar and furnishings for the children's corner; a sanctuary lamp and silver crucifix; a wardrobe of surplices; and a private communion set from the early nineteenth century. Parish accounts show that Leonard was also a regular contributor to church funds.

With the return of war with Germany in 1939 Leonard and Maud offered up the Nymans grounds to Canadian soldiers billeted in the area and turned over the Great Hall to be a dormitory for pupils and masters evacuated from Buckingham Gate School in London. Leonard used to lead the evacuees in morning prayers and treated them with a warmth he had rarely shown his own sons when they were growing up. Interviewed seventy years later, one of the boys recalled that they were spoilt during their time at Nymans and 'didn't want for anything'.

> There were twelve boys, and we all slept in the baronial hall, and the two masters slept in the minstrels' gallery. It had tapestries round the wall and armour and all that sort of stuff. Wood panelling and very little central heating, as far as I can remember, but the warmth came from a massive great fire, one of those big fires you could actually sit in, you know? And some woodman or someone used to produce these massive great logs. And that's where we slept. We had two refectory-type tables in the middle with benches, and that's where we did our homework and carried out our hobbies. One of our hobbies was making model aeroplanes, and the idea was you made your model aeroplane and you sneaked up to the minstrels' gallery when the teachers weren't there. You tried to fly it off the gallery to try to get it to the far end of the room. Hardly ever did it.[22]

Leonard took a keen interest in advancing the evacuees' future prospects, and several were offered positions at L. Messel and Co. after they left Nymans. At least one of those so favoured, Cecil Elliott, eventually rose to become a partner in the firm. In the case of Philip Hatch, the boy whose recollections are cited above, Leonard secured him an interview at the merchant bank Barings when he turned sixteen, leading to his first job as a junior clerk on a wage of thirty-five shillings a week. Hatch remained at Barings throughout his career and was forever grateful to Leonard for starting him off with a helping hand.

Fire-fighters tackling
the blaze at Nymans,
19 February 1947

The Triumph of Hope 13

T HE SECOND WORLD War brought new tragedy to the Messel family. Leonard's
elder son Linley was mentioned in dispatches while on active service in Palestine
and returned home safe at the end of the war with the rank of colonel. Yet three
of his Messel cousins lost their lives in the conflict. Ruth's son John Parker, a
squadron leader in the Royal Air Force, was killed when his flying boat crashed in
Malta in September 1942. Two years later his brother Christopher was killed in
action during the Italian Campaign; he had previously been awarded the Military
Cross for gallantry during the Second Battle of El Alamein. Hilda's elder son
Nigel Gibbes also took part in the Desert Campaign and died of wounds received
at the Battle of Gazala in May 1942.[1] Away from the fighting, both of Leonard's
surviving sisters, Ottilie and Hilda, died during the war, while Maud's brother
Roy Sambourne died shortly after, on 15 July 1946. Maud donated the Staplefield
cricket pavilion in his memory.

Just as Leonard and Maud were beginning to pick up the pieces after so many
losses, disaster struck Nymans. At 3 a.m. on the morning of his seventy-fifth
birthday, 19 February 1947, Leonard was awoken by the smell of smoke to find
flames coming through the ceiling outside his bedroom. He had been bedridden
for several days by a minor operation to remove a growth but managed to rouse
the household by ringing the main bell while Maud telephoned for the fire brigade.
All eight occupants were forced to escape in their nightclothes, but no one was
injured in the blaze. There was no water supply with which the fire crews who
rushed to the scene might bring the flames under control, so their hoses had to be
dragged to a pond a quarter of a mile away. The fire raged for over three hours,
consuming all the main rooms in the south and east of the building and sending
showers of stone tiles crashing down from the roof. Once it had taken hold of
the wooden floors, beams and panelling it was impossible for fire crews to gain
an entry.

Coverage of the disaster in the national press sacrificed accuracy for sensation,
with *The Times* reporting that all the Messel furniture, tapestries and paintings
were destroyed in the flames.[2] In reality, the butler Wells joined forces with the
Nymans gardeners and the village policeman and managed to rescue many of the

most valuable objects, which were piled up unceremoniously in the snow. In the days that followed, Leonard and Maud's daughter Anne compiled an inventory of items salvaged from the fire which ran to over forty pages, but there was no hiding the scale of the losses. The Velázquez that had hung over the fireplace in the library was just one of many treasures to perish in the flames.

The cause of the fire was never established. The winter of 1947 had been particularly cold, and the pipes of the medieval manor house had to be warmed to prevent them from freezing. It is believed that the use of a blowtorch to heat the pipes may have caused some of the wood panelling to smoulder and that this then burst into flames during the early hours of the morning. Fire crews had to smash through four inches of ice on the pond that supplied them with water to fight the flames, and their hoses had to be broken up afterwards once the water had frozen within them.

The loss of the dream house they had built so painstakingly just twenty years earlier was a crushing blow to Maud and Leonard, and they would never live at Nymans again. The fire had destroyed almost all the main rooms in the building, and there could be no thought of rebuilding again from scratch. Maud and Leonard were given temporary accommodation by their friends the Cadogans and then moved to the Birch Hotel at Haywards Heath. Soon afterwards their son Linley saw that Holmsted Manor in Staplefield, just down the hill from Nymans, had come on the market – by coincidence the very house John Dearden had built in 1891 after selling Nymans to Ludwig Messel. Leonard bought it, and they

James Comber (left) and Leonard Messel at Nymans

moved in soon after. As Leonard confided to his diary at the end of 1947, 'So ends a year of many blessings and some severe trials.'[3]

Leonard and Maud celebrated their golden wedding anniversary on 28 April 1948 in their new home surrounded by their children and grandchildren – 'a wonderful day for which we are truly thankful', Leonard wrote in his diary. They soon felt able to visit Nymans once more, and Leonard started returning on a daily basis to discuss the development of the garden with Comber, no longer acting as head gardener but still very much the senior authority on the estate. Now in her mid-seventies Maud busied herself once more in the Handcross Shakespeare Society, directing its November 1951 production of *Much Ado About Nothing* in two performances in the Handcross Parish Hall, with a repeat performance at Cuckfield the following March. It was clearly a comfort to her to be involved in these familiar activities with friends she had known for so many years, just as it would be when she took up the reins again in March 1954 to direct two performances of *The Winter's Tale*.[4]

By this time Maud was a widow. Leonard's health had been in decline from the beginning of the decade, and, while he still delighted in being pushed round Nymans garden in a bath chair, he was increasingly unable to take part in the social functions which had been such a feature of his life. He died on 4 February 1953 at the age of eighty, the cause of death given as pneumonia arising from influenza. His funeral took place three days later in the packed parish church of St Mark's, Staplefield. His coffin was carried out at the end of the service by six employees from the Nymans estate, including the new head gardener Cecil Nice. Giving the eulogy on behalf of the Bishop of Chichester, the Archdeacon of Lewes paid tribute to Leonard's long service to both God and country and drew attention to his 'continuous love of flowers and of all growing things'. Leonard's old friend and colleague at the Royal Horticultural Society, Lord Aberconway, writing his tribute in *The Times*, also remembered him first and foremost as a gardener:

> Leonard Messel was a most generous friend and anything that he could give to another good garden from his treasury of plants he gave generously and willingly. A walk round the garden with him in the late afternoon, followed by dinner in the beautiful dining hall that he had constructed, was a pleasure never to be forgotten.

Many more tributes would come in over the following days drawing out particular aspects of Leonard's life and career. Yet perhaps the most telling obituary was the local tribute published in the *Mid-Sussex Times* of 11 February 1953 and reprinted as a memorial leaflet afterwards. Along with a moving account of the funeral service and a list of the principal mourners, the paper spoke of the memories and the reputation that Leonard would leave behind him:

> For a long period the Colonel had been an invalid, and of late had only occasionally been seen outdoors, but at all times did he retain his concern for local affairs, his devotion to the Church and his interest in the wide circle of friends, among whom he will always be remembered as A FINE OLD ENGLISH GENTLEMAN.

The capital letters are there in the original, and they bear witness to the transformation of the Messel family within a single generation. In contrast to his father, the heavily accented German-Jewish immigrant who first bought Nymans in 1890, Leonard had sloughed off any suspicion of not belonging in the society they had made their own. While the family journey still had several twists and turns ahead of it, one thing was clear: the Messels had succeeded in their aim of integrating into their adopted country and had prospered.

The fate of Nymans after Leonard's death had been of great concern to Leonard and Maud for years. It was not felt that Linley, their eldest son, would be able to take on the responsibility of the estate, while Anne and Oliver each had their own interests to pursue. This left the option of finding a public body to take over Nymans, a possibility Leonard raised in a codicil to his will at the end of 1947. The most obvious choice was the National Trust, but it had never taken on gardens except when they were an adjunct to an historic house. Now, however, a joint committee had been formed with the Royal Horticultural Society to consider accepting historic gardens on their own account. The committee was chaired by Leonard's friend Lord Aberconway, who had just finalized arrangements for transferring his own estate of Bodnant in North Wales to the National Trust. Following a visit by representatives of the committee to ensure that the property was up to the standard required of such a gift, Leonard was able to add a second codicil to his will in February 1949 bequeathing Nymans to the National Trust 'to be held by it inalienably for the public benefit in such manner as they may think fit'.

On 16 May 1953, three months after Leonard's death, James Comber passed away. While he had officially stepped down from the position of head gardener some years earlier, he still lived on the estate and his influence remained unmistakable. It is safe to say that Nymans would never have developed into the famous garden that it is today had it not been for Comber's skill and commitment over a period of almost sixty years. Anne paid him a touching tribute in the *Journal of the Royal Horticultural Society* as 'one of the finest gardeners and most loyal of friends that a garden and family could ever have' and added some personal memories:

> As children we were terrified of Comber. He would round the corner here and pop up there, like a Mr Macgregor, ready to pounce on anyone not doing his utmost. I can remember him making me spend a whole day tying and retying a wall-plant in order to get the job perfect, reef knots and all. There was a reason why each thing had to be done, just so, and you had to learn it. But Comber had some secrets too, I fear, in his art of cultivation, which now we shall have to learn for ourselves.[5]

Comber's dedication set a powerful example to his successors, with the result that Nymans was managed by just three head gardeners in its first hundred years. The next to take on the role was Cecil Nice, who had started as a junior gardener under Comber in January 1925 on an hourly wage of 8d.; this rose to 9d. when he became foreman of the kitchen garden, responsible for growing the fresh fruit and vegetables that had to be packed in hampers and sent up by train to the Messels' home in London every other day when they were not down in the country.[6] Once he had taken over the management of the garden as a whole, Nice continued the tradition of raising new plants for exhibition at the Royal Horticultural Society and succeeded in winning a fresh array of honours for cultivars named in memory of those who had made Nymans great. One of the most celebrated, *Magnolia x loebneri* 'Leonard Messel', saw its 1955 Award of Merit upgraded to First Class Certificate in 1969; the following year, the equally famous *Camellia* 'Leonard Messel' was upgraded to First Class Certificate and won the Cory Cup.[7]

While horticultural activity continued, much would change at Nymans once the garden was formally opened to the public. Colonel Sir Ralph Stephenson Clarke from nearby Borde Hill and Vita Sackville-West from Sissinghurst presided over the ceremony on 26 March 1954 to mark the transfer of ownership to the National Trust. Maud and her three children represented the Messel family, with Anne delivering a speech in which she declared it a 'happy day' that the future of the garden was now assured.[8] While Nymans had previously held dedicated open days for enthusiasts, under the new dispensation visitors would be admitted from 2 p.m. to 7 p.m. (or dusk, if earlier) on Tuesdays, Wednesdays, Thursdays and Sundays from April to October for an entrance fee of two shillings. In contrast to today's relaxed regime no picnics were allowed.

Oliver, Anne, Linley and Maud Messel at Nymans on the day of its transfer to the National Trust

The early years of National Trust ownership were not always easy. The Messel family had agreed to pay a substantial endowment of £20,000 out of Leonard's estate to help finance the running of the property; yet even with the income from this investment it soon became clear that sales of produce from the kitchen garden and revenue from entrance fees could not meet the cost of maintaining Nymans on a professional basis. There were no facilities in the early years, and cars had to be parked on the grass verges of the garden, with predictably negative consequences. Visitor numbers remained disappointing and raised fears that there might never be more than limited interest in a garden that had been designed for horticultural specialists rather than the general public. As a result of continuing financial pressures, the decision was taken to close the kitchen garden and relieve some of the staff costs associated with having so many gardeners working on the estate. It would take many years for Nymans to become the success story that it is today.[9]

The last link to the creative genius behind Nymans was broken when Maud died at Holmsted Manor on 8 March 1960, aged eighty-four. Her funeral service followed three days later in the Staplefield parish church where she and Leonard had worshipped together for so many years. She had done as much as he had to establish the Messel presence in the Sussex countryside, and the design of the new house at Nymans had been very much her personal creation. The obituarist for *The Times* celebrated Maud's strength of character, her courage and her 'insatiable fund of interest in all around her' but could not resist a horticultural metaphor in suggesting that her 'iridescent, almost gossamer-like beauty was that of the tenderly nurtured exotic rather than of the wild hedgerow flower'.[10] Maud had an other-worldliness which could infuriate those who tried to persuade her to do anything she didn't want to do; her strong will had made her accustomed to getting her own way from an early age, and – like many of those who had been born a Messel – she could be difficult when crossed. Yet her capacity for getting things done is amply borne out by the many achievements of her full and creative life.

The position of Messel family representative at Nymans now passed to Maud's daughter Anne, although she had effectively been acting in that role for several years with her second husband Michael Parsons, Sixth Earl of Rosse. Anne's first marriage, to the successful Welsh barrister Ronald Armstrong-Jones, had been solemnized in a glittering society wedding at St Margaret's, Westminster, on 22 July 1925, followed by a reception at the Messels' London home at 104 Lancaster Gate. The bride, who wore 'a dress of white satin beauté, embroidered with pearls', was attended by no fewer than eight bridesmaids and three child attendants. In recognition of her service as their captain the Staplefield Girl Guides and Brownies provided her with a guard of honour at the church.[11]

Anne was an instantly recognizable figure in London high society from the time of her presentation at court on 8 June 1922, constantly featuring as one of the supreme beauties of the age in portraits for *The Tatler*, *Bystander* and *Vogue*. Nor did this change when she became mother of the two Armstrong-Jones children: Susan, on 12 February 1927, and Antony, on 7 March 1930. The latter was celebrated in *The Sphere* as the child of the 'most beautiful woman in London', and both daughter and son were regularly photographed alongside Anne in society portraits throughout their childhood.[12] Yet Anne's first marriage soon degenerated into unhappiness, and she came to resent the children in later years as a reminder of her time with Ronald Armstrong-Jones. The couple separated in 1933 before divorcing two years later.

Michael Parsons had succeeded to the title of Earl of Rosse before reaching his twelfth birthday, as his father had died of wounds received on active service in the First World War. The young earl progressed through Eton – where he

Anne Armstrong-Jones, née Messel, the 'most beautiful woman in London'

was a couple of years behind Anne's younger brother Oliver – to Christ Church, Oxford. He would then go on to have a full career in public life on both sides of the Irish Sea, his success attributed to a personal blend of efficiency, charm and good looks.[13] Usefully, Michael was active in the highest echelons of the National Trust, chairing its important Historic Buildings Committee from 1954 to 1969. He was also vice-president of the Royal Horticultural Society, which awarded him the Victoria Medal of Honour in 1974, and he joined Leonard Messel as a member of the exclusive Garden Society from 1949. Michael's accomplishments on the other side of the water were equally impressive, although his dual loyalties sometimes landed him in trouble: he was forced to stand down from his role as president of the Royal Horticultural Society of Ireland in 1969 for rashly proposing a toast to the Queen of England at the society's annual dinner.

Anne's second marriage marks a definitive stage in the Messel family's passage into high society. Marrying into the nobility was never part of Ludwig's plan for his children or grandchildren, and Leonard was deeply disappointed when Anne's first marriage to Ronald Armstrong-Jones came to a premature end. From a social perspective, however, the move from *Burke's Landed Gentry* to *Burke's Peerage* was a considerable step up and one that Anne relished.[14] After a private wedding at the City church of St Ethelburga's on 19 September 1935, Anne and Michael embarked on a five-month honeymoon, including a stay with Michael's brother Desmond in China. They returned to Birr Castle in Ireland in February 1936, where Anne quickly settled into her new position as Countess of Rosse.

Although she and Michael spent the greater part of their married life in Ireland, Anne was given the title of garden director at Nymans when her mother died. When she was there she exercised an autocratic authority that did not make things easy for the professional staff. There was bound to be a clash of cultures between a National Trust that had to make the garden financially viable and a family representative keen to preserve the past at all costs, and tensions often rose to the surface. At one point the Trust's head of gardens John Sales recalls Lord Rosse taking him to one side and saying, 'You may think my wife is difficult, John, but you should have met her mother.'[15]

Gradually the first modernizations to the garden began to take place. The open field that Ludwig Messel had provided to the Handcross Cricket Club fifty years earlier was converted into a car park with outside lavatories, and a new entrance area was constructed leading directly into the Top Garden. Visitor numbers began to rise, helped greatly in 1971 when Britain's most famous horticulturalist Percy Thrower presented two programmes on Nymans as part of the BBC's popular television series *Gardeners' World*. Management of the garden was rejuvenated when Cecil Nice retired as head gardener in 1980, after more than fifty years' service. He was succeeded by David Masters, a young and enthusiastic gardener who continued the tradition of cultivating new varieties of plants at Nymans. When Anne's husband died in 1979 his contribution to the garden would be honoured in the newly raised honeysuckle *Lonicera etrusca* 'Michael Rosse'.

Once her son William had inherited the Rosses' ancestral seat of Birr Castle, Anne retired to the west wing of the house at Nymans, the only part to have been restored to habitable order following the 1947 fire. In bequeathing the estate to the National Trust, Leonard had stipulated that the next generation of his family

The ruins at Nymans today

should retain the right to live in the house if they so wished, and Anne now availed herself of this privilege.[16] Accustomed to the grandeur of Birr, she referred to Nymans as her 'potting shed'; yet she did not permit her reduced circumstances to silence her voice on matters related to the garden or to the broader issues of heritage conservation. True to her own experience of Nymans as a family home, Anne argued the importance of maintaining the individual identities of National Trust properties so that the visiting public could feel they had a proper insight into what had made them the way they are. Her letter to this effect, published in the National Trust magazine in autumn 1983, warned against turning the heritage industry into an 'immense supermarket' where every property was so impersonal and homogenized as to be indistinguishable from the next:

> How well I recall, when at my much-loved home of Birr, looking like nothing on earth, in an old mackintosh on top of a ladder, pruning the plants on the castle walls and wall tying. Along came a party of American tourists. With a welcoming smile I said I hoped they had enjoyed the garden. 'Do you work here? Tell me about the people who live here.' 'Well – actually, I do' was my obvious reply. 'Oh, you just can't tell me *you* are Lady Rosse, for God's sake? Do you mind if we get out cameras because *this* is the *real* thing – you mean to say you actually *garden yourself* – now we feel part of this place.'

By the time she came back to Nymans, Anne's years of pruning on top of ladders were behind her. As her health began to fail, she agreed to pass on the role of Messel family representative to the next generation, and Alistair Buchanan, elder son of Anne's cousin Phoebe Messel, officially took over from her on 13 October 1987. Three days later the Great Storm hit south-east England with a ferocity unseen in three hundred years. Nymans lost 486 mature trees, including twenty of its twenty-eight national champions. Of the 260 conifers that stood in the garden the day before the storm, just seven survived the morning after. The monkey puzzle tree that had stood in front of the house at Nymans for more than a century, and which had just been adjudged the tallest specimen in the country, was destroyed. The tree had embodied the garden for Anne, and she was bitterly hurt by its loss. 'There was always a chair, a seat, under the Monkey Puzzle. It was a sort of meeting place. And it was a friend. And when it came down, it really was like a friend dying.'[17]

Many shrubs in the Wall Garden were crushed by falling timber, as was the Japanese pergola that had stood since the beginning of the century. Yet for all the heartache caused by the devastation, it was soon clear that nature had created the perfect opportunity for a rebirth of the garden. The mass of high trees which had been planted at Nymans over the years had become so dense that most of the original views were blocked by thick screens of foliage, and plans had already been laid to thin out the pinetum. Acting without sentimentality or restraint, the Great Storm did a more radical job than any human could have done. Nymans still boasts many national champions, but the views are restored and the garden can breathe once more.

Nymans has always been a gardener's garden and not to everyone's taste. James Lees-Milne, visiting Anne there in 1979, reflected in his diary, 'Not a sympathetic garden; still the stockbroker's, with too much colour, great clumps of herbaceous pink, and those metallic blue hydrangeas in the woods.'[18] Nymans was also treated critically in the 1980 television series *The English Garden* presented by Sir John Gielgud, who had known the Messel family personally from his earliest years. The programme, which looked back wistfully to the grand designs of the eighteenth century, acknowledged that 'many magnificent new varieties of plants and shrubs' had been bred at Nymans but concluded that the focus on horticultural innovation had come at the expense of the garden's layout.

> Gardens like Nymans certainly owe something to the Surrey style conceived by Gertrude Jekyll. This style deliberately denies any feeling of the grand. Often with no apparent overall plan, the sheer number of different flowers and shrubs are more important than the design. Even in a large garden, this style is fundamentally suburban.[19]

Rhododendron cerasinum
'Herbert Mitchell', painted
by Victoria Messel

The patrician tone of Gielgud's voice is unmistakable; yet even he admits that the focus on interesting plants that ordinary mortals can grow in their own gardens is what makes a visit to Nymans so appealing to the general public. Today Nymans is still one of the National Trust's most popular properties. The connection with the Messel family continues. Ludwig's great-grandson Alistair Buchanan celebrated thirty years as family representative in 2017. The Nymans Florilegium established in 2006 by Leonard's granddaughter Victoria Messel maintains the link between art and gardening started by Ludwig Messel himself. Yet the last word on Nymans should go to Muriel Messel, who concluded her foreword to *A Garden Flora* with a reflection made all the more poignant by her untimely death soon after.

I think that the garden may be fitly described as the triumph of hope. It was always full of experiments, it gave endless pleasure, and, if you walk through it, you will see the careful thought that was bestowed on each plant.

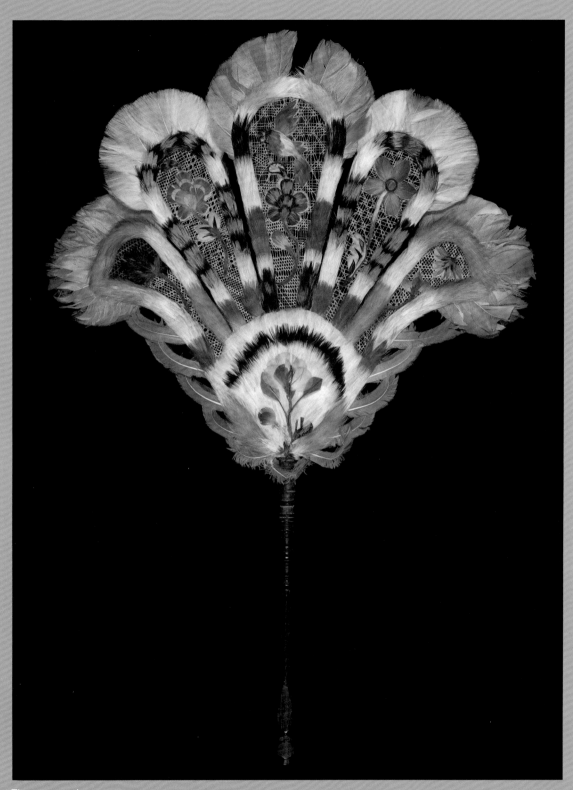

The seventeenth-century
Messel Standing Feather Fan

Serious Collecting 14

THE FIRE THAT destroyed the house at Nymans in 1947 was a personal tragedy for Leonard and Maud Messel, who had poured so much energy into redesigning it. But perhaps the greatest blow for Leonard was the irreparable loss of his collection of herbals and other botanical books, which were kept in the library at Nymans and which went up in the flames. The collection contained several rare incunabula from the fifteenth century, as well as early printed works from continental Europe and a set of all the notable English herbals from the sixteenth century onwards. Among its many treasures the library held the only known copy of the 1512 Nuremberg edition of Walafrid Strabo's *Hortulus*, the earliest medieval gardening book to have survived to modern times. Leonard had built up his collection steadily from the 1920s onwards, paying large sums for the most important works from specialist antiquarian booksellers.[1] The description of the library written by garden historian Eleanour Sinclair Rohde in 1933 shows just how seriously Leonard approached the task.[2]

The Victorian era had seen an explosion in the popularity of collecting, as the expanding middle classes aspired to create their own collections to rival those that the aristocracy had inherited from their ancestors on the Grand Tour. Instead of Greek and Roman antiquities, Sèvres porcelain or Old Master paintings, newcomers were content to amass collections of more accessible commodities such as old English pewter, Staffordshire ware or playing cards. To some, this democratization cast suspicion on the whole practice of collecting; to others, collectors were no more than solitary hoarders disconnected from society. So how could the aspiring collector still express self and status through collecting, yet in a socially acceptable manner beyond any hint of crass consumerism?

The founding of magazines such as *The Connoisseur: An Illustrated Magazine for Collectors* in 1901 and *The Burlington Magazine for Connoisseurs* in 1903 signalled a concerted attempt to move beyond the negative image of the Victorian collector and to redeem collecting for a new generation of socially conscious individuals. The badge of 'connoisseur' allowed Edwardian collectors to transcend any suspicion of base materialism by connecting with the higher world of scholarship as well as with other experts in their chosen field. The precondition

The 1542 herbal, *De Historia Stirpium*, a rare survival from Leonard Messel's botanical library

of this compact was that the collector must devote time and effort to studying the social, historical and artistic contexts in which their acquisitions had originally come into being and to work towards a level of expertise that would set them apart from the casual enthusiast. Thus was established the figure of the 'serious collector', whose elevated status gave them 'not only a sense of purpose', as Russell Belk puts it, 'but a sense of *noble* purpose in supposedly generating knowledge, preserving fragile art, or providing those who see it with a richer sense of history'.[3]

Leonard Messel certainly lived up to the ideal of a serious collector; in the words of his daughter Anne, 'My father was the true collector, who not only loved to show and to share but had a profound knowledge of all that he collected.'[4] Supported by the wealth he inherited from his father and the fortune he made from his own career as a stockbroker, Leonard channelled his energies into constructing multiple collections and developing his own expertise across a range of disciplines. Leonard never spoke of the cold world of business at home but would talk only of art and cultural affairs. The joy he experienced in collecting offered him a channel of release from the emotionally constricted world of upper-class society, not least when it came to the thrill of closing a purchase. Writing home from honeymoon, Leonard's newly married wife Maud recounted how he was 'perfectly mad' in his enthusiasm for beating down the prices demanded by Italian tradesmen and 'jumps about like a baby school boy when he gets anything cheap'.[5]

Leonard and Maud's shared passion for collecting was a central feature of their life together. They paid regular visits to the art galleries, antique dealers and silversmiths of London, and Leonard recorded their purchases meticulously in his personal inventory. As they became known as collectors, dealers would visit 104 Lancaster Gate at breakfast time and leave potential purchases for unhurried consideration so that Leonard could return to them after his day's work in the City. Nor was their collecting in any way confined to British shores. Decades later Anne would recall the thrill experienced when treasures collected on the couple's travels in Europe were delivered to their London home:

> Lancaster Gate was filled as the years went by with the spoils of the visits of my parents to Italy, Spain, Germany and Holland. How well I recollect the arrival of the vans, months later, and the childish excitement of my dear parents unpacking them. Those were the days when you were able to import what you fancied, and by the First World War the house had become a treasure house of the widest possible range of art and beauty.

Maud made the interior design of 104 Lancaster Gate a personal priority, taking Leonard to visit stately homes and palaces in order to hunt down styles that could be emulated in their own domain. As she wrote to her mother after one visit in early 1905, they decided to model their interiors after the rooms in the Baroque extension to Hampton Court Palace built by Sir Christopher Wren in the latter years of the seventeenth century.[6] Maud sought professional assistance from period recreation specialists Lenygon and Morant, interior designers to the Royal Family, who supplied the main rooms at Lancaster Gate with what Anne described as 'the finest brocade curtains in the Italian style'.

While the hall, the dining-room and the drawing-room were hung with tapestries and paintings, the walls of the museum room were lined with patterned damask and glass-fronted display cabinets filled with choice examples from Leonard's various collections. Those spanned a broad range including English and continental silver, European and Chinese glass, ancient coins, ivories, porcelain and Japanese netsuke as well as old English furniture, arms and armour, tapestries and bronzes; there were also more recherché items such as antique toys and seventeenth-century silver-mounted coconut cups. The overall effect was that of a connoisseur's art gallery, harking back to the tradition of the *Kunstkammer* that Leonard would have known from his time in Germany.

Leonard also collected paintings, with several of the most notable pieces coming via Sir Hugh Lane, the Anglo-Irish art dealer who had previously helped Ludwig Messel put together his own collection of Old Masters. In November 1909 Leonard paid the considerable sum of £1,700 for six seventeenth-century

Leonard Messel, 'the true collector'

paintings from Lane, including William Dobson's portrait of Richard Weston, First Earl of Portland, and Sir Godfrey Kneller's portrait of Queen Mary II, from the collection of the Duke of Leeds. He purchased many more paintings from Lane and from other London dealers over the years, one of the most significant being the portrait of Barbara Villiers by the Dutch artist Willem Wissing. Leonard's active preference for such aristocratic portraits may reflect a latent desire to associate himself with the great and the good from past generations, hinting at an English pedigree he never possessed. Yet his artistic purchases were also driven by other considerations, as with the James Tissot oil *The Gardener* he bought from the retrospective of the artist's work held at the Leicester Galleries in January 1937.[7]

Leonard was an early member of the Walpole Society, a subscription scheme founded in 1911 to promote the study of British art. Like his father before him, he commissioned portraits of members of the Messel family from contemporary artists, the most celebrated of which was the oil painting of Maud by the Scottish artist Robert Brough. One of Brough's last paintings before his untimely death in a railway accident in January 1905, the large portrait was well received when it was shown posthumously at London's New Gallery in April of that year and later when Leonard lent it out for exhibition at the dedicated retrospective of Brough's work held at the Burlington Fine Arts Club in 1907. While the original painting was lost in the fire that destroyed the main house at Nymans, the copy Oliver Messel painted in his own style hung in the kitchen at Old House until its sale in 2002.[8]

Maud was also the subject of a portrait by the miniaturist Annie Jane Harrison, a pupil of the Solomon J. Solomon whom Ludwig Messel had commissioned to paint his wife Annie in 1885. Harrison's portrait was shown alongside other miniatures in the Watercolour Room at the Royal Academy's 1910 exhibition, and the artist was further commissioned to paint a watercolour of Maud with two of the Messel children.[9] Leonard himself was depicted in a small bronze bust from 1905 by the sculptor Francis Derwent Wood, best known today for his statue of the Boy David atop the Machine Gun Corps Memorial on the north side of Hyde Park Corner. The sculpture portrays Leonard as an eighteenth-century gentleman in powdered wig and cravat, in keeping with the family's passion for recreating the romantic history of Elizabeth Linley and the Irish dramatist Richard Sheridan. Maud claimed a family connection to Elizabeth Linley through her father and revelled in the romance of the couple's elopement and secret marriage. Leonard was happy to play the part of Sheridan, donning wig and costume to accompany Maud, as Mrs Sheridan, to the fancy-dress Arts Club Ball in December 1911.

Likenesses of the Messel children were also commissioned, the most significant being the portraits painted by Glyn Philpot between 1911 and 1912. Philpot, a family friend who would go on to become a mentor to Oliver Messel in his own career, painted individual portraits of Maud and Linley plus a joint portrait of the two younger children together, receiving £350 as his fee for the three works. Both Anne and Oliver treasured fond memories of sitting for their portrait at Philpot's Tite Street studio. 'After he had finished working he would scrape the paint from his pallet on to paper, fold it, and make us butterflies,' Oliver recalled.[10] Philpot's painting of them was destroyed in the fire at Nymans, but photographic reproductions show it to have been a charming portrayal.[11] Anne also sat for a portrait by the Victorian artist Herbert Draper, best known today for his large canvases of water nymphs.[12] In 1921 the society painter W.B.E. Ranken was paid £75 for individual heads of Linley, Anne and Oliver; the two boys' portraits came up for sale in separate auctions in September 2020, each fetching many thousands of pounds.

Maud shared her husband's passion for collecting, delighting in the purchases that they made together and building her own historical collection of textiles, cushions and woven silks. That she approached collecting with the same seriousness as Leonard is clear from the record she kept of purchases made in Britain and on the Continent over a thirty-year period from 1902 to 1935. The inventory stretches to hundreds of pieces of lace, brocade, damask and other fabrics, as well as the business cards of textile merchants from whom she bought the items. She also collected antique embroidery, sometimes spending

The Museum Room at 104 Lancaster Gate

significant sums to acquire older pieces, such as the £60 paid in 1903 for 'two large panels of seventeenth-century embroidery and a chasuble in old needlework' in a shop in Naples.[13] These samples could also double up as patterns for the needlework classes Maud ran in Balcombe and at Nymans.

Maud's most significant legacy comes in the form of the dress collection she bequeathed to her daughter Anne and which has since been expanded so that it spans six generations of women from the Messel family. All the items of clothing and accessories now in the collection were originally designed to be worn, carried or otherwise used, sometimes for special occasions such as weddings or parties, in other cases for regular wear. Unlike impersonal objects purchased in order to build a collection, their preservation is an act of remembrance that perpetuates the memory of the individual Messel family women and the circumstances in which each of the outfits was worn. The garments also reflect each woman's personal style and the social context in which she found herself. Maud's taste in clothes was 'conventionally elegant and feminine', even if she kept abreast of changing fashions and allowed herself the occasional flourish such as the use of ammonite buttons or gold scarab clasps to embellish her outfits.[14] For her trousseau and for many years after her marriage she ordered her dresses from the Grosvenor Square salon of Sarah Fullerton Monteith Young, as well as from court dressmakers Reville and Rossiter and other London fashion houses. Before marrying into the Messel family Maud and her mother had shopped at department stores such as Woollands, Whiteleys and Harvey Nichols. With the superior purchasing power that came with her marriage Maud gained access to the highest-quality dressmakers working in England at that time.

The dresses Anne added to the Messel collection are more individualistic and daring than Maud's, a reflection of her flamboyant character. Before her marriage to Ronald Armstrong-Jones, Anne had worked at the exclusive dressmakers Victoire on Sloane Street, where she learnt to cut and sew to a professional standard. She would later use the skill to assist her brother Oliver with stage costumes and to make her daughter Susan's wedding dress. She developed personal friendships with emerging designers such as Norman Hartnell and Charles James, whose bespoke creations for Anne in the 1930s form a centrepiece of the Messel dress collection today. Anne remembered the 'whimsical and impetuous' Charlie James with affection in the tribute she wrote for the Brooklyn Museum's retrospective of his work in 1982.

> Everything he designed was a masterpiece of style and elegance. He laced daring originality with an unfailing flair of the best possible taste for the occasion for which the dresses had to be worn. But – the wearer if she wanted to enjoy his creations had sometimes to be sacrificed for the designs! To begin with, there could be a mystery as to how to get into the clothes when they arrived! Or which was the front or the back, which he might have altered at the last moment! With some, walking might be difficult – or sitting down tricky! But an appreciative wearer would gladly cooperate.[15]

In the post-war period Anne turned to London couturiers such as John Cavanagh, whose dress for Anne to wear at the Coronation Ball in 1953 incorporated patterned silks that Oliver Messel had designed for the Hungarian émigré Nicholas Sekers. As she spent more time at Birr, Anne also patronized Irish designers such as Sybil Connolly and Irene Gilbert, whose close twenty-year collaboration with the Countess was based on mutual inspiration and respect.

'She is never slow to disagree with me,' Gilbert commented, 'but I always welcome it because she is a woman of exceptional talent with a needle. When I make something for her it combines the best of our ideas.'[16] Anne also turned to continental designers who had made their home in Ireland, such as the Danish couturier Ib Jorgensen and the German master tailor Thomas Wolfangel. Above all, Anne remained faithful to Maud's conception of the dress collection as a living record of the past, and she was the driving force behind its preservation. Now held by Brighton Museum's costume department, the collection comprises more than five hundred garments and accessories from the 1870s through to the earliest years of the twenty-first century.

Anne Messel, 'a collector's daughter'

While the Messel dress collection is a record of a feminine world, it would be wrong to divide Leonard and Maud's collecting along strictly gendered lines. Beyond his contribution to the garden at Nymans and the botanical library that was lost in the fire of 1947, Leonard is chiefly remembered today for the collection of ornamental fans he built up over his lifetime, which now forms the Messel-Rosse Collection at the Fitzwilliam Museum in Cambridge. With their connection to ladies' fashion and court intrigues, fans have traditionally been objects of interest for female collectors; the collection donated to the British Museum in 1891 by the indefatigable Charlotte Schreiber was the most famous example from the nineteenth century, while the royal collection curated by Queen Mary – who became a friend of Leonard's – originated in fans collected by Queen Victoria herself. As with his other pursuits, however, Leonard's fan collection was primarily a scholarly endeavour in line with the Edwardian ideal of the collector as connoisseur. His guiding principle was to create an ensemble that was representative of the finest examples of fans throughout the ages from both European and Asian contexts.

Some of the fans Leonard managed to acquire are remarkable rarities. The Messel Mica Fan is one of only four recorded specimens of the type known to exist in the world. Made at the time of the Restoration, it is a folding fan composed of three bands of transparent mica panels mounted in paper, painted in body colour and gilt, with sticks and guards of ivory. The Messel Standing Feather Fan is an even more precious survival from the second half of the seventeenth century; made in South America for the European market, it is decorated with brilliant blue, orange, yellow and purple feathers arranged to resemble the purple-breasted cotinga bird, a native of the rainforests of Central and South America. Most poignant of all Leonard's collection is the simple English fan manufactured to

The Messel Mica Fan

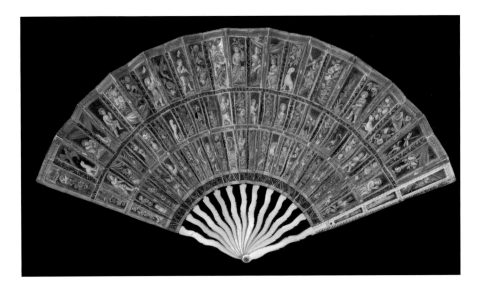

celebrate George III's recovery from his first major bout of mental illness, which may have been used in the service of thanksgiving for the King's return to health held at St Paul's Cathedral on 23 April 1789.

Leonard would host occasional 'Fan Evenings' at Lancaster Gate, at which chosen friends and fellow connoisseurs could examine the specimens in his collection and discuss the finer points of their significance. He had risen through the ranks of the Worshipful Company of Fan Makers to become free warden in 1919 and master in 1920 and was well known among the community of fan collectors. Several Messel fans were included in the comprehensive *History of the Fan* published by George Woolliscroft Rhead in 1910, and the same author later contributed two dedicated articles on Leonard's collection to *The Connoisseur*.[17] The opening paragraph of the first illustrates the Edwardian thesis that scholarship and erudition allow the serious collector to transcend any charge of frivolous consumerism and even the bounds of gender itself.

It is not usual in the countries of the Occident to associate the fan with the masculine gender, neither with regard to its use nor as forming the material for a collection, the prevailing idea being to invest this dainty article of feminine attire with a certain sense of triviality. Lt.-Col. Messel, however, whose very extensive collection of fans is here in part under review, understands his subject thoroughly, and knows that, properly regarded, so far from being trivial, it is as serious as anything that could occupy the attention of a collector.

Leonard lent seventeen fans from his collection to the spectacular Japan–British Exhibition held at London's White City in 1910; with other loans from Queen Mary, the *Daily Graphic* concluded that it was 'a collection of fans such as have never before been shown in any exhibition in the world'.[18] Ten years after Leonard's death 130 pieces were selected to form the Victoria and Albert Museum's dedicated exhibition 'Fans from the Leonard Messel Collection'. Its curator Peter Thornton's illustrated review affirmed it to be 'one of the most important fan collections in Europe'.[19] Yet the collection's ultimate transfer into public hands was a virtue born of necessity. Anne inherited the fans on her father's death and kept them together for the next thirty years. As she became frailer towards the end of her life it was clear that she would require increasing levels of care if she wished to continue living at Nymans. The fan collection was recognized as an immediately realizable asset that would enable her to enjoy the home assistance she needed, and its sale to the Fitzwilliam Museum was eventually agreed in 1984 for the sum of £100,000, four-fifths of which came from the National Heritage Memorial Fund. In the foreword she wrote to Nancy Armstrong's guide to the collection in its new setting, Anne declared:

> That the matchless collection of fans formed by my father, Leonard Messel, finds its lasting home in the Fitzwilliam is my lasting delight. This transfer of responsibility of ownership from family inheritance to a museum in this country, especially to a great university museum, fulfils, I know, my father's wishes, as well as my own.

The truth was a little more complicated, as Anne had recoiled from the loss of the family collection at the last minute and almost intervened to stop the deal from going through. Yet reality prevailed, and the transfer of over 400 individual pieces went ahead at the beginning of 1985. Anne's personal copy of the Fitzwilliam's annual report for that year has been preserved in the Messel family archive at Nymans, with her lament scrawled across the front cover: 'Oh, the pang it gave me parting with my father's world collection of fans.' Yet the result is more perfect than either she or Leonard could ever have imagined, for the collection is beautifully presented in its own permanent gallery as a national treasure for future generations to admire. As the art historian Sir David Piper put it in his review for the *Financial Times*:

> The rustle and crepitation of fans that once enlivened the chatter and froth of parties may have been silenced for ever, but there remain among the intricacies and conceits of the Messel collection many masterpieces of visual lyricism and craftsmen's skill. Their presence in the Fitzwilliam adds a further grace note to the museum's range.[20]

Anne, Countess of Rosse,
photographed by Bassano in 1936

Preserving the Past 15

T HE PRINCIPLE OF conservation was the inspiration for much of Anne Messel's life. It was one which she applied to each of the family homes with which she came into contact, whether on her own side or through her marriage to her second husband Michael Parsons, Sixth Earl of Rosse. The Rosse family seat is Birr Castle in the Irish county of Offaly, originally acquired in 1620 and handed down through the generations ever since. Anne went to live there on her return from honeymoon in 1936 and fell in love with the romantic castle and its extensive grounds. Over the years she helped restore and redesign several of the most impressive rooms in the castle, lining the walls of the saloon and drawing-room with the opulent damasks she knew from her childhood at Lancaster Gate.

The couple spent less time at the Rosses' English seat of Womersley Park in Yorkshire, which had passed into the family's ownership through marriage in the second half of the nineteenth century but which lay abandoned for the fifteen years prior to 1935. The floor in the drawing-room had been ripped up and the contents sold off, so that Michael had all but resolved to put the house up for sale, but Anne was determined to restore it and quickly set about buying back pieces of furniture from dealers in nearby Pontefract. The decision proved timely, as Anne would move to Womersley with her four children for the duration of the Second World War while Michael was away serving with the Irish Guards. It is a testament to the power of Anne's personality that the soldiers billeted with them were prepared to devote their spare time to creating a box-hedge parterre for her.[1]

Of all the properties associated with Anne during her life it is 18 Stafford Terrace in Kensington that saw her greatest hour. Anne's mother Maud had entrusted her with the care of the former Sambourne family home, a magical time capsule in the Aesthetic style that had been left untouched since the 1890s. Anne continued to use it for parties when she was in London, even though she had been given the more practical Belgravia residence of 25 Eaton Terrace by her father as a first-wedding present back in 1925. The soirées soon became legendary. 'Although the Stafford Terrace drawing-room is still very much with us,' recalls the architectural historian Mark Girouard, 'it is hard to put over the glamour imparted to it by the personality of Lady Rosse and the parties that she gave there.'

His description goes some way towards recreating the effect:

> The enfolding glamour of evenings in her drawing-room, of the soft lighting from low lamps picking out the violets (were they real or crystallized, I can't remember) in Paul de Lamerie silver, while white-gloved footmen handed round drinks, remains enshrined in my memory in a golden glow. The presence of Princess Margaret could give the parties extra cachet, but the guests were always varied and amusing, among them John Betjeman, Harold Acton, Osbert Lancaster – and I remember, not having caught his name, asking Compton Mackenzie what he did – another remark that was not well received.[2]

It was at Stafford Terrace that Anne accomplished what is perhaps her most enduring legacy: the founding of the Victorian Society. Her husband Michael was a leading light in the Georgian Group, which had been so successful in raising awareness of the importance of preserving Britain's greatest eighteenth-century buildings.[3] Yet there was still a strong resistance to extending the same respect to the Victorian era, so that more and more nineteenth-century buildings were falling under threat of demolition. After its partial destruction by fire in 1947 Sir George Gilbert Scott's Preston Town Hall was condemned to wholesale demolition despite a public campaign to restore it. Plans to remove A.W.N. Pugin's Bishop's House in Birmingham to make way for the city's new inner ring road were already under way by 1952, and 'thus it came about that one of the most extraordinary buildings in Britain was replaced by a traffic island', as Timothy Brittain-Catlin lamented afterwards.[4] The decision – kept secret for years by the government – to demolish Thomas Collcutt's Imperial Institute in South Kensington was the final straw. Something had to be done.

Anne hosted the preliminary gathering to discuss the formation of a society 'to save the Victorian century' at 18 Stafford Terrace on Bonfire Night 1957. She had planned the evening in advance with the poet and champion of Victorian architecture John Betjeman, who had first proposed the idea back in the summer and who looked to Anne to draw together a group of enthusiasts for the task. Invitations duly went out to around thirty of Anne's friends who were known to share her concern for the preservation of Victorian heritage, some of whom were already influential figures within the world of architecture. The historian Asa (later Lord) Briggs attended out of his interest in Victoriana and because he was already friends with Anne, whom he considered to be 'one of the most formidable social hostesses'. He was not above admitting to a secondary motive: 'I knew also that if you went to 18 Stafford Terrace, you'd get the best champagne in London.'[5]

In addition to Briggs, Betjeman and the Rosses, those present included Anne's brother Oliver and other well-known figures such as James Pope-Hennessy,

Henri Cartier-Bresson's photograph of Anne entertaining at 18 Stafford Terrace in 1959

John Piper, Osbert Lancaster, Sir Hugh and Lady Casson, Christopher Hussey, Rosamond Lehmann and Peter Clarke, who immortalized the occasion in verse.[6] Nikolaus Pevsner was unable to attend owing to 'a long-standing engagement with Guy Fawkes', but he sent Anne a letter in advance outlining what he saw as the main tasks that the society should set itself, which Betjeman read out to the assembled gathering. Pevsner's strategic vision was a driving force behind the Victorian Society's success in securing a formal role for itself in the national planning system, so that today it has to be consulted on all applications of listed building consent that involve any element of demolition.

Sir Kenneth Clark had written his own letter to the November meeting to point out the importance of preserving decorative objects from the Victorian era as well as famous buildings. 'Lady Rosse,' recalled Briggs, 'who was surrounded at 18 Stafford Terrace by a multitude – a plethora – of objects, couldn't help but agree.' *The Times* reported two days later, 'A society is to be formed to protect, and foster interest in, Victorian and Edwardian buildings and their contents. It will probably be modelled on the existing Georgian Group, except that it is likely to pay as much attention to furniture, textiles and similar products of the nineteenth and early twentieth centuries as to architecture.'[7]

The first formal meeting of the Victorian Society took place at Stafford Terrace on 25 February 1958, and this time Pevsner was very much in attendance. Mark Girouard recalls an incident from early in the evening as the aristocratic and academic wings of the fledgling association experienced a clash of cultures:

> During the preliminary drinks Nikolaus Pevsner advanced on our hostess, Lady Rosse, with the benign air of someone who was going to give her a treat. He was sure she would be interested to know, he said, that there was a house in the suburbs of Birmingham that was exactly like Stafford Terrace in preserving its Victorian décor and contents complete. Lady Rosse was not at all pleased: Stafford Terrace was, in her view, unique, and Birmingham was a place to which one did not go.[8]

The initial years of the Victorian Society left Anne and her fellow campaigners in no doubt as to the struggle they faced. Their first two major battles both ended in defeat, even if they did much to put the society on the map. The fight to save the monumental Euston Arch that had formed part of the original entrance to the London train station since 1837 received considerable (although far from universal) public support, and the Victorian Society offered to launch a fundraising campaign to move the massive Doric propylaeum on rollers so that it could be relocated nearer to the Euston Road. The Conservative government of Harold Macmillan had no interest in the scheme, however, and it was demolished in 1961. Insult would follow injury when the silver model of the Euston Arch donated to the Victorian Society by the demolition contractors was stolen from the society's headquarters in 1968.

The second battle that the Victorian Society took on was to save James Bunning's 1849 Coal Exchange in the City of London, famed for its multi-storey cast-iron rotunda. The building had suffered bomb damage in the Second World War and ceased to operate as an exchange on the Attlee government's nationalization of coal production in 1947, leaving it vulnerable to the Corporation of London's road-widening schemes. Despite the fact that Pevsner had identified the Coal Exchange among 'the twelve irreplaceable buildings of nineteenth-century England', the Corporation refused to entertain any of the alternatives that the Victorian Society proposed in place of demolition. Bunning's masterpiece was torn down in 1962.

While the 1960s were to see the further loss of Eaton Hall in Cheshire, Bayons Manor in Lincolnshire and important examples of nineteenth-century commercial architecture in cities such as London, Leeds and Edinburgh, the Victorian Society was soon able to mount stronger resistance in favour of preservation. Early victories included saving Sir Charles Barry's magnificent

Anne with Sir John
Betjeman, photographed
by Desmond O'Neill

Bridgewater House on London's Green Park, which was slated for demolition
in 1961; the University Museum and Broad Street front of Balliol College in
Oxford; and the Tower House that the architect of Cardiff Castle, William Burges,
had built for himself in Kensington. Yet the most spectacular success of these
years was the Victorian Society's campaign to halt the proposed demolition of
the Foreign Office, the Italianate creation of Sir George Gilbert Scott and Sir
Matthew Digby Wyatt at the heart of Whitehall. A second government proposal
in 1965 envisaged the wholesale destruction of all buildings below Downing
Street, and the Victorian Society fought off these plans, too. The victories laid
the foundations for future triumphs such as the preservation of the Albert Dock
in Liverpool and the successful Grade I listing of St Pancras Station, which also
prevented the destruction of the Midland Grand Hotel adjoining it.

Anne was midwife to the Victorian Society's birth and a regular presence at
its meetings, but she was never engaged in its day-to-day activities. In truth, she
had her hands full with her own properties, and the need to secure their future
was made all the more pressing as her husband Michael's health declined in the
second half of the 1970s. Nymans was safe with the National Trust, Birr would
pass to the elder Parsons son, William, while his younger brother Martin would
inherit Womersley, but arrangements still had to be made for the museum house
of 18 Stafford Terrace, which had been the Sambourne family home. With a
view to its preservation, Anne and Michael decided to offer the property to the
nation, and the Greater London Council agreed in 1979 to buy house and contents

Anne handing the keys of 18 Stafford Terrace to Willie Bell, Chair of the Greater London Council's Historic Buildings Committee

for £225,000 on the condition that the Victorian Society would be responsible for opening it to the public.[9] The property was duly opened the following autumn as a museum displaying what life was like in a middle-class home in the late nineteenth century, and Anne's personal contribution was recognized when she received the London Conservation Award from the Greater London Council in 1983.[10] Ownership of 18 Stafford Terrace has now passed to the Royal Borough of Kensington and Chelsea, but the house owes its survival to Anne and the Victorian Society that she founded there over sixty years ago.

On 1 July 1979, not long after agreement had been reached on the future of the house, Michael collapsed on the steps of 18 Stafford Terrace and died shortly afterwards in Anne's arms. He had been unwell for some months following an operation the previous year, and Anne found it difficult to come to terms with the visible deterioration in his health. The couple had enjoyed over forty years of 'supremely happy' marriage, as John Cornforth described it – 'one of those very rare marriages that give real pleasure to their friends'.[11] Another of those friends, James Lees-Milne, pronounced them 'the most blissfully happy couple I have known'.[12] For all her outward bravery Anne was devastated when Michael died and struggled to rebuild her life without him. The fact that she managed to do so with such aplomb is further evidence of her strength of character, as she dedicated the final decade of her own life to preserving the memory of her husband, her family and others whom she held dear.

Anne, Countess of Rosse died at Nymans on 3 July 1992, aged ninety. She had enjoyed a charmed life spanning almost the entire twentieth century and had witnessed momentous social changes, especially in the wake of the Second World War. Those who knew her leave no doubt that she was an extraordinary woman. She had a personality that could light up a room, and even though she had received no formal education she possessed a sparkling intellect and a sharp wit. Yet the historical record has not always been kind to her: she has been portrayed as a social climber and as an uncaring mother to the children of her unhappy first marriage. Anne could be wilfully obdurate, as has often been pointed out; yet it was her determination to get things done according to her own creative vision that won her the freedom to express herself. Any critical observer must be conscious of the double standards which have traditionally depicted such strong-minded women as manipulative, even heartless, while applauding their male equivalents for their force of character. Anne could be inconsiderate, just as she could be charming, but ultimately it was her strength of will that enabled her to make her mark in what was very much a man's world.

Anne was reunited in death with her husband Michael, and both lie buried at Womersley, where her funeral took place. She had organized the service herself 'in great theatrical style', as James Lees-Milne wrote approvingly in his diary.

> Two priests, one Irish swinging a censer. Anne's coffin invisible under a golden pall smothered with wreaths and raised on a catafalque . . . Six young men, one a grandson wearing ponytail, carried the coffin slowly down the nave through the west door, across the graveyard into the grounds of the house, where they put it into the hearse, a handsome, streamlined, modern motor. From her own front door Anne was driven away for the last time, with great dignity and in total silence. Moving moment.[13]

John Cornforth's eulogy highlighted Anne's artistic and creative achievements, drawing out her lifetime's contribution 'as a preserver of the beautiful and the romantic'. Marrying into the nobility had impressed upon her an obligation to build continuity between the past and the future; certainly, centuries of Rosse tradition weighed more heavily than the history of her own family with its German-Jewish wanderings. Yet Anne embraced her Messel heritage with enthusiasm, revelling in the achievements of her father and grandfather and in the artistic legacy which had been handed down to her from earlier generations. John Cornforth declared that she was 'proud of the Jewish elements in her background and in her own personality', an indication that the positive overtones of such a heritage now outweighed any fear of being seen as an alien presence in British society.

Even Anne's talent for preservation could not prevent the dispersal of Messel possessions after her death. Her parents' passion for collecting had been fuelled by the double fortune of inherited wealth (very lightly taxed) and a stockbroker's income. Without the income, and with the top rate of estate duty touching 80 per cent in the 1950s, Anne remained determined to keep the major collections together, even when forced to hand them over to public institutions. Her children's generation, by contrast, would have to sell off individual items in order to meet debts, death duties and the need for ready cash. Sotheby's held a sale of the residual contents of Nymans on 27 June 1994 featuring over 460 lots of ceramics, glass, paintings, artworks, textiles, clocks and furniture. The house at Nymans was permanently opened to the public three years later.

Oliver Messel photographed
in his studio by Angus McBean

Bright Young Things 16

OLIVER HILARY SAMBOURNE Messel was born on 13 January 1904 in his parents' Tyburnia home of 27 Gloucester Terrace. He was the youngest of Maud and Leonard's three children, and Maud's mother Marion pronounced him 'a clean, strong, happy baby' as well as 'very Hebrew-looking'.[1] The following year the family moved to their new home at 104 Lancaster Gate, an environment that gave Oliver the best possible start in a life devoted to the arts. By dint of hard work and commitment coupled with a sunny disposition and a considerable appetite for fun, Oliver would rise to become Britain's leading stage designer from the 1930s to 1950s, with a glittering career encompassing theatre, ballet, opera and cinema on both sides of the Atlantic.

Oliver spent his earliest years between Lancaster Gate and the eighteenth-century elegance of Balcombe House in Sussex. He found the London home overwhelming. 'As a child I was terrified of climbing the dark stairs and spooky landings which I was convinced were filled with goblins.'[2] He loved the family's pretty country house far more. Here Oliver was surrounded by beautiful treasures and 'very special toys, only to be peeped at as a great treat'. These included painted Hungarian peasant dolls 'with many petticoats in layers' and finely carved German toys from Nuremberg depicting village scenes that could be rearranged at will. 'These gave me infinite delight & I think influenced my interest in making detailed models.' Most presciently of all:

> My Father had also given me one of the Pollocks of Hoxton penny plain & twopence coloured toy theatres, with a great variety of scenes & figures to cut out. This I adored, & soon began innovating miniature stage settings myself, with tiny figures which I jointed & weighted so that they could move on strings like marionettes.

While his elder brother Linley was sent off to boarding-school in preparation for a career in the Messel family's stockbroking firm, Oliver and his sister Anne were allowed to inhabit their own private fantasies. As Anne later recalled, 'We lived in a world of imagination and making things from our earliest childhood.

Oliver and Anne posing for an article on children's games by Gladys Beattie Crozier in *Every Woman's Encyclopaedia*

If we had a mouse that died we'd have a lovely funeral and make wreaths for it and Oliver would make a glorious coffin out of a soap box. But beautiful, absurd childish things.'[3]

The children were showered with love by their mother, and Oliver responded by making imaginative presents for her as well as crocheting hats for his sister. When the time came for him to go off to his prep school he devised any number of imaginary illnesses to avoid having to leave home. His dislike of the institution was made all the worse during the First World War when fellow schoolboys discovered his surname was German and bullied him accordingly. Oliver was not a strong child and was forced to wear callipers to support his legs when small, but he soon discovered that he could get out of most things by pleading with his mother that he was unwell. Anne acted as his conspirator, as she loved having him at home with her, and the two forged a bond that would last the rest of their lives. Oliver would later write, telegram or phone Anne with florid displays of affection almost every day they were apart from each other, and she reciprocated with equally effusive letters of her own.

Oliver went up to Eton in the Michaelmas term of 1917 and found it more to his liking than his earlier experiences of school. Here he was able to mix with the cohort of brilliant young men who from an early age challenged the accepted canon of artistic and literary taste that had been handed down to them by previous generations. The leading lights of this cultural revolution were Harold Acton and Brian Howard, both of whom brought with them the influences of their rarefied upbringings: Acton in the Anglo-Italian splendour of his parents' villa at La Pietra, outside Florence; Howard as the only son of an American-Jewish family living in London, with a European-educated father who was a prominent art dealer. Oliver was friends with both Acton and Howard and a member of the Eton Society of the Arts which they founded as a forum for weekly discussions on avant-garde literature and aesthetics. The brilliance of these privileged young men was rejected by contemporaries such as George Orwell as 'unmanly', but it appealed to Oliver as exactly the type of free thinking he wished to develop in his own life.[4]

Oliver was petite and, like previous generations of Messel males, dark in hair and complexion with dark-brown eyes; his friend, the Welsh writer Emlyn Williams, assumed him to be Italian when he first set eyes on him. Many contemporaries remarked on his good looks, but no better physical description of him exists than from the pen of novelist Barbara Cartland, who knew him as a young man: 'He had a round forehead, satanic eyebrows, pointed ears, flashing white teeth, curly hair, and looked like a fawn.'[5] Oliver was always immaculately attired and refused to relax his standards even when working; as he explained some years later, 'I always dress in my smartest London clothes when I have any painting to do. I think the effort of trying not to make them dirty is an excellent form of self-discipline.'[6]

This devotion to sartorial elegance was one of the many traits that Oliver had confirmed in him by his mentor Glyn Philpot, whom he first met when Philpot was commissioned to paint the Messel children before the First World War. Philpot was a major influence on Oliver's decision to pursue a career as an artist, and Oliver revered him for several reasons. Not only was he a champion of traditional painting techniques at

Oliver Messel at Eton

a time when fashions were racing off in other directions, but as a homosexual convert to Roman Catholicism he was driven by a strong spiritual impulse, as well as an infectious sense of fun. 'I felt as if he had been borrowed from another age,' said Oliver. 'His sense of values was the truest I have ever known.'[7]

At Philpot's suggestion Oliver left Eton early and enrolled at the Slade under its legendary teacher Professor Henry Tonks. While the discipline of the art school would eventually prove too much for his independent character, he formed friendships there of lasting importance for his future career. Foremost among these was his collaboration with fellow student Rex Whistler, a kindred spirit with whom Oliver began to experiment making papier-mâché masks during their free time. It was characteristic of Oliver's good fortune that these extracurricular creations should turn out to be the catalyst for his success. Dr W.A. Propert, a family friend and an authority on Russian ballet, offered to display the masks alongside designs for the Ballets Russes by the young Catalan artist Pedro Pruna in a summer 1925 exhibition at the Claridge Gallery, a Brook Street establishment he had set up to foster emerging artistic talent.[8] This was an unparalleled opportunity for a young man of twenty-one, and Oliver remained grateful to Propert for giving his career such an initial boost.

The effect was immediate. The great impresario of the Ballets Russes, Sergei Diaghilev, saw the exhibition and commissioned Oliver to make a set of masks for the ballet *Zéphire et Flore* which was due to open at the London Coliseum in November 1925.[9] Oliver was asked to produce the masks in double-quick time and clearly impressed Diaghilev, who thanked him for his contribution and invited him to stop by the Hôtel de Paris in Monte Carlo should he happen to be passing at any point over the winter. Otherwise, he wrote, he looked forward to catching up with Oliver's new creations in Paris or London the following spring.

Receiving an accreditation on the programme of a work by the Ballets Russes was an astonishing coup for a hitherto unknown artist. Yet it was courtesy of his designs for the theatrical revues staged by the British impresario Charles B. Cochran, universally known as Cockie, that Oliver broke through into the public consciousness. Put on each springtime at the London Pavilion in Piccadilly Circus, the annual revues were a sophisticated mix of songs, sketches and dances, and the first night of a new production was a major social occasion on the London scene. Like Diaghilev, Cochran had seen Oliver's masks at the Claridge Gallery exhibition and was struck by their originality. His first commission for Oliver was to create the masks and costumes for a dance number in his 1926 revue entitled simply *The Masks*, and before long Oliver's creations had become a regular feature of the Cochran shows.

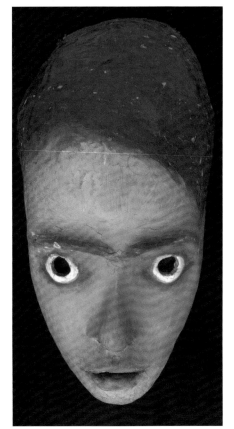

The Oliver Messel mask which inspired Noël Coward's 1928 revue number 'Dance Little Lady'

The impact of Oliver's masks is evident in the numerous references to them in the society magazines of the period. On their first appearance in the Manchester pre-season of 1926, *The Sphere* thought them 'distinguished by a strange *bizarrerie*, which should prove of great interest to London audiences'.[10] Once they had hit the capital *The Bystander* carried a cartoon suggesting that Messel masks should be made generally available outside the theatre so as to enhance the physical appearance of the travelling public and 'make our daily journeyings vastly more cheerful and entertaining'.[11] Before long Messel masks had become cultural references in their own right. Taking a look back over the heavy schedule of balls and other social events in Commem Week at Oxford, one writer commiserated with those who had been partying so hard that they ended up looking 'like an Oliver Messel mask'. 'But', the reviewer reflected philosophically, 'the more Messely you look the more of a compliment you pay to your host of the evening.'[12]

Oliver would have appreciated this reference, as much of his free time during this period was spent at such parties himself. This was the heyday of the Bright Young Things, when upper-class socialites sought to banish the horrors of the First World War and embrace a world of unbridled fun and entertainment. Oliver took an active part in organizing the parties, where the challenge was to find venues that were increasingly *outré*: 'We chose unusual, unexpectedly tatty settings like St George's Swimming Baths, Victoria; some unknown pub on the way to the East End; or dinners arranged on a railway train on a journey to nowhere in particular.'[13] Nor were the parties confined to British shores. At one point Oliver had to rush back to London to attend a débutante's coming-out party as he had 'just been over to Paris to dance at Princess Faucigny-Lucinge's fancy-dress ball'.[14] The Bright Young Things would regularly decamp for Venice in the summer, taking over the Lido and behaving even more outrageously than at home. At Lady Diana Cooper's birthday party on the island of Murano in August 1932 a fracas broke out 'involving the choir of fifteen gondoliers and an audience of fifty interested bystanders'.

> Cecil Beaton lobbed Prosecco bottles on to the heads of the protagonists and was promptly thrown to the ground by Oliver Messel. Duff Cooper waded in, and a rolling scrum of some eight men fought their way across the floor, dragging linen and crockery from the tables and overturning the furniture. Stepping over the prone body of a baronet in the doorway, Emerald Cunard made her customary late entrance. 'What a lovely party!' she trilled.[15]

Oliver's professional breakthrough came with the designs he created for Cochran's 1932 production of *Helen*, the operetta based on Offenbach's *La Belle Hélène*. The greatest coup came with the white-on-white set that Oliver designed for the bedroom scene, in which the only hint of colour is Helen's pale flesh as she languishes on her giant bed in expectation of Paris's arrival. Yet the intricacies of Oliver's design went deeper, as he projected Helen's bedroom out through the proscenium arch to draw the audience into the dramatic moment of seduction that would lead to the Trojan War. The sequence of costumes throughout the drama was intended as a humorous commentary on fashion down the ages, including the short skirts that had just come into vogue. As theatre historian Sybil Rosenfeld described it, 'On a revolving stage Messel designed three scenes for the three acts. Steeped in period atmosphere, he created an elaborate pastiche in which seventeenth-century perspective principles were used in a kind of mocking fantasy. Wit had entered scene design.'[16]

The triumph of *Helen* established Oliver as the leading theatre designer in Britain. He scored another hit three months later with his costumes for Cochran's production of *The Miracle*, a 'wordless spectacle' choreographed by Léonide Massine of the Ballets Russes. Oliver next returned to the London stage with sets and costumes for the Old Vic production of *The Country Wife*, the Restoration sex comedy considered so unsuitable for public consumption that its original version was not performed once between 1753 and 1924. While its revival stimulated a lengthy battle in the media as to whether such bawdy subject matter could be called 'art', there was no disputing that the Old Vic had excelled itself visually: 'Never before has the Waterloo Road seen such charming settings and lovely dresses as those devised by Oliver Messel.'[17] The production transferred to New York, making this the first substantial creation of Oliver's to be seen on Broadway. 'It is sugary, gay, the sets and costumes candy-coloured, the work of Oliver Messel, who must have been frightened by a birthday cake when he was very young.'[18]

The following year Oliver received his first full ballet commission to design costumes and sets for Tchaikovsky's fantasia *Francesca da Rimini* at Covent Garden. The reviewer for *Country Life* noted, 'Mr Messel has drawn on Fra Angelico, Botticelli, Carpaccio and most of the more decorative Florentines for his *mise-en-scène*, and quite ravishing it is.'[19] Oliver was soon designing the set and costumes for the Christmas 1937 production of *A Midsummer Night's Dream* at the Old Vic, with a stellar cast including Robert Helpmann as Oberon, Vivien Leigh as Titania, Ralph Richardson as Bottom and Ninette de Valois directing the ballet scenes. As Richardson recalled, 'The whole production was a deliberate harking back to the Victorians, with Mendelssohn's music, Taglioni fairies and the spirit of "tuppence coloured" pervading everywhere.'[20]

The spirit of 'tuppence coloured' is a direct reminder of the toy theatre Oliver's father had bought him as a child, but it could be applied to much of his creative design. Titania's headdress worn by Vivien Leigh in the Old Vic production provides a perfect example of how the most visually arresting item could be composed of the most banal ingredients: the flowers are a fabrication of metallic paper, chandelier drops, silver discs and cellophane held together on a framework of strong wire and masking tape. Oliver would also recycle costumes from the theatre for use in fancy dress, the most famous example being Cecil Beaton's photograph of him kneeling before his sister Anne in the all-white costume of Paris from the 1932 performance of *Helen*, complete with outrageously plumed helmet, trident and breast plate. The actor Peter Glenville wore the same costume to Lady Jersey's ball at Osterley House in July 1939, the last of the great fancy-dress extravaganzas before the Second World War. Oliver had helped organize the ball in aid of the Georgian Group, designing several of the costumes as well as the marquee in which the dancing took place. His own costume was a close imitation of the eighteenth-century outfit that his father Leonard had worn to the Arts Club Ball in 1911, although with noticeably more lace.[21]

Peter Glenville was to be an important figure in Oliver's career as well as his private life. The two met at a party in Oxford in 1934, and Glenville soon moved

Anne in the Pearl of Beauty costume designed for her by Oliver, 1930

A PEARL OF BEAUTY.

THE DAUGHTER-IN-LAW OF SIR ROBERT ARMSTRONG-JONES: MRS. RONALD ARMSTRONG-JONES.

Mrs. Ronald Armstrong-Jones is shown in a costume designed by her brother, Mr. Oliver Messel. It has a high headdress and a floating iridescent veil and represents pearls. Mrs. Armstrong-Jones is the wife of Mr. Ronald Armstrong-Jones, son of the celebrated physician.

PHOTOGRAPH BY CECIL BEATON.

in to Oliver's Chelsea studio at 16 Yeoman's Row.[22] Oliver had previously had a stormy relationship with Peter Watson, a wealthy contemporary from Eton who would later become a significant patron of the arts. The two travelled through Europe together in the summer of 1930, and Watson at one point presented Oliver with the impromptu gift of a Rolls-Royce. Oliver drove the car down to Nymans and received a 'tremendous roasting' from his father, who ordered him to return it immediately.[23]

Homosexuality would remain illegal until 1967, but the openly gay members of the Brideshead generation were able to conduct their affairs in relative freedom. Oliver was part of the social circle around Gerald Tyrwhitt-Wilson, a.k.a. Lord Berners, the eccentric composer, painter and writer who provided the inspiration for the aesthete Lord Merlin in Nancy Mitford's classic novel *The Pursuit of Love*. Under the pseudonym Adela Quebec, Berners lampooned the young men who swarmed around him in his own novella *The Girls of Radcliff Hall*, a transposed *roman à clef* in which the members of his entourage are thinly disguised as the residents of a girls' boarding-school.[24] The work was printed in 1932 for private circulation only; not only was the subject matter likely to fall foul of the obscenity laws but the jokes would mean nothing outside the immediate circle of those who could recognize the references in it. Oliver created masks in order for Berners to scare people when being driven around in his car, as discovered by the writer Beverley Nichols: 'In the back of the motor-car there was a strange object; a white, hideous mask, the mask of an idiot, fashioned by Oliver Messel. I once tried it on, in Oliver's studio, and the memory of it still gives me nightmares.'[25]

Oliver was himself involved in the world of publishing around this time. He contributed the illustrations to another privately printed book from 1932, the long and mildly surrealist poem *The Venetian Glass Omnibus* by his friend Edward James. With an eye to a wider readership Oliver also created the decorations for the eccentric *Lady Sysonby's Cook Book*, including a birthday cake in the form of an ocean liner. More serious was the publication in 1933 of Oliver's compendium of his own *Stage Designs and Costumes*; with a generous foreword by Charles Cochran and text by the fashion writer James Laver the book featured sixty-four monochrome and ten colour illustrations to showcase the breadth of Oliver's theatrical work to date.

The other publication to demonstrate Oliver's artistry during these years was the folio edition of *Romeo and Juliet* produced as a record of the 1936 Metro-Goldwyn-Mayer film starring screen idols Leslie Howard and Norma Shearer in the title roles. The treatment Oliver was accorded by the American studio shows how highly he was regarded on the international scene at this time. In a BBC interview ten years later he described how he was flown over to Hollywood for three days' discussion with the studio before embarking on a three-week tour of Italy to gather inspiration and materials for the production, all at top rates of pay. Having amassed a wealth of images of Renaissance embroidery, furniture and paintings, he then crossed back to Hollywood to work on the film.[26] The film received four Oscar nominations, and Oliver loved the experience. 'It gave me the greatest pleasure to imagine myself a painter in Renaissance Italy, designing a masque for some Sforza or Medici. In reading again and again the famous story and knowing at each time there would be revealed to me some new beauty that I had overlooked before.'[27]

Romeo and Juliet was Oliver's first contact with Hollywood, but he had already worked as costume designer on two British films with the celebrated director Alexander Korda, both released in 1934. The first was the historical comedy *The Private Life of Don Juan*, with the swashbuckling Douglas Fairbanks starring opposite Korda's future wife Merle Oberon. The second and more successful film was *The Scarlet Pimpernel*, with Leslie Howard in the title role. Oliver was once more engaged in designing the costumes for Merle Oberon, who starred opposite Howard, but the effects were muted in that the picture was shot in black and white. It was only when Oliver teamed up with Korda on the Technicolor extravaganza *The Thief of Bagdad* that cinema audiences could appreciate his imagination in all its glory. Released at the height of the Blitz in December 1940, the film's lavish sets and dazzling costumes provided a much-needed escape for British viewers having to deal with the daily realities of German bombing. The film won three Oscars and sowed the seed for Oliver's triumphant return to cinema at the end of the Second World War.

Oliver's costume design for Don Juan in *The Private Life of Don Juan*, 1934

The war interrupted Oliver's rise to stardom, as he spent most of it serving as a camouflage officer in the Royal Engineers. He joined the army as a second lieutenant in August 1940, just two months after the defeat of British forces at Dunkirk and at a time when the threat of a German invasion of mainland Britain was considered imminent. The need for home defences was pressing, and camouflage quickly became an essential part of the war effort. Oliver approached his new role with characteristic energy and within a month had sent off a letter with accompanying sketches to Winston Churchill's son Randolph outlining a novel means he had devised for trapping enemy tanks.[28]

Oliver was stationed at Taunton with responsibility for camouflaging the line of pillboxes that had been built across Somerset to block a German invasion from the west. According to the artist Julian Trevelyan, who took over the post from him, Oliver was 'in his element' disguising the concrete bunkers as caravans, haystacks and wayside cafés, 'always with great attention to detail'.[29] Promoted to Captain Messel, Oliver was next ordered to set up a camouflage school in Norwich and chanced upon the Assembly House, a deserted Georgian gem that was serving as a storage facility for packing boxes. Oliver requisitioned the building and turned it into the headquarters of the Eastern Command Camouflage School, enlisting the help of skilled workers to restore the dilapidated plasterwork and prevent the

Oliver fraternizing with the American military during the Second World War

house from falling further into disrepair. Harold Acton visited him and enthused later over the use to which Oliver's artistic talents were employed:

> For once camouflage had become artistic as well as imaginative. Hangars and gun batteries became pointillist paintings or tapestries woven with chameleon colours, a pleasure to the eye. Not only branches of trees and netting and splotches worthy of the Fauves but Victorian monuments, lych-gates and other constructions of deceptive ingenuity were designed like Oliver's theatrical scenery.[30]

Oliver managed to obtain occasional periods of leave during the war to work on new stage projects. He had already completed the costume and set designs for the Old Vic's 1940 production of *The Tempest* with John Gielgud, Jessica Tandy and Alec Guinness before embarking on his military career and was given a few days' leave to put the finishing touches to Jean Cocteau's *The Infernal Machine* starring Peter Glenville as Oedipus.[31] Oliver also designed the costumes and sets for the Sadler's Wells Ballet wartime production of Milton's *Comus* by working day and night over the course of a week in 1941. The performances by Margot Fonteyn and Robert Helpmann were well received, but the décor stole the show. 'It is Oliver Messel who emerges as the presiding genius of this lovely fragment. His backcloth, however derived, should be bought for the nation and housed in a new national gallery for the preservation and exhibition of scenic art.'[32]

Oliver was finally released from military service in 1944 so that he could work on the film version of George Bernard Shaw's *Caesar and Cleopatra* under the direction of Gabriel Pascal. Vivien Leigh had written to Oliver with news of the production, noting, 'I have of course told Pascal that nobody in the world must do the costumes except you.'[33] Buoyed up by this recommendation, Oliver demanded the enormous sum of £10,000 as his fee for the design of costumes and interiors and made the mistake of asking his rival Cecil Beaton whether this might have been too ambitious. In a sign of how covetous he had become of Oliver's fame, Beaton assured him that it was a perfectly reasonable request – and then promptly tried to undercut him by offering Pascal a set of similar designs for a lower fee.[34] Oliver was able to laugh off the incident as he retained the commission, becoming in the process the highest-paid set designer in the world.

At just under £1.3 million, the final budget for *Caesar and Cleopatra* was the largest in British cinematic history to that time. Filming began at Gainsborough Studios before moving to Buckinghamshire in order to reconstruct the city of Alexandria on the banks of the River Colne.[35] For Oliver, recreating the splendours of Ptolemaic Egypt in wartime Britain brought its own headaches:

> *Caesar and Cleopatra* in Technicolor, with Vivien Leigh as Cleopatra, sounds like every dress-designer's dream assignment. The dearth of fabrics and decorative materials, and the appalling shortage of workroom staff, must have transformed the dream into something more like an actual nightmare for Oliver Messel; but in spite of every deprivation and drawback, his costumes and décor somehow achieved the gossamer dreamlike quality of an Egyptian fairy-tale.[36]

The film's visual magnificence ensured that it was a box office success when it was released in December 1945, but the vast sums that had been spent on its production meant it would never make a profit. It was not well received by the

Claude Rains and Vivien Leigh in *Caesar and Cleopatra*, with costumes by Oliver Messel

British critics, who considered it 'devoid of style' or at best 'a singularly cold triumph'.[37] Oliver's contribution met with widespread praise, with Maurice Cowan declaring it 'breathtakingly beautiful' and 'the best work this brilliant young designer has done'.[38] George VI asked for a copy to be sent to Sandringham so that the Royal Family could watch it over the Christmas holidays.[39]

The colour of Oliver's costumes for *Caesar and Cleopatra* kindled the hope that Britain was finally emerging from the dark days of the Second World War. Yet it was his spectacular designs for Tchaikovsky's *The Sleeping Beauty*, the first production to reopen the Royal Opera House, that signalled the true reawakening. The opera house had been converted into a Mecca dance hall during the war, and reclaiming it for the performing arts was an important moment in the reassertion of normality. The Sadler's Wells Ballet founded by Ninette de Valois was given the honour of staging the inaugural production, the first step on its path to becoming the Royal Ballet ten years later. Wartime rationing, still in place despite the ending of hostilities, meant that many essential materials remained in short supply, and clothing coupons had to be pooled in order to obtain even the most basic fabrics. In a throwback to Oliver's military service, camouflage paint and army canvas were used to create the sets, with parachute silk for the more delicate drapery. The whole was a triumph of human inventiveness, and de Valois recalled the frantic last-minute preparations to have everything ready on time.

> Oliver Messel's lovely designs set us, with our restrictions, many a problem. He himself worked as hard as the smallest seamstress . . . up to the moment of the rise of the curtain, in the tradition of the true theatre, the last stitches were being put into the new costumes, the final flower sewn on the fairies' costumes: all was turmoil behind and curiosity in front.[40]

The first night on 20 February 1946 was a defining moment in the cultural history of post-war Britain. The entire Royal Family attended the performance, as did numerous foreign dignitaries and anyone associated with the arts. The rainbow of colours splashed across sets and costumes was a reminder of all that had been lost during the grim years of conflict and austerity, and the romantic beauty of the whole would be remembered for years to come. Every subsequent revival of the Messel Production has paid homage to the original, including Covent Garden's seventieth anniversary restaging in 2016. When the ballet transferred to the Met in New York in 1949, Margot Fonteyn reported, 'As the curtain rose, applause greeted the Oliver Messel décor before anyone danced a step.'[41]

Inside the Oliver Messel
Suite at the Dorchester

Fame and Fortune 17

THE YEARS IMMEDIATELY after the Second World War saw Oliver at the height of his career as a stage designer, with numerous commissions for the theatre and opera. Each added to his reputation, and each had its own story to tell. The tropical set that Oliver designed for *The Little Hut*, a risqué comedy adapted for the London stage by Nancy Mitford, was such a challenge for the technicians that its director Peter Brook begged him to come and sort out the last details while it was still on its preparatory tour around the country. When the production finally opened at the Lyric on Shaftesbury Avenue on 23 August 1950 *The Times* knowingly quipped that the play was set on 'a desert island so wittily exotic it might have been designed by Mr Oliver Messel'.[1] The production ran for over three years, with many people returning to see it more than once.

Oliver was too much in demand to spend time on fancy dress as he had in earlier days, but he could not resist the call to act as designer for the Beistegui Ball in Venice in September 1951. This was the most lavish costume ball to be seen in Europe since the war; the one thousand guests received their invitations six months in advance to give them enough time to prepare costumes that would faithfully reproduce the chosen year of 1743. The multi-millionaire art collector Don Carlos de Beistegui wished the masque to be hosted by Antony and Cleopatra as they had been depicted by Tiepolo on the walls of the Beistegui palazzo in Venice, with Baron Alfred de Cabrol in the role of Antony and Lady Diana Cooper as Cleopatra. Oliver was commissioned to create the Egyptian queen's dress, which he modelled closely on the Tiepolo original. He also made the outfit for the Aga Khan, who appeared as an Oriental potentate, as well as his own costume of a red velvet uniform coat that had once belonged to a Bohemian prince. Guests could arrive at the ball by gondola only, and the Grand Canal was awash with onlookers trying to identify each new arrival, not least because Beistegui had laid on free wine and salami for those watching outside.[2]

London was also striving to throw off the gloom of the post-war years, and when it came to magical fantasies Oliver was the designer of choice. In March 1950 he was commissioned to transform the Royal Opera House for a state performance in honour of the visiting French President and his wife, for which he expanded the Royal Box, festooned the Crush Bar with garlands and turned the foyer into a tented pavilion. 'The Royal Opera House can rarely, if ever, have presented so sumptuous an appearance,' cooed *Country Life*.[3] The Queen sent word to Covent Garden next morning requesting that the decorations be kept up for a week so that she could return and savour the experience all over again.[4]

Oliver was called on to redesign the Royal Opera House anew for the week of gala performances to celebrate the Coronation of Queen Elizabeth II in June 1953. For this he swathed the Royal Box in fabric of pure gold thread and filled it with three thousand roses. The successful blend of pageantry and visual beauty was lauded on all sides, and Oliver was commissioned to repeat the effect the following year for the state visit of the King of Sweden. Yet the designs he created for Tivoli-styled gardens as part of the 1951 Festival of Britain had been rejected by the organizing committee – a first sign that, outside the make-believe world of the Royal Opera House, Oliver's brand of nostalgic romanticism was out of step with the forward-looking spirit of the age.

Coronation year brought Oliver further engagements, including a contract to transform the Park Lane façade of the Dorchester Hotel into tiers of Coronation boxes. This in turn led to his most celebrated interior design commission: the creation of two new suites at the Dorchester. The Messel Suite, as it is now known, is on the seventh floor with views over Hyde Park and was the first new hotel apartment to be built in Britain since the beginning of the Second World War. A sequence of anterooms leads into a large drawing-room with a double bedroom, a single bedroom and two bathrooms, all fitted out with eighteenth-century furniture and Oliver's own paintings to create a feel of homely elegance. 'What I had in mind when I designed this new suite was to produce the kind of rooms I myself would like to live in,' said Oliver on the day of the launch. 'What I hope we have achieved is a hotel suite that is warm and friendly, a home in the best sense of the word.'[5] The Penthouse Suite above offers a selection of rooms for entertaining, culminating in a mirrored reception room that leads out on to the roof terrace. The theatrical effect is enhanced by a plaster figure of Bacchus on the mantelpiece and by models of Oliver's set designs embedded in the walls.[6]

Oliver received several new commissions on the strength of his Dorchester creations, which led to his redesigning Bond Street shops, theatre interiors and country houses.[7] He lavished the same care on his own home at 17 Pelham Place in South Kensington, which he had purchased after the Second World War and then enlarged into a 24-room residence by buying up the house next door and knocking the two together. This was to be home for him and his partner Vagn Riis-Hansen until they moved to Barbados in 1966. Vagn was a six-foot-tall Danish war hero who had fought in the resistance and three times escaped from German prison camps; predictably, he was universally known as the Great Dane.

He had been involved in the fashion industry as a young man, opening a dress shop in Copenhagen and travelling a great deal between Paris, London and the USA in search of clothes. In 1930, when still in his early twenties, he had married a Scottish actress called Zoe Gordon, whom he met while she was appearing in the Broadway production of Noël Coward's *Bitter Sweet*; she was twenty years older than Vagn and lived in London until her death in December 1958.

Vagn and Oliver were devoted to each other, and the Great Dane took over responsibility for managing Oliver's affairs for the rest of their life together, not least his hopeless inability to deal with money. Often, having negotiated the most lucrative terms for a commission, Oliver would omit to bank the cheque he was given at the end of it and then wonder why he found himself permanently in the red. Vagn also ran the household at Pelham Place, which took on a decidedly Scandinavian feel when he employed three fellow Danes as live-in staff (including cook and butler) in addition to Oliver's assistant Carl Toms, his secretary Brenda Haydon and the long-suffering gardener Mr Potter. In an idiosyncratic throwback to a bygone age, the male staff wore a livery designed by Oliver himself. 'Ordinary clothes look slovenly and white uniforms are expensive to keep clean,' he reasoned, 'so I invented a black tunic with brass buttons and striped sleeves, rather like the valets wear in France.'[8]

The view to the roof terrace from the Penthouse Suite at the Dorchester

Oliver's partner Vagn
Riis-Hansen, the
'Great Dane'

Vagn's other talent was as a chef, and he contributed a short series of food-related features to *Harper's Bazaar* between November 1961 and February 1962. The articles were more combative than usual in the cookery genre; his Christmas offering, for example, was an uncompromising attack on turkey as 'the dullest and most over-rated dish there is'. Yet his final article provided a nice description of the Pelham Place dining-room as a theatrical setting for parties: 'Silver and spring flowers (with an opened tulip flat by every place) . . . candlelight and comfort . . . pretty china on an organdie cloth, together with little *bibelots* for cigarettes and tiny coloured mints.' In similar vein Sir John Gielgud recalled a dinner party there shortly after the Second World War:

> The dining-room was a dream of beauty, as well as *gourmandise*. Marble tables without cloths, cabinets and shelves were spread or filled with wonderful dishes, sent from Denmark, such as one had not seen for many years. Shrimps, lobsters, vegetables and salads, all displayed and set out with the most exquisite elegance and graded colour schemes. How charmed I was and how lucky to see it in such

pristine splendour, before the other guests arrived to make speedy havoc of its delights, and how I should have loved to have had a photograph to remind me of its beauty.[9]

Visual records do exist courtesy of *Vogue*, which included a photograph of the garlanded Pelham Place dining-room in its October 1963 British edition. Two months later American *Vogue* featured more pictures in a longer interview with Vagn, in which he held forth on the best way to run a successful dinner party. Keeping the focus on Oliver as host, Vagn explained, 'He doesn't plan big dinners for fifteen or twenty people at a rectangular table. The boring person next to you might find you as boring. So you're both stuck through the whole dinner. A round table is much better, and eight or ten people are enough for dinner. Naturally, Oliver Messel knows a great number of people in the theatre. He knows, too, a great number of people in other fields. So he mixes them.'[10] The visitors' book for Pelham Place shows what a star-studded array of guests Oliver and Vagn hosted in the eighteen years they lived there, including Charlie Chaplin, Margot Fonteyn, Vivien Leigh, Laurence Olivier, Princess Margaret and HRH Queen Elizabeth, the Queen Mother.[11] Nor did their celebrity friends always stand on ceremony, as one visitor remembered: 'I went into his kitchen to get another bottle of wine. In the kitchen was a lady with an apron on and a scarf in her hair furiously scrubbing the floors. On my return I said to Oliver, "Your cleaner is a hard worker." He just laughed. A while later a ravishing beauty came in and Oliver called me over to meet his "cleaner". It was Marlene Dietrich.'[12]

Oliver was keeping equally illustrious company in his working life, being one of twenty British artists commissioned by Steuben Glass to create a collection of artworks on crystal; the finished designs were displayed at a dedicated New York exhibition opened by the wife of the British ambassador in April 1954. The others included in the show were established British artists such as Jacob Epstein, John Nash, Frank Dobson, John Piper and Graham Sutherland, as well as a somewhat younger Lucian Freud. Oliver's contribution was an engraving of the Puss in Boots from his triumphant *Sleeping Beauty* at Covent Garden, who 'towers in Baroque magnificence' over the pedestal and lilies that complete the design.[13]

Oliver had visited New York before the Second World War, but his first experience of producing work directly for Broadway was as set and costume designer for his old friend Peter Glenville in his production of *Romeo and Juliet*, which opened at the Broadhurst Theatre in March 1951. Comparing the costumes for this stage production with those Oliver had created for the Hollywood film version before the war shows how tastes had simplified in the intervening fifteen years, even if there is much continuity in the style of his drawings. Still on Broadway, Oliver won the 1955 Tony Award for best scenic design for the set of

Oliver's costume design for Puss in Boots from *The Sleeping Beauty*, 1946

the Truman Capote musical *House of Flowers*, which ran for 165 performances at the Alvin Theatre. Oliver loved working with Capote, and the show's hit number 'Bamboo Cage' was one of his musical choices when he guested as castaway on the BBC's *Desert Island Discs* on 5 May 1958.

No account of Oliver's career would be complete without mentioning his productions at Glyndebourne, the magical Sussex opera house run by the Christie family not far from the Messels' home of Nymans. Oliver was in his element, his whimsical designs fitting in perfectly with the surreal romanticism of the rural setting in which guests take to the lawns during intervals to picnic with the sheep. He had redesigned the proscenium arch for the opera house when it reopened after the Second World War, and during the 1950s he effectively became Glyndebourne's in-house designer, creating sets and costumes for ten separate productions over the decade – 'Rococo fantasies full of warm colour', in the words of the music critic Ronald Crichton.[14] Oliver was responsible for designing four of the six operas staged at Glyndebourne during the Mozart bicentenary festival in 1956 – two of them premièred that year – as well as the commemorative programme. His description of the variety between the four productions reveals the sophistication which he brought to each new design.

> *Idomeneo* was intended to be an eighteenth-century eye view of Crete, as in the frescos of Tiepolo with the echo of Tintoretto and Veronese . . . *Figaro* was an Italian conception of Spain. I chose the mid-eighteenth century rather than the late, because the style was more becoming to the artists. *Entführung*, being particularly light and artificial in mood, is designed with a less realistic approach. The eighteenth-century decorations on an Oriental theme in the Residenz at Munich, the lacelike pavilions in the Soho Tapestries, or Meissen porcelain groups, are the sources on which the designs are based. The technique is entirely different to the other operas. The last, *The Magic Flute*, presented far the most problems.[15]

The critics responded with enthusiasm. Andrew Porter acclaimed how organically Oliver's settings complemented the composer's operatic style: 'The great merit of his themes is that they impose nothing on the music but seem to spring from it. Although intensely personal they reflect and decorate Mozart, whereas less sensitive designers try to interpret him.' The art critic Eric Newton, reviewing Oliver's décor for *Die Entführung aus dem Serail*, concurred that 'not only is the stage a delight to the eye but the music has more meaning for the ear'.[16] Perhaps the greatest accolade is to be found in Salzburg, where the

Mozart Museum installed a model of Oliver's Glyndebourne sets as a tribute to the lasting importance of his scenic interpretations.[17]

Oliver was much in demand for stage and cinema work during the 1950s, but he managed to find time for one-off design projects such as his murals and menu cards for Fortnum and Mason and the wedding dress of his niece, Elizabeth Messel, on her marriage in 1955. He worked hard to fulfil each of his many commissions to the highest possible standard. Oliver was a driven man when committed to a project and would regularly work through the night to five or six in the morning on the basis that after midnight he would not be disturbed by telephone calls or visitors. He would then retire to bed and sleep until the early afternoon, a pattern he continued for most of his life. He was not a smoker and drank little in the way of alcohol, so that he was able to leave a party late at night and go straight to work after it.

Oliver's costume design for Don Magnifico in the Glyndebourne production of *La Cenerentola*, 1952

Oliver was awarded the CBE in the 1958 New Year's Honours for services to theatrical design. Even then fame did not spoil the warmth of his personality. As Barbara Cartland noted, 'His success has never gone to his head, he is still "a little boy" – shy, modest, charming and loved by everyone who works with him.'[18] Like many of his Messel relatives, however, Oliver could be difficult at times and confessed to having by nature 'an uncontrollable temper', especially when he found himself unable to get his own way. Yet this single-minded determination was a major part of his success in professional life. Arthur Boys, one of Oliver's team of artists on *Caesar and Cleopatra*, observed in a warm tribute, 'He is not an easy person to work with. He appears to be tireless, and he spares no one, himself least of all. He is a perfectionist. Nothing will "do"; everything must be right in design, construction, colour and material, and if it's not right it must be worked on till perfection is achieved.'[19]

Fashions were changing, however, and the failure of the inauspiciously titled *Twang!!* was a sign that Oliver's time as a stage designer had come to an end. Having triumphed with his musical rendition of *Oliver Twist*, the composer Lionel Bart conceived a spoof on the Robin Hood legend that would bring together the comic talents of Ronnie Corbett, Barbara Windsor and James Booth under the experimental direction of Joan Littlewood. How Oliver Messel came to be mixed up in such an unlikely production at the age of sixty-one is unclear, but the show was a disaster. Its preparatory run in Birmingham was cancelled under the pretext that the sets and costumes would not be ready on time – a calumny which Oliver indignantly rejected. The musical transferred to London in time for Christmas 1965 but was savaged by the press. Generous critics were prepared to consider individual elements in isolation. 'The Oliver Messel sets are the night's real pleasures,' said the *Illustrated London News*, 'and we must regret the evolutions in front of them.'[20] Others feared that no one involved in the production would escape with their reputations intact. *Twang!!* went down in theatrical history as the West End's most expensive flop to date, and Oliver never designed for the British stage again.

Within a year Oliver and Vagn had moved to Barbados, where they would live the rest of their lives. Oliver had inherited severe arthritis from his mother, and previous winter stays in the Caribbean had shown how much better the climate was for his condition. In 1964 he bought Maddox, a derelict eighteenth-century house overlooking the sea on the island's west coast, for the princely sum of £25,000. Oliver redesigned the property over several months, selling the lease on the Pelham Place home in which he and Vagn had lived for eighteen years, and at the end of 1966, as the ever-faithful *Tatler* reported, the 'Toymaker Extraordinary' left London for good.[21] Little did he know it, but the move would launch a new phase in Oliver's career as an architectural designer, creating bijou residences for the rich and famous not only in Barbados but elsewhere in the Caribbean as well.

Oliver's own home at Maddox was the prototype for many of his subsequent creations, which play to the strengths of the Barbadian climate through the use of open loggias with vistas over the Caribbean to achieve what he termed 'indoor-outdoor living'. The house at Maddox also displays many of Oliver's characteristic motifs. His most instantly recognizable signature is the elliptical arch which appears in fanlights above doorways and windows throughout the building, just as it did in the Regency interiors which he designed for Bond Street establishments in the 1950s. The second of Oliver's trademarks is the light shade of sage green he used on shutters, columns and balustrades for many of the properties he designed in Barbados. Now known simply as Messel Green, it evokes the colour of the Caribbean itself in the shallows of the island's sandy shores.

Oliver's career as an architectural designer began in earnest with his redesign of Leamington, a former plantation house on the 'golden mile' further up the coast from Maddox. Oliver persuaded Jack Heinz, president of the baked beans empire, to buy the property so that he could redecorate it and proceeded to transform it into a luxury Caribbean hideaway. Equipped with a new garden pavilion to serve as guest house and banqueting hall, Leamington would subsequently become the residence of the US ambassador. The majestic Fustic House, set in eleven acres in the north of the island, and Cockade House with its neoclassical pediments represent two of his other notable developments. Oliver was also commissioned by the Prime Minister of Barbados to redesign the interior of Queen's Park House in the capital Bridgetown, the former residence of the British military commander. He appreciated the opportunity to create solid monuments that would outlast him. 'The theatre is a toy, an ephemeral thing, and I adored working with it; but it's so marvellous here to see things grow and change, to know they are here to stay, and not wrapped up and thrown away at the end of a run.'[22]

On the back of his success in Barbados, Oliver received requests to redesign properties in St Lucia, Dominica, Guyana and Venezuela. Yet it was his unique relationship with the island of Mustique that would dominate the last phase of his new career. One of the string of islands that make up the Grenadines a hundred miles west of Barbados, Mustique was privately owned by the millionaire Colin Tennant, who had bought it in 1958 for £45,000. Tennant famously gave Princess Margaret a ten-acre plot of land as a wedding present on her marriage to Oliver's nephew Tony Armstrong-Jones, but the island lay undeveloped until the end of the 1960s. Princess Margaret had already stayed with Oliver at Maddox and loved the sympathetic way in which he had embraced the ideal of Caribbean living. She

Fustic House on Barbados, one of Oliver's most stylish architectural designs

now suggested that Oliver be invited to design a house for her land on Mustique, and Tennant responded by inviting him over to the island with a brief to turn the old Cotton House into a hotel, with two guest cottages near by. Oliver's plans for the redevelopment were so appealing that Tennant commissioned him to design all future properties on the island, and a partnership was born that would last the rest of Oliver's life.

Oliver would go on to build more than fifteen houses on Mustique, at a fee of £1,000 each. They were individualistic in style, with a nod to the traditions of French colonial architecture rather than the Georgian heritage of Barbados. Oliver's trademarks are still visible in the use of elliptical fanlights and the occasional splash of Messel Green, although he favoured a warm yellow as his signature colour on Mustique. The house he designed for Princess Margaret was completed in February 1973 and christened by her Les Jolies Eaux, a play on the name of the nearby beach at Gelliceaux Bay. As in Barbados, Oliver's emphasis was on providing people with the framework for an idyllic sub-tropical

Above
Les Jolies Eaux,
Princess Margaret's
Mustique hideaway

Right
Blue Waters, one
of the luxury villas
designed by Oliver
on Mustique

existence in harmony with the Caribbean. In Hamish Bowles's neat phrase, Oliver reinterpreted 'architecture as theatre, where the house sets the scene and the happy owners and their guests are players'.[23]

Mustique is a playground for the super-rich, as shown by the succession of billionaire celebrities who have owned homes there over the years. Having been brought up in wealth himself, Oliver was able to hold his own in such company, even when his own finances were in a parlous state. Yet he was equally at ease with the Bajan people among whom he lived in Barbados and made a point of challenging racial distinctions in his own household. Leaving England for a country where labour was comparatively inexpensive meant that Oliver could afford to employ several domestic staff at Maddox, but he treated them like family 'and always insisted that they eat with him when he was not entertaining', according to his close friend Nick Paravicino.[24] He worked closely with Bajan artists such as the sculptor James Massiah and his own assistant Carl Chandler, who collaborated with Oliver throughout his time in Barbados.

Racial prejudice incensed Oliver, and he took a conscious stand against it at several times over the years. In 1935 the infamous Diana Mitford brought the British Union of Fascists' leader Oswald Mosley with her to stay at Faringdon House, the country seat of Lord Berners. This was a time when many members of the British aristocracy were flirting with fascism or, in the case of two Mitford sisters, supporting it openly. Oliver found the movement's racist ideology abhorrent, not least because the Messels were at that moment trying to help their German cousins escape from Nazi-controlled Berlin. Oliver added the provocative tag under Mosley's signature in the Faringdon visitors' book: 'F.S.P.M.B.W.N.R. – Founder of the Society for the Propagation of Marriage Between the White and Negro Races.'[25] Mosley would publicly call for a ban on mixed marriages when he mounted his failed attempt to return to British politics in the 1950s. He would have been unamused to learn that he was being mocked behind his back in this earlier period when he was supposedly at the height of his powers.

The issue of interracial marriage was central to the first of two cases of injustice in which Oliver became involved after the Second World War. This was the notorious treatment of Seretse Khama, the deposed King of Bechuanaland. Khama had married a white English woman, Ruth Williams, in September 1948 while training as a barrister in London, and the couple soon faced a storm of racist opposition. Bechuanaland was a British protectorate, and South Africa's newly elected apartheid government joined with white settlers in Rhodesia in protesting to the British authorities that the union of a black African leader with a white woman would undermine the very basis of white supremacy on which their minority rule depended. To their shame, successive Labour and Conservative governments sided against Khama, and he was forced into exile in London.

Oliver with Mutesa II,
Kabaka of Buganda

The case soon became a *cause célèbre*, with public indignation at Khama's treatment bolstered by celebrity support from artists such as Augustus John and film stars such as Alec Guinness. Oliver Messel joined the campaign and wrote to the Foreign Secretary Anthony Eden on 2 April 1952 declaring himself 'wildly distressed' at the injustice that had been shown Khama and criticizing the British government for 'weakly pandering to the policy of South African colour discrimination'.[26] Despite the efforts on his behalf Khama remained in exile until 1956 and was barred from ruling over Bechuanaland for a further seven years thereafter. He was eventually elected in 1966 as the first President of the independent Republic of Botswana, as Bechuanaland was renamed.

Oliver was centrally involved in a second case involving racial discrimination against another African ruler, this time Kabaka Mutesa II of Buganda. Like Bechuanaland, Uganda was a protectorate under British rule, and Buganda was the largest traditional kingdom within it. The young Mutesa II had ruled as Kabaka under a council of regents since 1939, while completing his education at Cambridge and obtaining a commission in the Grenadier Guards. As he wrote in his memoirs, 'I was the first and I think the only black officer in the Grenadiers.'[27] Mutesa returned to Buganda to rule in person, and in 1953, amid growing hostility to colonial rule in East Africa, he called on the British government to prepare a timetable to move towards the independence of his kingdom. The new governor Sir Andrew Cohen rejected the call and declared a state of emergency, forcibly arresting the Kabaka and deporting him into exile in London.

Oliver had known Mutesa since his time at Cambridge and offered to help make arrangements for the Kabaka to take a flat on Park Lane at the beginning of 1954. Just as Mutesa was about to move in, however, the estate agent phoned to say that the offer had been withdrawn, 'the reason being given that the Kabaka was coloured'.[28] Oliver responded by holding an impromptu press conference with Mutesa at his own home in Pelham Place and managed to get the issue of a 'colour bar in Park Lane' into the national press. Oliver spoke of being 'ashamed and embarrassed' that his friend should have suffered such an indignity in London, and the Colonial Office was forced into a series of awkward denials as to why it had not heeded the Kabaka's request for help. A substitute flat was found in Eaton Place, and Oliver would go on to host dinner parties in South Kensington for the Kabaka throughout his time in exile.[29]

Perhaps the most powerful example of Oliver's willingness to take a stand against racism came in 1970, when he was asked by the Performing Arts Council of Transvaal for permission to stage *The Sleeping Beauty* in Johannesburg using his designs from the famous Covent Garden production of 1946. Oliver refused outright in light of South Africa's apartheid ban on mixed audiences, stating, 'I could not wish to accept any hospitality from a country whose laws and principles are to me so utterly abhorrent.' Oliver rejected out of hand the suggestion that separate performances could be put on for the benefit of the 'coloured peoples', declaring himself 'revolted' by the idea. 'When or if the day arrives that South Africa's white minority comes to its senses,' he concluded, 'then nothing would give me greater pleasure than to come over and help to put on the finest production possible.'[30]

Oliver's idyllic life in Barbados was shattered when his partner Vagn died of cancer on 2 December 1972. The loss was all the more devastating because Vagn had for so long taken care of the practical details of Oliver's life that he was unable to manage himself. The actress Lauren Bacall sent him a warm letter of condolence recalling that the only way she had coped with Humphrey Bogart's death fifteen years earlier was by immersing herself in her work, and she hoped that Oliver had enough to distract him from the pain of separation. As it happened, this period saw him start work on his last ever stage commission: to design the costumes for the musical *Gigi* that was due to open in San Francisco in May 1973 before touring across the USA to Broadway. Oliver's costumes for the production have

Oliver's costume design for Honoré in *Gigi*, 1973

been heralded as 'the most charming group he ever designed' and earned him another Tony Award nomination.[31] Yet just like *Twang!!*, his swan song on the other side of the Atlantic, *Gigi* was not a success.

Happily, this was not to be the note on which Oliver took his final bow, as the Met contacted him a couple of years later with a view to staging a full-length revival of the Messel production of *The Sleeping Beauty* in New York. Oliver was treated like royalty, receiving a fee of $12,000 to rework the scenery and costumes with the aid of two assistants who were sent to Barbados especially for the purpose. When the time came to oversee final preparations for the production, Oliver was flown first class to New York and provided with a healthy allowance for as long as he was there. He received top billing on the notices, his name appearing above that of Tchaikovsky himself, and was accompanied to the première by the former First Lady, Jackie Onassis.[32] Oliver revelled in being the centre of attention: 'All the thrilling first nights of my experience were nothing compared to this.'[33] Yet, ominously, he had collapsed with severe heart pains three days before the ballet opened and was rushed to hospital. He had already suffered a minor heart attack four years earlier, and his health now went into more serious decline. Back home in Barbados he had oxygen cylinders installed in his bedroom so that he could continue working on his final design project, Colin Tennant's Turkish Pavilion on Mustique.

Oliver died at Maddox on 13 July 1978, aged seventy-four. Following a funeral service at the Anglican parish church of St Peter's, his body was flown back to England for a second service at the Messel family church of St Mark's, Staplefield. In line with Oliver's instructions, his ashes were buried with Vagn's in the Wall Garden at Nymans where he had spent his teenage years. The memorial service of thanksgiving for Oliver's life was held four months later in London at St Martin-in-the-Fields. The altar steps were strewn with white flowers. Oliver's two closest nephews – Thomas Messel and Lord Snowdon – read the lessons, and Dame Ninette de Valois 'then ascended the pulpit and bereft of a single note delivered a remarkable tribute'.[34]

The obituaries that came out in the days following Oliver's death lionized him as 'one of the most gifted and influential designers of the century'.[35] *The Times* went further:

Messel's genius lay in his unique quality of bringing rightness, flair and great taste to enrich any period or situation, whether it be in play, opera, ballet, musical or film. By the late 1920s he was established as the foremost stage designer in Britain, and to have his name attached to any production was as great a draw as the stars appearing in it.[36]

History has also been kind to Oliver. While his personal brand of romantic escapism was eclipsed by the gritty realism of the 1960s, recent years have seen renewed interest in the florid effusion of his imagination. He naturally gravitated towards the eighteenth century as his preferred frame of reference, but Oliver was conversant with a wide range of cultural modes and demonstrated his versatility in the many different productions he worked on over the years. The impact of his sets and costumes generated an excited expectation that awaited each new production, so that every stage design was appreciated as an artistic creation in its own right. Sarah Woodcock summed up Oliver's contribution in the retrospective book of his career compiled by Thomas Messel:

> Twentieth-century theatre owed him an immeasurable debt, not just for his brilliance but for raising and consolidating the professional status of the stage designer: during his lifetime, stage design became a discipline and, though he never taught save by example, many of his principles became absorbed into the mainstream. Since Messel died, there have been many great designers, but no one has quite equalled his achievements.[37]

Like so many of the Messels, Oliver was a mix of insider and outsider elements. An openly gay man from an immigrant family, he was at the same time quintessentially English and one of the most recognizable figures in high society during the inter-war years. His Messel inheritance meant that he lived a life of immense privilege; yet, despite this early wealth and the high fees he commanded throughout his career as a designer, Oliver died in debt. While most of his life was spent among the jet set, he was equally keen to use his privilege to challenge racial prejudice. Yet he was a natural conservative and never showed any interest in confronting the structures that allowed prejudice and privilege to persist from generation to generation. It would require a more intellectual member of the Messel family, Oliver's beloved cousin Rudolph, to take that step.

Rudolph Putnam Messel
as a boy

Cinema and Socialism 18

Rudolph Putnam Messel was born on 28 November 1904, the eldest child of Harold and Nonie Messel. When he was five years old the family moved to the large Tyburnia mansion of 8 Gloucester Square, and the 1911 census reveals what a privileged life he and his younger sister Phoebe enjoyed there. In addition to a German governess for Rudolph and a Scottish nurse for Phoebe, the family employed eight domestic servants: a butler, a footman, a lady's maid, a cook, a kitchen maid, two housemaids and a between maid (or 'tweeny') who helped the housemaids in the morning and the cook in the afternoon. Sadly, the governess and the nurse did not get on, so brother and sister were taken for separate walks in Hyde Park and instructed to bow politely on the occasions that their paths crossed.[1]

Rudolph and Phoebe's early years were filled with love, remembered all the more fondly in view of the sadness that would later eclipse their childhood. Rudolph recalled his mother accompanying their 'baby games' with music from the piano, and there is a touching early photograph of Nonie reading with her two children, one arm around Phoebe while Rudolph peers over her shoulder from behind. Yet the children's lives would be shattered by the tragic deaths of both their parents in quick succession – their mother in childbirth and their father through suicide. Rudolph was thirteen when his mother died and fifteen when he lost his father, and the double bereavement left him deeply scarred. He and his sister Phoebe were entrusted to the care of their American grandmother, Jennie Gibson, who became their guardian. They moved back to London and into 3 Hyde Park Gardens, the property that Ludwig Messel had bought in the last years of his life. It was to remain their home until the end of the 1920s, when Phoebe married.

Rudolph started at Eton in the summer of 1918, just days before his mother's death. There he joined his cousin Oliver Messel, who was ten months his senior and who had started at the school the previous autumn. The two boys were devoted to each other. As Oliver recalled, 'All through childhood we had been more like brothers, so at Eton we were constant companions.'[2] Together they formed lasting friendships with other boys in their house such as Billy Clonmore,

Rudolph and Phoebe
Messel with their
mother Nonie

the future Eighth Earl of Wicklow, who would later be ordained deacon and assist at the wedding of Rudolph's sister Phoebe; and Robert Byron, who would find fame as author of the seminal travelogue *The Road to Oxiana*. As well as his academic interests, Rudolph was known for his devotion to Wagner and would sit 'closeted for hours hypnotized by the emotion of the music', according to Oliver. The 'extremely handsome' Rudolph also inherited his father's sporting prowess, being particularly good at rowing. It was a sport in which he continued to participate when he went up to Merton College, Oxford, in 1922.

Oxford was to prove a formative influence on Rudolph's life in more ways than one. Not least among these was his membership of the notorious Hypocrites Club, one of a number of social clubs designed to prevent Oxford undergraduates from getting into trouble by drinking in the town. It had originally been a sober establishment 'mainly for the purpose of discussion of subjects relating to music, art and literature'.[3] Yet it was irrevocably transformed by the new intake of Etonians who went up to Oxford together with Rudolph. Evelyn Waugh, who was introduced to the Hypocrites by Rudolph's close friend Terence Greenidge, described the change:

> Most of the original members were heavy-drinking, rather sombre Rugbeians and Wykehamists with vaguely artistic and literary interests, but it was, at the time I joined, in process of invasion and occupation by a group of wanton Etonians who brought it to speedy dissolution. It then became notorious not only for drunkenness but for flamboyance of dress and manner which was in some cases patently homosexual.[4]

It would be wrong to dismiss the club as a den of debauchery, even after its takeover by the Etonians. For its more cultured members the Hypocrites' appeal lay in the opportunity for elevated conversation above and beyond what was available in the common rooms of the university. Waugh was dazzled by other-worldly Bohemians such as Harold Acton and Brian Howard, Eton contemporaries of Rudolph who would together form the inspiration for Anthony Blanche in *Brideshead Revisited*. Other Hypocrites included literary figures such as Anthony Powell, Cyril Connolly and Robert Byron, Rudolph's friend from Eton days. Oliver Messel used to pay regular visits to the club from London, brightening up its two main rooms with murals he painted together with Byron. The Oxford newspaper *Isis* described the club's members as 'perhaps the most entertaining people in the university', even if they were rather alarming to talk to. 'They have succeeded in picking up a whole series of intellectual catch-phrases with which they proceed to dazzle their friends and frighten their acquaintances; and they are the only people I have ever met who have reduced rudeness to a fine art.'[5]

This rudeness, combined with the Hypocrites' increasingly riotous parties, eventually caught up with them. A dinner given by Billy Clonmore on the roof of the Oxford church of St Peter's in the East had already alerted the authorities, but the final straw came with a fancy-dress party organized at the Hypocrites Club in March 1924. Street musicians had been engaged to create a suitably exotic ambience, and Oliver Messel 'came expressly from the Slade to assist with the decorations', according to Acton.

> 'Still lifes' of lobsters, rabbits and poultry that might have been arranged by Landseer were suspended like chandeliers from the ceilings; and significant scenes of Victorian history were depicted on the walls: Queen Victoria – not amused; 'Mr Livingstone, I presume'; Alfred, Lord Tennyson nursing his whisky bottle; Baroness Lehzen with Stockmar – sketched with greater brio than fidelity.[6]

The camp décor was reflected in the costumes of the attendees, immortalized in a group photograph of the party retained by Anthony Powell. In addition to various *faux*-military dignitaries, these included a nun, several pirates, a choirboy and an eighteenth-century courtesan. Acton described the evening as having been 'uproariously gay', even if it was not quite the orgy it became in legend. Shortly after, the Hypocrites Club was shut down by the dean of Balliol, Francis Fortescue 'Sligger' Urquhart, who thereby earned the lasting enmity of Waugh and his friends. The closure failed to put an end to the Hypocrites' high jinks, however, as many of them continued the same lifestyle under the auspices of other drinking clubs. Nor did the fun cease once they had left Oxford, as a good number slipped seamlessly into the London scene of the Bright Young Things and lived a life of unbroken parties for much of the ensuing decade. Yet beneath the glamour lay a darker reality of substance abuse that left its own legacy of addiction and mental breakdown. As Paula Byrne remarks in her study of the Brideshead generation, 'Many of these young men ended up as alcoholics or suicides (or both).'[7]

The second influence that Oxford had on Rudolph's life was to instil in him a love of cinema. His friendship with Terence Greenidge was the catalyst for this, as for other pursuits. Greenidge was an eccentric who had been orphaned in infancy and brought up by his godfather. Openly homosexual, he was one of the leading lights in the Hypocrites along with Acton and Howard, and his 1930 study *Degenerate Oxford?*, which he dedicated to Rudolph, is a reflective record of their university years together. His later life was scarred by mental illness, with the result that he had 'large parts of his brain removed by a surgeon', according to Waugh's diary description of him in 1963.[8] Greenidge had bought himself a 16-millimetre camera and shot amateur films with fellow undergraduates in various risqué roles. The most enduring of these is *The Scarlet Woman*, an 'ecclesiastical melodrama' written by and starring Evelyn Waugh. The story fantasizes a papal plot to convert England to Roman Catholicism, which is foiled only when a priest confesses all to a cabaret queen played by the future Hollywood actress Elsa Lanchester.

Rudolph Messel's first foray into film-making came in 1924 with the 'burlesque drama' *Big Dog*, a two-reel 16-millimetre silent movie which he co-wrote with Greenidge. A preservation copy of the film survives in the archive of the British Film Institute, and the synopsis gives a sense of its dramatic potential. 'A spy is sent by his organization to the country to blow up a train carrying an important official. He stays with a local farmer and falls in love with his wife. He is distraught when he realizes that she is on the train under which he has planted the bomb. However, a St Bernard dog finds the bomb and puts it in a river.'

In addition to Rudolph's own St Bernard in the title role, the cast comprised just three actors: Peter Crowland as the spy, Terence Greenidge as the farmer and Rudolph's sister Phoebe Messel as Polly Lugg, the farmer's wife. The film enjoyed some exposure, being shown at a private screening in London together with Waugh's *Scarlet Woman*.[9] Rudolph's second film, *Next Gentleman Please*, is the story of a French fortune-teller who helps her beau steal jewels and then 'elopes with a local thug'. The film starred Joan Maude, who would go on to feature alongside David Niven in the 1946 classic *A Matter of Life and Death*. As well as its private viewings, *Next Gentleman Please* received a public screening at the Super Cinema on Charing Cross Road on 27 July 1927, prior to a showing of the 'mystery drama' *The Prey of the Wind*.[10]

Rudolph declared during his time at Oxford that he would write a full-length history of the cinema, and he spent much of 1927 in retreat on Lundy Island fulfilling this intention. The finished product, *This Film Business*, was published the following year. The book has rightly been described as 'eccentric'; yet it is a bold overview of the main trends in the history of film up to the 1920s, with informed comparisons of the industry in Germany, Britain and the USA.[11] Rudolph devotes admiring passages to films still recognized as masterpieces today, such as Robert Wiene's *Cabinet of Doctor Caligari* (1920) and Fritz Lang's newly released *Metropolis* (1927). He is effusive on the young Sergei Eisenstein – 'there

is no knowing to what heights he may not attain' –
but equally prepared to recognize the commercial
genius of Douglas Fairbanks, Charlie Chaplin and
the biblical blockbusters of Cecil B. de Mille. The
book ends with a hint at Rudolph's lasting belief
in film as a force for good, as he eulogizes on the
power of cinema to 'change the injustices of our
present social system and readjust our outworn
codes of values'.[12]

Phoebe Buchanan, née
Messel, with Towser

For the cinema was not to be the only legacy
of Rudolph's Oxford years. The other passion
he developed was for politics, and again his friendship with Terence Greenidge
played a decisive role. Although 1920s Oxford was a bastion of Conservatism,
there was a small Labour Club made up of dedicated students who maintained a
shared idealism in the face of privilege. Greenidge noted in *Degenerate Oxford?*
that their commitment to socialism was 'thoughtful, emotional and yet vague' but
praised this as a mark of genuine human conviction when compared to the cold
logic of the doctrinaire (and even smaller) Communist Party group.[13]

Nothing in his family background would have marked Rudolph out for a life
in socialist politics. His father Harold was elected a member of the Conservative
Club in 1908, while his Uncle Leonard was a member of the Carlton Club and
played an active role in his local Conservative Association. Most other members
of the Messel clan would have identified as Tories; even Rudolph's cousin Oliver
referred to himself as a 'staunch Conservative supporter' when writing to complain
to the Foreign Secretary about the treatment of Seretse Khama, the deposed King
of Bechuanaland. Yet Rudolph was to become a committed socialist, devoting
much of his life to radical political causes designed to further the common good
rather than the narrow class interests of the ruling élite.

According to his own account, Rudolph became involved in left-wing politics
as a result of witnessing the General Strike of May 1926. The strike pitted the
organized working class against the Conservative government in a test of strength
that lasted just nine days but cast a shadow over industrial relations for decades to
come. Four million workers from all sections of the trade-union movement walked
out in solidarity with the coal miners, who were being pressed by the (private)
mine owners to work longer hours for less pay. The strike brought the centre of
London to a standstill, with only a handful of buses and trains left running. As
deliveries ground to a halt Hyde Park was cordoned off by the government and
converted into a distribution centre for food and milk. Half a million members of
the upper and middle classes answered Prime Minister Stanley Baldwin's call for
volunteers to break the strike, the men acting as drivers and special constables, the

R. P. MESSEL.
PROSPECTIVE LABOUR CANDIDATE
SOUTH MOLTON PARLIAMENTARY DIVISION.

Printed and Published by Southwoods (Exeter) Ltd., 39-40, North St., Exeter.

Rudolph's campaign
leaflet for the
Devonian constituency
of South Molton

women working as telephone operators or helping to staff impromptu canteens.[14]

It is a mark of his commitment that Rudolph sided with the workers against his peers in this open declaration of class war. His sister Phoebe reacted similarly. As well as voting Labour in future elections, she became a Quaker, was actively engaged in social welfare and followed a vegetarian diet for the rest of her life. Yet this should not suggest that brother and sister were killjoys. On the contrary, both Rudolph and Phoebe took great pleasure in the opportunities inherited wealth made available to them. In 1928 their American grandmother took a lease for them on a house at Bridestowe on the edge of Dartmoor, beginning a love affair with Devon that would last the rest of their lives, and the two siblings cut a fine figure when they used to waltz and tango together at local village dances.

Rudolph stood as a Labour candidate for the Devonian constituency of South Molton in the General Election of 1929 at the age of twenty-four. His candidature came about by accident as the original Labour candidate had to move suddenly to Birmingham, and the local party elected Rudolph unanimously in his place. Rudolph went to it with a will, enlisting his sister and grandmother to campaign on his behalf.[15] Yet this was the first time the Labour Party had put forward a candidate for the constituency of South Molton, and Rudolph came a distant third behind the Liberal and Conservative candidates. As he himself admitted, it was always going to be a hopeless seat.[16] His Messel family background was brought into play when he was heckled as a German on the campaign trail and forced to make a 'vigorous denial' of false accusations concerning his nationality at a meeting held at Crediton Town Hall.[17] Rudolph's good looks provided local journalists with colour throughout the campaign, as in the description of his reception after the announcement of the results: 'Mr Messel was subjected to much attention by the women folk, some of whom saluted him with kisses.'[18] Rudolph increased his share of the vote when he ran again for South Molton in the General Election of 1931, but there was never any hope of the Labour Party's winning such a rural seat. He stood for Labour in the Croydon South by-election held in February 1932, where he reduced the Conservative majority, and in the seat of Birmingham Aston in the General Election of November 1935, where he again lost out to the Conservative candidate. Clearly fate had never intended Rudolph Messel for an MP.

Instead of entering parliamentary politics Rudolph channelled his energies into a wide range of educational outputs designed to build appreciation of the

Rudolph Messel (left) shaking hands with the Conservative candidate in the 1932 Croydon South by-election

socialist cause. The first of these can be found in the summer 1932 edition of the *Socialist Review*. Rudolph's friends Terence and John Greenidge both wrote regularly for the journal, which covered cultural as well as political issues; Terence was its film critic. Rudolph's initial contribution, 'Socialism Five Hundred Years Ago', was an enthusiastic description of the socio-economic system in Peru prior to the Spanish invasion of 1532. Drawn from the accounts of two sixteenth-century Spanish visitors, the article extols the socialized system in which land was held as communal property, with each family assigned a portion sufficient for its sustenance. In contrast to the social cohesion of this primitive socialism, Rudolph described the plight of the modern Peruvian peasant farmer in uncompromising terms. 'The remnants of a broken road, and beside it perhaps the figure of a Peruvian of today caught in the circle of unremitting toil as he tills no longer *his* land but the property of some settler from Europe. In short, capitalism draining a country which Socialism had once stocked with abundance.'[19]

In May 1933 Rudolph took over as joint editor of the *Socialist Review* with Terence Greenidge and Francis Streeten, revitalizing it from a quarterly to a monthly publication and securing contributions from internationally recognized authors such as Sylvia Pankhurst and Upton Sinclair. The period coincided with Hitler's consolidation of power in Germany, and the journal's monthly news coverage is full of calls for action against 'Nazi terrorism' as well as concern for

Jews and fellow socialists already singled out for persecution at the regime's hands. Rudolph continued to write book reviews for the journal and commissioned further contributions from friends such as the Fabian writer Raymond Postgate and the novelist Naomi Mitchison. Nor was he above drawing on Messel family talent in supplementing the political content of the journal with cultural fare: the translation of Heinrich Heine's poem 'The Lotus Flower', credited to a mysterious P.B. in the June 1933 issue, is doubtless from the pen of Rudolph's sister Phoebe, who had acquired those initials through her marriage to John Buchanan and who was a keen translator of German poetry.[20]

Shortly after the appearance of his article on Peruvian socialism Rudolph joined a group of artists and intellectuals on a research mission to the Soviet Union organized by the New Fabian Research Bureau. The delegation included the Labour MPs Frederick Pethick-Lawrence and Hugh Dalton, the Fabian theorists Margaret and George Cole, as well as Naomi Mitchison, her brother Graeme Haldane and Raymond Postgate. Each member of the delegation was expected to meet their own expenses (including £1 a day for board and lodging while in the Soviet Union) and was entrusted with a specific research focus. Given his acknowledged expertise, Rudolph was tasked with investigating the state of Russian cinema. His chapter in the publication that resulted from the visit, *Twelve Studies in Soviet Russia*, highlighted the Soviet conception of film as an instrument in the service of ideological education, rather than the medium of entertainment it is normally understood to be in the West.

Rudolph also wrote a lighter account of his Russian visit for the *New Clarion*, the weekly newspaper of the Labour left.[21] The article led directly to the first of his regular film columns in the paper. Filling a full page of newsprint, Rudolph published reviews that encompassed anything from Laurel and Hardy to the latest expressionistic German masterpieces, all from a stridently socialist perspective. By way of example, Rudolph's review of the film *Cavalcade* concludes that 'it is an insult to all people of intelligence and will therefore be acclaimed with eulogy by all sections of the capitalist Press'.[22]

At the same time as writing his weekly film column, Rudolph was working on his first novel, *High Pressure*, published by the Fortune Press in 1934. Dedicated to Terence Greenidge, the book is a curious mix of social commentary, modernist experimentation and left politics. The plot is based around the parallel lives of five young men trapped in their respective settings who end up being thrown together by a series of chance incidents. Tom and Harry are rural labourers from north Devon, with dreams beyond the confines of their narrow existence. By contrast, Jim is a musician trying to square a faltering career in London with his unhappy engagement to a wealthy fiancée, while Olaf is a young ship's captain seeking to escape the loneliness of life at sea. The final protagonist, Charles, is an aspiring

American poet whose father pays for him to visit Europe, where he undergoes a dramatic conversion to Roman Catholicism through an accidental encounter with a mass in Venice, one of the book's most delirious passages.

Rudolph's literary powers grow more assured as the novel progresses, and there is genuine menace in the description of the alcohol-fuelled parties frequented by its heroes, surely drawn from the author's own experiences. Other passages are authentically poetic; the sixth chapter opens with a description of a London 'languishing under its biannual heat-wave' which blends social observation with a delicate colour palette:

> The sun went on shining, and a few of the bolder spirits discarded ties; river picnics
> for those who could afford them, and in the slum areas knitting on the doorsteps
> and conversations shouted across the streets . . . Michaelmas daisies opened a
> few shy petals in the green calm of Lincoln's Inn Fields. Actors addressed rows of
> empty stalls, and the nights were blue and beautiful.[23]

The novel reaches its climax when the lead character, Tom, vows to take action against the uncaring capitalist system that has driven one of his new-found friends to suicide. He joins the Communist Party and confronts his brother Harry with his new socialist convictions in a London pub. In the final scene Tom stumbles across the Aldwych to a Soviet travel agency emblazoned with the words 'Visit the USSR'. Face to face with the image of a man with a peaked cap and a hand outstretched towards him, Tom falls into a reverie. 'The Union of Socialist Soviet Republics. Socialist Republics; the words mean something, for they were real and they stood for something that was there, someone who had won . . .'[24]

Whatever its political merits *High Pressure* did not meet with critical acclaim. The reviewer for the *Birmingham Gazette* complained that it was 'an extraordinarily difficult novel to read', while the *Dundee Courier* called it 'an outlet of volcanically violent experience of life in the jazzy mood'. The Devonian *Western Morning News* felt that it was 'powerful and original' as a novel but 'unsatisfying' as a political tract.[25] In an interview with the *Daily Herald* even Rudolph seemed to lose confidence. 'My hero would have shown more sense if he had joined the Labour Party, but as he has shown no sense all through the book I couldn't make him come to his senses all at once without seeming utterly unconvincing.'[26]

Rudolph Messel in South America

A Pacifist at War 19

Rudolph Messel channelled the same political convictions into his next creative venture: the development of educational cinema for a mass audience. He had used his *New Clarion* column of 11 March 1933 to castigate the film industry of his day for existing 'to make capitalism seem attractive to the working classes'. In order to counter the propaganda pouring out of Hollywood, Rudolph concluded, 'There is only one effective thing which we can do, and that is to produce our own films; and I suggest that we should do it.' He was true to his word, and that month set about the birth of the first film-making collective devoted to the production of socialist cinema for the use of Labour groups and radical film societies across Britain.

Working within the left of the Labour Party, Rudolph set up a film committee consisting of himself and Terence Greenidge along with Raymond Postgate and his wife Daisy, daughter of the Labour leader George Lansbury. The committee adopted the name of the Socialist Film Council, and Lansbury agreed to be its president – the beginning of a relationship that was to be a major influence on Rudolph until the end of the older man's life. The focus was on producing films that would educate as well as entertain, making use of the medium's mass appeal in much the same way as Rudolph had witnessed in the Soviet Union. As he quipped in *This Film Business* five years earlier, 'Everyone is averse to learning, but no one is averse to going to the cinema.'[1]

The inaugural film produced by the Socialist Film Council was intended to be the first in a series of bulletins to counter the propaganda newsreels shown to millions of people each week in cinemas up and down the country. *What the Newsreel Does Not Show* was a single-reel production designed to be made available for local viewing at Labour Party meetings. It included footage shot in the Soviet Union by Rudolph himself depicting aspects of the Five-Year Plan such as the construction and opening of the Dnieperstroy Dam; a section contrasting London slum dwellings with working-class housing in Germany (an echo of Alfred Messel's social reform architecture); and footage of May Day celebrations from around Britain sent in by readers of the *New Clarion*. Terence Greenidge may have been overly optimistic when he suggested, 'The truth of the Labour newsreel should ensure its popularity.'[2] While there was some interest from local groups around the country, it was too ambitious to hope that such alternative newsreels could be repeated on a regular basis, and no more editions were produced.[3]

The Socialist Film Council's other opening venture was more successful: a stand-alone drama on the social impact of the hated means test, entitled *The Road to Hell*. The National Government formed by Ramsay MacDonald in 1931 had introduced means testing as a way of restricting access to unemployment benefit, with claimants forced to undergo intrusive investigation into their household means before being granted any payments. Rudolph's film, written and directed with Raymond Postgate, was an attempt to draw out the human cost of means testing through the dramatic representation of a family brought to its knees by a series of accidents. The father (played by Postgate) is hit by a car driven by a drunken playboy (Rudolph Messel) and left unable to work, yet he cannot claim the benefits due to him because the elder of his two sons (Terence Greenidge) is earning a wage. The mother of the family (Naomi Mitchison) pleads her case before the Public Assistance Board but is rejected, upon which the younger son takes his own life while his brother ends up in gaol. The ending is marked by an impassioned speech from the mother, who declares, 'All over London there's thousands of people suffering just as we have, starving on the means test and doing nothing about it.' The final frames are of a fluttering flag adorned with the closing words of the *Communist Manifesto*: 'Workers of the World, UNITE.'

The Road to Hell was very much an amateur enterprise. All the actors were friends and relatives, and a good proportion of the filming took place in the Lansbury family home in east London. It was a silent film, despite the fact that 'talkies' were by now established as the future of cinema, and cost the grand total of £66 to make, which Rudolph paid out of his own pocket. *The Road to Hell* was greeted by a standing ovation and 'much cheering' when it was shown at the 1933 Labour Party conference in Hastings, and George Lansbury expressed his wish that it be seen by all in the House of Commons. It was praised by the *Cinema Quarterly* as 'a first-class object lesson to every film group or independent amateur in the country . . . well constructed, well acted, well cut, well lit and well directed'.[4] The review by the young critic John Grierson in Rudolph's own paper, the *New Clarion*, was less complimentary. While acknowledging that 'in every technical respect the film was well enough made', Grierson – who was to become the father of documentary film-making in Britain – denounced its story line for failing to portray the true causes of unemployment and omitting to suggest more definitive action to deal with the issues raised.[5] Fortunately *The Road to Hell* has survived the passage of time and is now freely available online courtesy of the British Film Institute, so readers can make up their own minds.

Buoyed up by their initial experiences, the members of the Socialist Film Council embarked on a more ambitious project for their next venture. Taking its title from a Walt Whitman poem, *Blow, Bugles, Blow* was a strident anti-war film written by Raymond Postgate (who had been imprisoned during the First World War for his pacifist beliefs) and directed by Rudolph. Once again the actors were drawn from friends and family, but this time the film was shot in 35-millimetre rather than 16-millimetre format and was no longer silent; the budget of £1,500 – again financed by Rudolph – was considerably larger than that of the Socialist Film Council's previous two films. The story tells of a young editor's rebellion against his newspaper's jingoistic support for British war plans against France. He publishes a leader article calling for a general strike to prevent the war, but the Trades Union Congress will only do so if the French unions do the same. Here the sub-plot comes into play, as the editor's wife has been having a listless affair with an army officer, whose

Rudolph in the role of film director

own wife Marguerite is sister to a French trade unionist (played by Rudolph). Marguerite smuggles through a message from the French unions arranging for a general strike in both countries simultaneously, and war is prevented. Workers persuade soldiers to give up their weapons, the British government is overthrown and the Red Flag is raised over Downing Street to the strains of the 'Internationale'.

Blow, Bugles, Blow was completed in the summer of 1934 but soon fell foul of the authorities. While 16-millimetre films did not have to comply with censorship restrictions, 35-millimetre productions were required to obtain a certificate from the British Board of Film Censors before they could be released. Yet the Board was determined to block the release of any film dealing with political issues from a subversive perspective, and there could be few more subversive prospects than the threat of a general strike overturning the nation's decision to go to war. The film was denied a certificate and suffered accordingly. One working men's institute in the South Wales mining community of Maerdy was severely censured for putting on an illicit screening of *Blow, Bugles, Blow* in 1935 and threatened with legal action if it ever showed an uncertified film again.

The experience of *Blow, Bugles, Blow* was a disappointment for Rudolph, who had been the driving force behind the Socialist Film Council. The reviewer of

Rudolph at his typewriter

trade paper *Kine Weekly*, who saw the film at the 1934 Labour Party conference, praised it as 'an excellent example of the economically produced propaganda picture', but it never fulfilled the hopes its makers had invested in it.[6] While private screenings continued to take place, the £5 cost of hiring *Blow, Bugles, Blow* (compared to £1 10s. for the earlier two films together) discouraged wider uptake. Rudolph handed the film over to the Independent Labour Party in 1938, which organized its first public screening in conjunction with the Port Talbot Cooperative Society.[7]

Rudolph continued to provide financial support to other leftist cinematic ventures, such as the Film and Photo League's production of *March Against Starvation*, a record of the National Unemployed Workers' Movement protest march of 1936. His own film-making days were behind him, however, and the Socialist Film Council was allowed to fade out quietly. Critics have been ambivalent in their appreciation of its efforts, accusing Rudolph and his fellow enthusiasts of dilettantism at a time when the true challenge to commercial cinema was to be found in the documentary film movement. Yet the Socialist Film Council is acknowledged to have pioneered the use of 16-millimetre film as a medium of political education in Britain and for that reason has held its place in cinematic history.

Rudolph was still keen to fund other socialist education initiatives, just as he financed the activities of old friends from outside politics, such as the excavation of the Myrelaion monastery in Istanbul led by his Eton and Oxford contemporary David Talbot Rice.[8] On the political front Rudolph supplied the financial backing for a new socialist monthly, *Fact*, the first edition of which appeared in April 1937. The idea for the venture was based on the Penguin pocket-book format recently brought out by publishers Allen Lane. Each issue of *Fact* would be a stand-alone treatment of a particular theme running to a hundred pages at just sixpence a copy.[9] The series was edited by Raymond Postgate with support from some of the most eminent figures on the left at that time, including Stephen Spender, Joseph Needham and H.G. Wells. Margaret Cole wrote the main essay for the inaugural edition, to which Rudolph contributed a quirky review of three novels based on the theme of boxing. *Fact* ran for twenty-seven issues, its most notable editions featuring Ernest Hemingway's essay on the Spanish Civil War and C.L.R. James's radical history of black African revolt. Yet with the Second World War looming other priorities took precedence. As Postgate's children recalled in their biography of their father:

> By the spring of 1939, Messel had decided that he could use his wealth more effectively by helping the ever-increasing flood of refugees from European fascism and he withdrew his financial backing – and who could say he was mistaken? Efforts were made to find another backer from within the publishing trade, but they failed and in June, much praised but with insufficient sales, *Fact* 'folded'.[10]

Friendship with the Postgates brought Rudolph closer to George Lansbury and his deeply held Christian pacifism. Lansbury had been forced to relinquish the Labour leadership in 1935 as a result of his anti-war views, which he acknowledged were now out of step with the party's desire for mobilization to confront the rising threat of fascism. While many on the left had opposed 'imperialist' war in 1914, few were prepared to maintain the same stance in the face of Mussolini's aggression against Abyssinia or Hitler's declaration that he was rebuilding the German military machine in defiance of the Treaty of Versailles.

Freed from the responsibility of representing the official Labour Party line, Lansbury embarked on a personal crusade for peace that would see him criss-cross Europe and the USA for the remaining five years of his life. His travels included private meetings with Hitler and Mussolini, in which Lansbury pleaded his case for an international conference to remove the causes of conflict and forestall the coming war. Rudolph provided the funding for these ventures, accompanying Lansbury on several of his European journeys. Rudolph had been one of the early signatories of the Peace Pledge Union, the British section of the War Resisters' International, and he was valued by Lansbury for his pacifist convictions as well as his practical support. The description of their sea voyage to an anti-war conference in Copenhagen in Lansbury's published memoir, *My Quest for Peace*, paints a picture of their comradeship.

Rudolph working in the refugee settlement, Colombia

Rudolph Messel was my companion, acting as usual as guide, protector, and friend. He and I occupied ourselves on the journey in playing chess, much to the amusement of more serious and skilled players who could not understand how we could talk and play at the same time. It was an extremely pleasant journey out to Denmark and back; the sea was like a pond with just a ripple of movement and some sun. The voyage itself did us a great deal of good.[11]

Rudolph's engagement with the peace movement was to take him further afield when he was appointed special representative of the War Resisters' International to the Colombian settlement established for Jewish and other refugees fleeing fascism. The scheme had originally been devised by the International Christian Council for German Refugees, which had supported the creation of a small agricultural colony in a high mountain valley forty miles from the Colombian town of Popayán. The War Resisters' International agreed to assist with the development of the colony, and Rudolph was entrusted with the project.

Most of the existing records of the settlement come from Rudolph's own reports, especially the account he wrote of his visit to Colombia, *Refuge in the Andes*. Published on the eve of war in 1939, the story starts with Rudolph being asked to go and 'look for some refugees who seem to have got lost'. The book describes his sea passage to South America and his journey inland to the colony, but it soon becomes clear that there is serious conflict between the settlers, largely owing to the need for further funds to secure their access to land. Rudolph and his travelling companion Robert Proctor agree to return to England and raise the necessary finance, embarking on the round trip in March 1938 and returning with the money in July. They then spend the next three months working on the colony as manual labourers, before taking their final leave of Colombia and arriving back in England at the beginning of November.

As with his other books, Rudolph's character shines through *Refuge in the Andes* in a distinctive way. The descriptions of his journeys are always engaging, with a constant eye to humour and often self-deprecation. Yet there is a sensitivity in his observations that is by no means found in all European writing on Latin America, as shown in his description of the Ecuadorian capital Quito and the life of poverty that you can expect to live as a member of the indigenous non-Spanish majority:

You can sit along with other Indians in the street markets, and if you are lucky you may sell as much as sixpenceworth of fruit or maize in a day. If you have been very lucky, you may be able to sell a blanket which has taken you months to weave for as much as three-and-sixpence. But when the market is over you have to go home, and very probably you live fifteen or twenty miles away from Quito. You can't afford a mule, so you have to walk it, and when you get home the sixpence you have earned will not buy so very much for your children, nor will it go very far towards meeting the demands of the landlord or the rent collector.[12]

Reports sent back from the refugee colony after Rudolph left confirmed that it continued to prosper, but there were tensions with the Colombian authorities, who stipulated that any further settlers to join the colony must be skilled agriculturalists. In a more sinister vein, they also stated that newcomers must not be of Semitic origin – a condition that those running the programme from Britain protested against vigorously.[13] Rudolph had detected a Nazi presence among the Germans who lived in the towns surrounding the colony, and their influence may have been behind the Colombian government's change of heart. Eventually the refugee settlement proved unsustainable as a permanent venture, but it had served its purpose in providing a safe haven until the improving international situation removed the need for it. The project was wound up in 1951 as one of many schemes to have provided asylum for those fleeing fascism in Europe.[14]

The effort to help refugees from Nazi Germany took on an added urgency for Rudolph and the wider family in the years leading up to the Second World War, as their Messel cousins still lived in Berlin and found themselves at growing risk of persecution. All three of Alfred Messel's children had been baptized and brought up in the Protestant faith; yet under the 1935 Nuremberg Laws it was enough to have three Jewish grandparents to be defined as a 'full Jew' in Nazi terminology, with all the consequences this entailed. Alfred's only surviving child, Irene, had three Jewish grandparents, and the situation grew ever more precarious as the net tightened around those of Jewish heritage who had not yet left the country. Irene had visited Nymans in her youth and was personally known to her English relatives, and they now acted together as sponsors to provide the financial security necessary for her and her husband Wolfgang to flee Germany. They were finally brought over to England with their two children, Ena and Harro, before the outbreak of war.

What they escaped is shown all too clearly in the fate of Wolfgang's parents and his sister Vera, who stayed behind in the German city of Kiel. Wolfgang's father, Dr Wilhelm Bruck, was an appeal court judge from a Jewish family background who had won the Iron Cross for distinguished service during the First World War. Despite the fact that he had been brought up a Protestant and, as a war veteran,

Rudolph's wife Judy
Messel, née Birdwood

was supposed to enjoy protected status under the Third Reich, Dr Bruck and his wife Elisabeth were evicted from their home in April 1942. Shortly after, the dreaded order came for their daughter Vera to be deported to the concentration camp at Theresienstadt, by now little more than a staging post on the way to Auschwitz. Father, mother and daughter committed suicide together on 7 July 1942. Three brass cobblestones now stand in their memory on the pavement in front of their family home.

The return of peace brought hope of new beginnings, some of them in unexpected directions. Like many of his Oxford contemporaries, Rudolph had always been known as a homosexual or, as the euphemism of the day put it, 'unlikely to get married'. Yet he did now get married, to an old friend he had known from his film-making days. The Honourable Judith Birdwood was the daughter of Field-Marshal Lord William Birdwood, hero of the Gallipoli campaign and later commander-in-chief of the British Army in India. Despite these patrician origins, Judy had acted with Rudolph in the Socialist Film Council's 1933 picture *The Road to Hell* and in the anti-war film *Blow, Bugles, Blow*. Off screen she was a figure of great theatrical presence: as a young woman she had been warned by her doctors to stop eating so compulsively if she wished to avoid an early death – a warning she disregarded entirely, enjoying life fully to the age of seventy-seven. She designed costumes for Sadler's Wells in the 1930s and in later years moved to live near Cambridge, where she took charge of the Arts Theatre wardrobe, 'very, very large and always smiling', according to one admirer.[15]

The wedding of this unlikely couple took place on 23 October 1947. Although it was a lavender marriage, it was obviously based on affection and both parties recognized that it would not be a conventional union. Judy had previously been married to the stage manager Roger Colville-Wallis and by all accounts had not enjoyed the experience, divorcing him after eight years together. In Rudolph she saw a kindred spirit, and they formed a happy partnership on a number of projects in the years that followed.

One of these was a characteristically generous expression of Rudolph's pacifist sympathies: an attempt to resurrect the career of the Hungarian-Jewish conductor Charles Brill. A classical violinist before becoming a conductor, Brill had been a regular presence on the wireless during the 1930s with his own Charles Brill Orchestra, often playing light music but also making première recordings of works by Benjamin Britten. Already in his forties at the outbreak of the Second World War, Brill had been called to serve as a driver in the Royal Army Service Corps. Rather than register as a conscientious objector, he deserted and proceeded to wait out the rest of the war in semi-hiding in London before turning himself in. He was interned in Dartmoor Prison, just twenty miles from Rudolph's house outside the village of Drewsteignton. My mother remembers being driven across

Rudolph with his wife Judy, sister Phoebe and nieces (from left) Judith, Celia and Phoebe Buchanan

Dartmoor by her Uncle Rudolph so that they could hide cigarettes for Brill in chinks in the prison wall.

Brill was released and back in circulation by the end of 1947, and Rudolph provided the finance for three London concerts the following summer to revive his conducting career. Two years later Rudolph undertook a grander project: the première of Brian Easdale's opera *The Corn King*, based on the book by his old friend Naomi Mitchison. The work was performed in a run of five nights at the New Paddington Hall Theatre, and Charles Brill was again the conductor. Rudolph Messel was credited as producer, while Judy provided the costumes and décor.

Any stability that Rudolph found with Judy was likely to be short-lived, but the decisive blow came with the death of his beloved sister Phoebe. Phoebe and her husband John Buchanan had five children, but her sixth confinement had ended tragically with the birth of a still-born son, Andrew, in 1946. The trauma compromised Phoebe's own health, leaving her with dangerously high blood pressure. She suffered a stroke while on a weekend visit to Rudolph and died in Devon on 3 May 1952. She was just forty-four. There exists a long and poignant letter which Rudolph wrote to Phoebe's youngest son, Ronald Buchanan, to paint a picture of what his mother had been like when they were growing up together. Rudolph reflects on the fact that, at nine years old, Ronald is even younger than he was when he lost his own mother, and the letter is an outpouring of love for the sister with whom he had shared so many happy memories over the years.

In the end Rudolph was unable to escape his demons. Like his father before him he had been prone to bouts of depression, on top of which he suffered from night terrors as a result of excessive alcohol consumption over many years. His life came to an end on 3 May 1958, the sixth anniversary of his sister Phoebe's death, while he was in Spain. The Spanish coroner's report gives the cause of death as arteriosclerosis, but it is understood within the family that he committed suicide as his father had done. His final resting place is in the English cemetery of Málaga. Like Charles in his novel *High Pressure* Rudolph had been received into the Roman Catholic Church in his later years, and a Requiem Mass was held for him in the Lady Chapel of Westminster Cathedral four days after his death. As well as his widow and many other members of the wider Messel family, the service was attended by friends such as Terence Greenidge, Brian Easdale and Charles Brill.[16]

It would be easy to dismiss Rudolph as the quintessential 'champagne socialist'. In his youth he enjoyed fast cars and flying, sometimes turning up at Labour Party meetings in his own plane. He travelled extensively in Europe, North Africa and the Americas at a time when overseas voyages were the preserve of a tiny minority. The value of the estate he left his wife Judy on his death was £119,583 3s. 6d. – the equivalent of £6 million in today's earnings – and he clearly enjoyed the most privileged of existences. Yet he chose to devote much of his life to causes beyond his own self-interest, many of which made him deeply unpopular. His personal creed may be summed up in the fundraising appeal he wrote for the refugee settlement in the Andes: 'It is not enough today to say that we believe in peace and freedom – we must do something to make peace and freedom possible for those who have been denied them.'[17]

Harold Acton, Rudolph's contemporary at Eton and Oxford, recalled him as 'strikingly handsome, sociable and popular' but felt that his story was ultimately a tragic one.[18] Yet Rudolph enjoyed a purposeful and varied life that allowed him to express his creative energies in many forms. The last word can go to Evelyn Waugh, who continued to meet Rudolph occasionally in the years after they left Oxford. Looking back on his university experiences in his autobiography, Waugh composed a 'necrology' of those friends who had frequented the Hypocrites Club in the heady summer of 1923 but who had predeceased him. Among them he listed Rudolph Messel, with the simple epitaph: 'cadaverous, wayward, generous'.[19]

Princess Margaret and Tony
Armstrong-Jones in the official
engagement photograph released by
Buckingham Palace in February 1960

Royal Wedding 20

THE MOST FAMOUS of all the Messels is not widely known to be a Messel at all. Yet Tony Armstrong-Jones's marriage to Princess Margaret in 1960 brings the family story full circle, as it represents the moment at which the immigrant outsiders attained the status of ultimate insiders. While it was widely noted that Tony was the first commoner to marry into the Royal Family in over four centuries, his German-Jewish ancestry was less publicly remarked upon. The wedding marked the conclusion of a remarkable journey that began two hundred years earlier with the expulsion of the Messel family by Princess Margaret's ancestor George III.

Antony Charles Robert Armstrong-Jones was born on 7 March 1930 at 25 Eaton Terrace, the Belgravia home that his mother had been given as a wedding present by her father Leonard Messel five years before. The privileged circumstances of Tony's birth were offset by the breakdown of his parents' marriage when he was still in his infancy. The impact on Tony and his elder sister Susan of Ronald and Anne's separation in 1933 and their divorce two years later was most immediately felt in the nomadic lifestyle caused by constantly moving between their parents' various homes. Yet the deeper psychological effect on the children came from Anne's desire to put her time with Ronald Armstrong-Jones behind her as she moved on to her second and far happier marriage to Michael, Sixth Earl of Rosse. Brought up largely by their nanny, both children would find it hard to come to terms with their mother's coldness towards them. Anne would always be hostile to Tony, complaining that he had taken after his father and was 'not a Messel'.[1]

At his prep school Tony was 'outdoorsy' and 'loved drama and acting', according to his classmate Tony Atkinson. Despite being short, Tony proved himself to be good at boxing and became featherweight champion at the age of eleven. The school was infamous for its headmaster, Hugh Ozanne, who used to take pleasure, according to Atkinson, in beating boys in front of the assembled school with his prized collection of bamboo canes. To put an end to this practice, the rebellious young Atkinson stole the headmaster's canes and buried them in a nearby wood but slipped up by confiding in Tony:

I made the mistake of telling Armstrong-Jones where I'd hidden them. Ozanne didn't like him much, so, anxious to gain favour, Armstrong-Jones sneaked on me. Ozanne made a great ceremony of taking me into the woods and, with the solemnity devoted to exhuming a body, making me dig up the canes. My reward was a caning with the 'swishiest' cane.[2]

Tony did not excel academically, regularly coming near the bottom of the class in Latin, English, French and mathematics, so that the headmaster concluded despairingly in his report to Tony's parents, 'Armstrong-Jones may be interested in something, but it is not anything we teach here.' Yet he managed to pass the Common Entrance examination to Eton and started there in Michaelmas 1943. While his academic performance improved, he was still more interested in the extracurricular activities that the college had to offer and was soon boxing for Eton against other schools. His passion for inventiveness betrays the influence of his much-loved uncle Oliver Messel: Tony rigged up any number of ingenious contraptions in his study, including a radiogram, a series of intruder alarms and an electric toaster. As a precursor of his future career, he swapped a microscope that he had been given by his grandfather for a camera from another boy, set up a makeshift enlarger and revived the Eton Photographic Society.

Tony's progress through adolescence was dealt a severe blow when he contracted polio in the summer of 1946. This was the eve of the outbreak which gripped England and Wales in 1947 and turned into an epidemic throughout the following decade, with thousands of cases in 'polio season' every summer. Tony was critically ill for days and his left side paralysed; once his life was no longer in danger he was transferred to the Liverpool Royal Infirmary to spend six months in rehabilitation learning to walk again. Long hours in bed were broken up by an intensive regime of exercise, baths and physiotherapy, as well as copious free time to indulge in model-making and other creative pursuits. Oliver Messel arranged for thespian friends who were performing in Liverpool to drop in on Tony and cheer him up, and surely no other teenage patient could boast personal visits from such celebrities as Marlene Dietrich, Noël Coward or Bea Lillie, dubbed 'the funniest woman in the world'. Tony's sister Susan was a more regular visitor, and in return he spent many lonely hours knitting her an enormous scarf.

By the summer of 1947 Tony was back at Eton again, coxing one of the boats at the annual Fourth of June festival held in celebration of the birthday of George III. He continued to cox throughout his final year at school, that being a position for which his weakened left leg was no impediment, while his diminutive stature was a distinct advantage. The effects of polio did, however, mean that Tony was exempted from military service, so that he went up to Jesus College, Cambridge, in 1948 ahead of his peers. He was originally meant to read natural sciences

Tony as cox of the
Cambridge eight

but switched to architecture after ten days. Yet the discipline of an architectural training was not in keeping with Tony's character. Following in the Messel family tradition he spent much of his time at university on the river and coxed the Cambridge eight which triumphed over Oxford in the 1950 Boat Race. In characteristic style he designed his own lightweight rudder for the boat out of laminated aluminium rather than the traditional mahogany.

Tony came down from Cambridge with a Blue but no degree, as he chose not to re-sit the second-year examinations which he had failed. His mother was deeply concerned at his proposal that he abandon architecture for photography, sending a hasty telegram: 'Do not agree suggestion changing career. Telephone this evening.' He was given lunch at the family firm L. Messel and Co. to see whether life as a stockbroker might appeal to him but according to his own account Tony was unable to see himself there and 'left immediately after pudding'.[3] Instead, with his mother won round, he embarked on the photography career that would make his name. He set up a makeshift darkroom in a mezzanine flat above the porter's lodge in Albany, the exclusive set of apartments on Piccadilly where Tony's father, Ronald Armstrong-Jones, was living at the time. From there he was able to take his first steps in commercial photography, producing portraits of family friends and their cats as Christmas cards which he made up by hand.

Tony's father paid £100 for him to be taken on as an apprentice of the society photographer Baron, whose Park Lane studio functioned as a production line for formal portraits of upper-class ladies and their daughters. Born Sterling Henry Nahum, Baron came from a family of Italian Jews who had emigrated from Libya to Manchester at much the same time that the Messels arrived in London from Germany. He had developed a lucrative business that by then employed around thirty people, and Tony was one of four trainee assistants who would acquire a working knowledge of all aspects of the photographer's art from lighting to finishing as well as indexing and filing of records. For this experience he would receive a gross weekly wage of £3, as shown by the first pay packet he proudly kept from the studio.[4] Baron would later be chosen to accompany Prince Philip on his 1956 tour of the Commonwealth, but he died suddenly in hospital when an operation for arthritis went wrong. Ironically, in view of his more significant entry into the Royal Family four years later, Tony was dismissed as a possible replacement for the Duke of Edinburgh on the grounds that he was 'too bohemian'.[5]

After serving six months' apprenticeship at Baron's studio Tony embarked on his own career as a photographer with glossy portraits for magazines such as *The Tatler*, which published his first picture – an arty shot of cockle-hunting at Blakeney Point in Norfolk – on 19 September 1951.[6] He followed it up a week later with a full-page portrait of his grandmother, Maud Messel, examining paintings given to her for her birthday by her son Oliver and in October with a portrait of his aunt and uncle on the other side of the family, the Honourable Denys and Mrs Buckley, with two of their three daughters.[7] Tony's family were members of the upper-middle class considered of interest to *The Tatler*, and he was not above exploiting these connections for all they were worth. Yet he was also keen to experiment with novel subjects and forms. In contrast to most photographers at the time, whose style was based on the conventional use of bulky equipment to achieve high-quality finishes, Tony would increasingly rely on a small 35-millimetre camera that he could transport and manoeuvre easily for more naturalistic results. While this meant that his photographs were often rejected as too grainy, he was able to pioneer a new style of reportage that captured the impromptu and unexpected rather than the staged and the 'safe'.

By 1952, at the age of just twenty-two, Tony was able to move into his first solo studio, a former ironmonger's premises at 20 Pimlico Road. Despite being on the fringes of Belgravia, this was not a fashionable area; the studio was underneath a block of Peabody flats and next door to a Sunlight laundry, with rent at £2 a week. When the plumber moved out of the basement two years later Tony converted that space into a living area connected to the ground floor by a spiral staircase he designed himself. He was still bringing in regular earnings with portraits of children and débutantes in society weeklies such as *The Tatler* and *The Sketch* and was also commissioned for sporting events such as the 1955 Henley Regatta.

Yet even here he pushed the boundaries of what was expected in such reportage, juxtaposing the obligatory river scenes with keenly observed shots of upper-class punters and working-class stall-holders at the fun fair.[8]

One of Tony's breakthroughs was to take the 21st-birthday photographs of the Duke of Kent in autumn 1956. In typically direct fashion he won the commission by writing to the Duke's mother and asking if he could do it. The portraits were released on the Duke's birthday, 9 October, and were swiftly followed by a far more important commission: a set of intimate photographs for Prince Charles's eighth birthday on 14 November 1956. In addition to a quirky solo shot of Charles reflected three ways in one of the state-room mirrors, Tony took several double portraits of the Prince and his sister Princess Anne, with an emphasis on catching their identity as children. The photographs were heralded as 'the most unconventional royal pictures ever' and harbingers of 'a new era in royal photography'.[9] The Queen valued the images highly enough to invite Tony to take follow-up photographs for Charles's ninth birthday as well.

Even more significantly, Tony was commissioned to record the Royal Family at Buckingham Palace in a series of formal and informal images designed to give an insight into the monarch's private life. Published in October 1957, the photograph that has gone down in history shows a relaxed Queen with Prince Philip looking down from a bridge in the grounds of Buckingham Palace, while their two children read together on the bank of the stream beneath. In photographic terms the solo portrait of the Queen taken at the same

Tony's 1957 portrait of Her Majesty the Queen

time is even more striking, capturing an animated intimacy in one of Tony's trademark 'over the shoulder' close-ups.[10] When compared to other royal portraits of the period – including those taken by his former employer Baron a year earlier – the freshness of Tony's approach is unmistakable.

Tony's instant success with these high-profile commissions won him his first contract with *Vogue*, which allowed him to experiment with fashion journalism as well as celebrity portraits. He approached the work with an irreverence that was largely unknown in the world of *haute couture*: 'His photographs were zany, they were tongue-in-cheek, they were witty, and he refused to take it seriously.'[11] Tony was also regularly commissioned to contribute photographs to *The Queen*, the society magazine that had been bought by his old school friend Jocelyn Stevens and was being relaunched to a new, younger audience. Tony held his first solo exhibition at Kodak House on Kingsway in June 1957, with portraits of well-known figures such as Prime Minister Harold Macmillan and the actress Ingrid Bergman alongside reportage from Madeira, Vienna and other locations. The journal of the Royal Photographic Society devoted six pages of its September 1957 edition to images from the exhibition, noting that Tony had designed the controversial mounting of the photographs himself, blowing up the largest shots into murals nineteen feet high.[12]

The following year saw the first of the major documentary publications that would secure Tony's reputation as a serious photographer. Simply entitled *London* and dedicated to his sister Susan, this was a visual essay in 140 photographs on life in the post-war capital across the class divide. Several pictures came from the affluent milieu into which Tony himself had been born, but others were from the other end of the social scale, such as a destitute family on a deserted east London bomb site and early-morning drinkers on the West India Dock Road. Some are arresting in their backstories, such as the girl having the word 'Mother' tattooed on her arm 'because she had had toothache very badly the night before and the pain of the tattooing would take the pain of the toothache away'. Several have

Tony's iconic photograph of nannies on Rotten Row from his 1958 publication *London*

become famous compositions in their own right, such as the phalanx of nannies pushing their prams down Rotten Row or the naked cabaret dancer performing at lunchtime in the Bridge House Hotel at Canning Town.

The photographs were taken with Tony's 35-millimetre Leica and without artificial light, so that when blown up to folio size they created a gritty atmosphere of naturalistic reportage. This was too revolutionary for the establishment – the *British Journal of Photography* dismissed the effect as 'squalid' – but it did much to inspire a younger generation of up-and-coming photographers:

> *London* particularly impressed contemporaries on account of the consistently grainy quality of the prints and the sustained down-to-earth informality of the whole. The antithesis of the dilute neo-romantic topographics that typified British 'travel' photography of the 1950s, *London* was both satirical and affectionate, a landmark in promulgating a crisper 35mm vision of the social landscape.[13]

The other book of Tony's published in 1958 was more conventional: a profile of the island of Malta produced in conjunction with cultural critic Sacheverell Sitwell. The book offers a respectful portrait of the British colony, as befits a work devised with the assistance of its Governor and Commissioner-General (Malta obtained its independence from Britain only in 1964). Tony's photographs are equally demure, with the exception of the head and shoulders of Queen Victoria's statue in Valletta's old Piazza Regina, her face peeping out from behind a troupe of distinctly disrespectful pigeons.[14] He adopted a similarly cautious approach over twenty-five years later in his book of photographs from a trip to Israel. Only his 1972 book on Venice, published privately by Italian typewriter manufacturers Olivetti, recreated the grainy edge of *London*, this time in colour so as to capture the full effects of the Venetian winter fog.

While his professional career was taking off, Tony's private life was about to undergo the transformation that would redefine him for ever, for 1958 was the year in which he first became involved with Princess Margaret and began the two-year romance that would end with him entering the Royal Family as brother-in-law to the Queen. Margaret's earlier love for the dashing fighter pilot and royal equerry Peter Townsend had entranced the nation, and official opposition to their desire to marry had generated enormous sympathy for the young Princess in Britain and around the world. Yet Margaret eventually accepted that she could not wed the divorced Townsend without forfeiting her royal privileges, and the two agreed to go their separate ways. Ever since that time there had been speculation as to which eligible bachelor she would marry out of the pack of aristocratic suitors who made up the 'Margaret set'. No one suspected that it would be an untitled photographer.

Princess Margaret was first introduced to Tony Armstrong-Jones at a dinner party given for her in February 1958 at the London home of her lady-in-waiting Lady Elizabeth Cavendish. Their paths had in fact crossed two years earlier at the wedding of Lady Anne Coke to Colin Tennant at the Earl of Leicester's family seat of Holkham Hall in Norfolk, but Tony – whom the Earl insisted on calling 'Tony Snapshot' – was merely the hired hand paid to take pictures and had not been introduced to Margaret. Worse still, Tennant (who knew Tony socially) had ordered him to use the servants' entrance – a gratuitous reminder of the photographer's lowly status that Tony would neither forgive nor forget in their subsequent meetings down the years.

At Lady Cavendish's dinner party, by contrast, Tony and Margaret were placed next to each other and discovered that they shared many artistic interests as well as numerous social acquaintances. They both enjoyed the good life and were physically well suited: Margaret was barely five feet tall, and Messel family genes meant that Tony was only a few inches taller. A few weeks later they were thrown together again in a professional context as Tony was asked to photograph Margaret for a new set of portraits at his studio in Pimlico. On home turf he took control of the sitting as if the Princess were any other client, and she was entranced. Despite the fact that he was already involved in relationships with two other women, a romance soon began in earnest.

Tony's courting of the Princess is the stuff of legend, told and retold in every royal biography to appear over the past sixty years. Clandestine visits to his Pimlico studio were an intoxicating transgression for someone like Margaret, who had been confined to the strictures and protocols of palace life. Even more thrilling was the experience of riding incognito through London on the back of Tony's motor cycle to the romantic but edgy setting of Rotherhithe, where he kept a ground-floor room overlooking the river courtesy of the journalist Bill Glenton. In this unlikely row of houses, all the more special for being so different from anything else in Margaret's life, she and Tony were able to get to know each other properly. It was, the Princess told Glenton later, 'one of the sweetest rooms I know'.[15]

Thoughts of marriage were already in the air when Tony joined Margaret at Balmoral in October 1959, and news of Peter Townsend's engagement to his young Belgian girlfriend confirmed the Princess in making the final commitment. It would be a couple of months before they asked the Queen for her approval, as Tony again joined the Royal Family at Sandringham for a flying Christmas visit. When Prime Minister Harold Macmillan arrived there he was met by a 'greatly disturbed' Duke of Gloucester who said, 'Thank Heavens you've come, Prime Minister. The Queen's in a terrible state. There's a fellow called Jones in the billiard room who wants to marry her sister, and Prince Philip's in the library wanting to change the family name to Mountbatten . . .'[16]

The engagement was announced on 26 February 1960 – and to universal surprise. Not only had the couple managed to keep their romance a secret from the press, but even good friends of the Princess had no inkling of how serious her relationship with Tony had become. The media made much of the fact that this was a genuine love match, not least because the memory of Margaret's doomed affection for Peter Townsend was still fresh in people's minds. The prospect of the Princess marrying a commoner was a cause of equal excitement. Cyril Hankinson, the editor of *Debrett's Peerage*, gave chapter and verse: 'Not for 457 years has an English Princess had a husband without a title. Not since 1503, when Cicely, third daughter of Edward IV, married Thomas Kymbe.'[17] Yet others pointed out that this was hardly a case of princess and the pauper, seeing that the groom had been born in Belgravia and educated at Eton and Cambridge. 'Tony might not have been a very common commoner,' his friend Bill Glenton conceded, 'but he was nearer to Windsor soup than Windsor Castle.'[18] The national and religious hinterland of Tony's family was considered no barrier: German ancestry was something that he and Margaret obviously had in common, while the Messels' relatively recent conversion from Judaism to Christianity was 'a genealogical fact that the royal family chose to disregard'.[19]

A certain section of the commentariat was unhappy at the announcement, again on grounds of Tony's commoner status rather than his ethnic background. Professional snobs confided their outrage to diaries or letters, Evelyn Waugh declaring himself 'appalled by the proposed mesalliance'.[20] Kingsley Amis, who harboured a personal grudge against Tony over a previous incident, laid in to the couple with venom, lambasting Princess Margaret 'for her devotion to all that is most vapid and mindless in the world of entertainment' and calling Tony 'a

Tony and Princess Margaret on the balcony of Buckingham Palace on their wedding day

dog-faced tight-jeaned fotog of fruitarian tastes such as can be found in dozens in any pseudo-arty drinking cellar in fashionable-unfashionable London'.[21] Cecil Beaton, whose old rivalry with Oliver Messel had been replaced by a new rivalry with Oliver's nephew, was downcast – but cheered up when his neighbour, Lord Pembroke, on hearing the news of the engagement, announced that he was going to go and live in Tibet.[22]

The reaction of the Royal Family was warmer. The Queen Mother took a shine to Tony from the start, referring to him as 'my dear and talented son-in-law'.[23] The Queen herself was also enthusiastic, not least because the union provided some form of closure to the bitter legacy of the Townsend affair. Those outside the innermost circle were less positive, however. Lunching with the Duchess of Kent and Princess Alexandra a couple of weeks after the announcement, Noël Coward wrote in his diary, 'They are *not* pleased over Princess Margaret's engagement. There was a distinct *froideur* when I mentioned it.' Coward himself liked Tony when he met him at the court ball given in the couple's honour at Buckingham Palace on the eve of the wedding. 'He is a charmer and I took a great shine to him, easy and unflurried and a sweet smile.'[24]

The wedding took place at Westminster Abbey on 6 May 1960. Two thousand guests attended the service, although few European royals came over for what was not, after all, a dynastic union. As well as the 100,000 onlookers who lined the streets between the Abbey and Buckingham Palace, millions more watched on television, this being the first royal wedding to be televised and, indeed, the first royal spectacular since the Coronation in 1953. Tony was applauded for his good taste in persuading Norman Hartnell to design an elegant but simple dress for Princess Margaret – a 'triumph' according to the editor of the *New Statesman*, Kingsley Martin, who further declared that Anne, Countess of Rosse 'looked about the best dressed woman in the Abbey'.[25] The *Evening Standard*'s Anne Sharpley summed up the significance of the occasion:

> In splendour, sunshine and great sweetness, Princess Margaret married Mr Antony Armstrong-Jones, the young man without title, without pretension, today in Westminster Abbey. It was something that could have happened only in the 20th century – a Sovereign's daughter marrying a photographer with all the force of the centuries of this ancient land bringing dignity, grace and deep approval.[26]

Among one thousand other wedding presents Tony and Margaret were given a black Rolls-Royce Silver Cloud with red-leather upholstery from the British motor manufacturers.[27] They were also granted the use of the royal yacht *Britannia* for their six-week honeymoon in the Caribbean, the first time it had been used by a member of the Royal Family for purely private purposes. The cost of the

Princess Margaret and Tony honeymooning on board the royal yacht *Britannia*

voyage, underwritten by the taxpayer to the tune of £10,000 per week, became a source of some discontent and not only in republican circles. Sir Alan 'Tommy' Lascelles, the Queen's former private secretary, told Harold Nicolson how much he lamented the whole thing, 'especially the yacht. He says that the boy Jones has led a very diversified and sometimes a wild life and that the danger of scandal and slander is never far off.'[28] During the honeymoon Tony's status as a commoner became the subject of good-humoured fun at the hands of Caribbean musicians. The calypso artist Fitzroy Alexander, better known as Lord Melody, recorded a single in May 1960 entitled 'Just Mrs Jones', a tribute to the power of love.

> I don't want to make the Hall of Fame,
> I just want to be Mrs Jones;
> I don't want to be Queen, over millions to reign,
> I just want to be Mrs Jones.
> Castles, fortune, power and glory,
> All these things mean nothing to me;
> I'm in love, I'm happy as the world can see,
> I just want to be Mrs Jones.

In reality, Princess Margaret loathed being referred to as Mrs Jones.[29] There was a further indignity awaiting the couple on the day they returned from honeymoon, as the waxwork model of Tony was stolen from Madame Tussaud's. It was found two days later in a phone box behind the Savoy with a sign round its neck bearing the words 'Welcome Home'. The media had a field day with photographs of Princess Margaret's new husband being returned to the museum from Bow Street police station, his head separated from his body for safe transit. A spokesman for Madame Tussaud's said, 'We are treating this fairly lightly, but if we catch the people responsible they will be charged.'[30]

Tony would soon meet with more serious opposition – and from unexpected quarters. Shortly after the couple had moved into their new flat at Kensington Palace there was a minor scandal when their butler, Thomas Cronin, left after just twenty-five days in service and sold his story to *The People*. According to Cronin's revelations, published as an exclusive by the Sunday paper over a six-week period, he had felt unable to continue in post owing to Tony's 'sudden elevation into the royal tradition', as the former photographer had failed to follow established protocol to the butler's satisfaction. 'Mr Jones', as Cronin pointedly called Tony, 'preferred to wear nothing more than a shirt, tight trousers and a sort of leisure-time jacket. I cannot say that I approved. Still less so when I found he was given to eating in his shirt sleeves, and, to do so, suspended his jacket from the back of his chair in the dining-room. Never before had I served a master in such garb.'[31]

Tony's status was enhanced when he agreed to accept a peerage in 1961. He had turned down the offer of a title prior to his marriage, but the issue raised its head with more urgency when Margaret discovered she was pregnant with their first child. The announcement on 3 October 1961 that Tony would henceforth be known as the Earl of Snowdon ensured that any children born to him and Princess Margaret would be titled, which was deemed appropriate given that they would be high in the line of succession to the throne. Tony's mother Anne looked back with distaste on her son's elevation to the peerage, which she dismissed as an arrangement 'for stud purposes'.[32] Others were similarly unimpressed. In a coruscating piece of journalistic prose *The People* derided the move as an example of outmoded monarchy.

> In Victorian times it would have been awkward for the Sovereign to have a brother-in-law who was plain Mr Jones, even with a hyphenated addition to his surname. It would have been embarrassing for the heir to the throne to have to entertain a first cousin who was plain Miss or Master Jones. But who in Britain worries about this kind of social distinction today? As the husband of the Queen's sister Tony Armstrong-Jones had one very big claim to the sympathy of the British people. He was, like most of us, without a handle to his name. He was, in fact, one of us, and we felt sorry for him having to join the royal roundabout. Now he has lost even that most precious asset that was his birthright. He is just another new peer – and he cannot even say that he had the title forced on him by inheritance or even that he earned it.[33]

The birth of Tony and Margaret's first child, David Albert Charles Armstrong-Jones, on 3 November 1961, gives a sense of just how far the Messel family had come since being expelled from their home in north-west Germany two hundred years earlier. The infant David, who assumed the courtesy title of Viscount Linley, was fifth in line to the British throne when he was born, behind Prince Charles, Prince Andrew, Princess Anne and his mother Princess Margaret. It is a pleasant thought to consider how his six-times great-grandfather Aharon Leib Bentheim, a refugee trudging his way to the village of Messel as a result of George III's anti-Jewish edict, would have taken the news. When Tony and Margaret had a second child on 1 May 1964 she became Lady Sarah Frances Elizabeth Armstrong-Jones. At her birth she was seventh in line to the throne.

Princess Margaret and Tony, now Earl of Snowdon, with the Queen Mother and their first child David

Lord Snowdon at Nymans

Disability Campaigner 21

TONY AND MARGARET were the new and exciting face of the Royal Family in the Swinging Sixties. They were photographed with the A-list celebrities of the day, including the Beatles and the Rolling Stones. They were friends with international figures such as the Aga Khan, with whom they would regularly holiday in Sardinia; actors Britt Ekland and Peter Sellers, who made an amateur home movie with them as a present for the Queen's thirty-ninth birthday; and Tony's uncle Oliver Messel, with whom they stayed together in Barbados. Yet it soon became clear that Tony would not be satisfied with life as an appendage to the Queen's sister, and it was agreed in early 1961 that he should be appointed as an unpaid adviser to the Council for Industrial Design. He took the role seriously, opening the Sixth Congress of the International Union of Architects that summer with a speech in which he decried the lack of inventiveness in Britain and challenged the profession to provide 'excitement in architecture, the excitement that comes from calculated boldness and originality'.[1]

As if to prove a point, Tony himself designed a wide variety of objects throughout his life, the most outlandish being a range of skiwear for women which, by his own admission, 'didn't sell at all'.[2] More successful by far was the radical new aviary he designed for London Zoo. Tony was asked to lead the project on the recommendation of his brother-in-law Prince Philip, following his previous work on a small aviary for the Royal Lodge in Windsor Great Park and a Gothic birdcage at Mereworth Castle in Kent. Tony enlisted the help of

The Snowdon Aviary at London Zoo

architect Cedric Price and structural engineer Frank Newby to work on a modernist design that would allow the exotic birds to fly free within the aviary while offering visitors to the zoo the opportunity to observe them at close quarters.[3] Dubbed 'a whopping great birdcage' by *Pathé News*, the Snowdon Aviary quickly established itself as an icon of architectural innovation.[4] Cecil Beaton described the official opening on 9 July 1965 with admiration, noting that it had taken an extraordinary mind to conceive 'such a curious mélange of struts and cantileverages'. He also relished the incongruity of the royal procession making its way among the zoo's emus, zebras and rhinoceroses, with Princess Margaret 'done up like Empress Josephine walking over hard ground'.[5]

Tony's second major design project lasted a couple of hours only: the ceremony for the investiture of the Prince of Wales on 1 July 1969. Tony was proud of his Welsh roots, serving as the first president of the Civic Trust for Wales as well as patron of other Welsh cultural associations. In 1963 the Queen had made him Constable of Caernarfon Castle, a sinecure held earlier in the century by David Lloyd George MP, and she now invited him to take charge of Prince Charles's investiture there. Tony was determined to stage the ceremony in a manner that brought the Royal Family into the modern age, not least because it was to be broadcast internationally to an expected audience of five hundred million people. In place of the usual paraphernalia that cluttered royal occasions, he stripped the ceremony down to its bare essentials 'to make it into a television production that was going to be viewed at home in people's sitting-rooms, so that when you were sitting alone watching it you thought you were there'. Discarding the medieval costume worn by previous Constables of Caernarfon Castle, Tony designed his own futuristic uniform for the ceremony in sleek blue-green barathea. Interviewed on the anniversary of the investiture forty years later by the BBC's Huw Edwards, he admitted that it made him look like 'a cinema usherette from the 1950s or the panto character Buttons'.[6] The Queen was pleased with the event's success and appointed Tony a Knight Grand Cross of the Royal Victorian Order (GCVO) in recognition of his services.[7]

Tony's professional career took another turn with his appointment as artistic adviser to the innovative colour magazine launched by the *Sunday Times* in 1962. The magazine was originally conceived as a glossy vehicle for bringing in advertising revenue, but under its new art director Michael Rand it quickly became a home for serious photojournalism. Rand had worked with Tony at the *Daily Express* and brought him over to the new venture, where he 'made a very valuable contribution, especially on social reportage'.[8] This is certainly the most memorable aspect of Tony's photographic career and the work he was proudest of in later life. Over the next fifteen years he contributed a series of hard-hitting photographic essays on the elderly, children, loneliness and psychiatric institutions, each accompanied by text from the magazine's investigative reporters.[9]

Tony adopted the same grainy realism in his overseas commissions, including features from Nigeria, Peru, Egypt, Thailand and India. His series for the *Sunday Times* on contemporary British artists led to the publication in 1965 of *Private View: The Lively World of British Art*. With four hundred of Tony's photographs documenting the working lives of artists such as Francis Bacon, Barbara Hepworth

and David Hockney, the folio-sized volume was 'the publishing sensation of the year'.[10] Looking back in the context of 1960s British photojournalism, art historian Martin Harrison singled out *Private View* for special praise. 'Large format, superbly printed, and skilfully designed by Germano Facetti, it was one of the most striking and informative photography books of the decade.'[11]

Following his social reportage in the *Sunday Times* Tony was commissioned by the US television network CBS to produce a documentary about loneliness and old age. Conscious of his own lack of experience in the medium, he joined forces with the British broadcaster Derek Hart, and the two worked together for over six months to create the film *Don't Count the Candles*. The documentary was an unflinching study of the challenges of growing old, arousing 'pity, sympathy, repulsion, despair and horror', according to one reviewer, although the *Daily Mirror* managed to find it 'quite cheerful'.[12] The film was premièred in New York and watched by over seven million people when it was broadcast on BBC1 on 4 April 1968. It won awards at the Prague International Television Festival and Venice Film Festival, as well as two Emmys – one for Tony's photography and one for production – in the USA.[13]

Tony went on to make several further films across a range of social issues, including *Peter, Tina and Steve*, a compassionate study of fostering as an alternative to the incarceration of young offenders. Yet it was his documentary

Born to Be Small that took on from where *Don't Count the Candles* had left off. Made again with Derek Hart, the film explored the condition of dwarfism and the stigma faced by those living with it; once again, it was watched by over seven million people when it was broadcast on 6 December 1971 and nominated for a BAFTA the following year. One member of the public, who identified herself as 'a 3 ft 9 in member of the Association for Research into Restricted Growth', wrote to express her gratitude. 'I pray that this film will have helped the small of stature (and those yet to come) to be accepted by society as human beings, not someone to be scoffed or scorned at.'[14]

Active engagement with issues of disability was a passion for Tony, stimulated by his own childhood experience of polio and the awareness it instilled in him. He used his maiden speech in the House of Lords on 10 April 1974 to draw attention to issues facing disabled people in Britain and was invited by the Labour government of Harold Wilson to chair an inquiry into the 'integration of the disabled' into society. The resulting Snowdon Working Party Report was hailed as a major step forward in challenging social barriers to disabled people's rights. Combining his campaigning energies with his enthusiasm for design, Tony created an indoor battery-powered mobility aid for his friend the journalist Quentin Crewe at roughly half the price of existing electric wheelchairs. Developed further by the engineering company Rubery Owen, the Chairmobile (as it was called) was adopted by the *Sunday Mirror*, which placed a bulk order through its parent company so that five thousand were manufactured for sale. The Science Museum holds a specimen model donated by Tony himself, but the design did not catch on.[15]

Tony was equally active in campaigning for safer mobility outside the home and expressed particular concern at the three-wheeled 'invalid carriages' that were provided at that time by the Ministry of Health. Specially adapted for wheelchair users, the motorized tricycles were notorious for their lack of stability; Tony recounted to the House of Lords his own experience of overturning in one and finding himself unable to escape, even though petrol was pouring on to the road beside him. 'Nothing will convince me that this lethal machine is intrinsically suitable for a disabled person', concluded Tony, 'or that its production should be allowed to continue for a moment longer.'[16] The invalid carriage was phased out shortly afterwards. Tony also campaigned for accessibility at popular cultural events, most notably in two high-profile spats with the Royal

The 'invalid carriage' against which Tony campaigned so vigorously

Horticultural Society over access to the Chelsea Flower Show. The first, in 1976, challenged the event's ban on guide dogs, while the second, five years later, sought to overturn its ban on wheelchair users; 1981 was, after all, the International Year of Disabled Persons, and Tony had been appointed its president for England. Both campaigns were ultimately successful and helped to normalize accessibility as a right rather than a concession.

More than anything, however, it was Tony's photographs that allowed him to promote recognition of disabled people's rights. The portraits he published in the *Sunday Times* of people in public institutions lifted the veil on an issue that has always touched a nerve in British society, although he was aware of the 'hairline between reportage and exploitation' in such images and was 'determined not to be a voyeur'.[17] Tony used the proceeds of his photographic success to provide financial support for disabled people. Not wishing to be seen to have profited professionally from his marriage to Princess Margaret, he had set up a trust into which all the fees from his royal portraits would be paid. The sum total of these commissions was boosted by other donations, and in 1981 Tony established the Snowdon Trust to provide grants to disabled students to overcome barriers to their further education.[18] Today the charity provides around a hundred grants a year and offers Snowdon Scholarships for postgraduate students in partnership with several universities and colleges.

While his professional life was full and successful, Tony's marriage had by this time disintegrated. Most accounts have ascribed responsibility for the breakdown to both parties, noting that they were two strong-willed characters unaccustomed to accommodating the needs of others and too similar to get on with each other in the long run. The force of their alienation was as intense as the passion of their coming together, and it brought out the worst in Tony's character. However difficult she may have been to live with, his treatment of Princess Margaret was cruel to the point of vicious. Constantly finding fault and undermining her in public, he would leave spiteful notes for her in private, including the infamous jibe: 'You look like a Jewish manicurist and I hate you.'[19]

As the marriage collapsed into acrimony, Tony and Margaret sought solace elsewhere. To begin with, their liaisons were kept out of the British media, which dutifully suppressed rumours that were given greater coverage in the foreign press. Yet it was Margaret's relationship with Roddy Llewellyn – a young Welshman who bore an uncanny resemblance to Tony – that opened the floodgates. On 22 February 1976 the *News of the World* published a front-page photograph showing Margaret and Roddy together in bathing suits on her Caribbean hideaway of Mustique. This quickly led to a storm of recriminations that the taxpayer was paying for a senior member of the Royal Family to swan around the Caribbean with a 'toy boy' rather than fulfil her public duties. The exposé also provided

Tony with an opportunity to seize the moral high ground, even though he had had extramarital affairs since the 1960s and had written to the Queen just three months earlier saying that the marriage must be brought to an end.

The royal couple separated in March 1976 and divorced two years later on grounds of 'irreconcilable differences', freeing Tony to marry his long-term lover Lucy Lindsay-Hogg a few months later. There was much media fanfare that this was the first royal divorce since Henry VIII rejected Anne of Cleves in 1540. In reality, the Queen's first cousin, the Earl of Harewood, had been divorced for adultery by his wife in 1967, while sixty-six years earlier Queen Victoria's granddaughter Princess Victoria Melita had divorced her husband Ernst Ludwig, Grand Duke of Hesse – the same man, as it happens, who commissioned Alfred Messel to design the State Museum in Darmstadt. Yet it was still a shock to the system for the monarch's own sister to end her marriage in this way, and Margaret's reputation was badly battered as the press set about unpicking every detail of her relationship with Roddy Llewellyn.

Tony had always managed to remain on good terms with other members of the Royal Family, so that when he and Margaret separated the Queen provided £70,000 for a house in Kensington for him to live in.[20] Tony was particularly valued for his discretion, in that he had consistently refused to divulge any secrets of his relationship with Princess Margaret or the other royals. He even attempted to prevent the publication of the book *My Queen and I* by the republican MP Willie Hamilton, who had for years railed against the large sums of taxpayers' money given to Princess Margaret in return for what he saw as very minor acts of public service. Tony tried in vain to stop the book's publication on grounds of factual inaccuracy, but his complaints were dismissed by the publisher as 'trivial'.[21] In fact, Hamilton was quite complimentary towards Tony in the book, calling him 'an impressive photographer with a professional eye for detail' and stating that 'in the entire Royal Family, he is the only one with any real creative talent of his own'.[22]

Tony's marriage to Lucy Lindsay-Hogg was soon blessed with a daughter, Frances, born on 17 July 1979. Yet he had already begun a secret affair with the journalist Ann Hills that would last, on and off, until her suicide on New Year's Eve in 1996. The following year Tony was asked to act as guest editor for a special London edition of *Country Life*, and this assignment brought him into contact with his next paramour, the magazine's features editor Melanie Cable-Alexander. The fruit of this relationship, a son called Jasper, was born on 30 April 1998, not long after Tony's sixty-eighth birthday; Melanie was thirty-four. Tony recognized his responsibility to Jasper, whom Melanie would bring up as a single parent, and included him as one of the principal beneficiaries of his will alongside the three children born to him in wedlock. Yet the arrival of the '*Country Life* baby', as

Jasper was known, was too much for the long-suffering Lucy, who called time on their marriage.

Tony continued to have further relationships with women into his seventies, all of which were paraded before the public by Anne de Courcy in the semi-authorized biography *Snowdon*, serialized in the *Daily Mail* over the summer of 2008. Tony collaborated with de Courcy on the book, stating that he wished 'to put the record straight', and he encouraged his friends to be similarly candid in providing her with information.[23] The most sensational revelation was that Tony had fathered another illegitimate child while he was courting Princess Margaret, at a time when he was already in relationships with two other women. The child in question was Polly Fry, daughter of Tony's friends Camilla and Jeremy Fry, with whom he had enjoyed many riotous evenings during the 1950s. Tony's paternity was confirmed only in 2004 when he agreed to take a DNA test. The scandal centred on the fact that his secret love-child had been born just three weeks after his glittering wedding to Princess Margaret in Westminster Abbey.

While Tony was always treated with greater deference than his female partners in media coverage of his life story, this latest revelation stretched public sympathy to breaking point. Anne de Courcy loyally sought to explain Tony's womanizing as a mechanism for coping with his mother's coldness towards him. The diarist and Messel family friend James Lees-Milne heard from Tony how badly he was treated by Anne after his separation from Princess Margaret: 'He invites his mother to luncheon, asks others to meet her, cooks delicious meal (has no servant), and Anne chucks at last moment on spurious grounds that she does not feel well, though he later finds she entertained sixty to drinks that evening.'[24] Even if they sympathized with him, other friends felt that self-pity must have its limits. Sir Roy Strong, dining with Tony and Melanie Cable-Alexander eight years after Anne had died, recorded in his diary:

> One thing is certain: Tony Snowdon does seem to like someone in attendance. The excuse he gives is how his mother, Anne Rosse, treated him, putting him down in favour of her children by Michael, a peer of the realm. Some time in life you have to get over this. Some time also you have to get over having been a married-in royal. He still even now has a touch of that Princess Margaret switch-on switch-off grandeur and distance, which will suddenly erupt during a hands-down conversation.[25]

Tony's sense of status was reinforced in 1999 when he was appointed a life peer in the newly reformed House of Lords, for which he took the additional title of Baron Armstrong-Jones of Nymans in the County of West Sussex. Paradoxically, Tony would sever ties with the Messel family home three years later when he sold off the lease on Old House, the cottage on the Nymans estate which he had taken over from his Uncle Oliver. His decision not to inform other members of the Messel family that he was selling the contents of the house, especially the portraits of his grandmother Maud, caused much unhappiness as relatives found themselves bidding against each other to buy back their own family possessions.[26] Tony did not appreciate the irony four years later when he tried to prevent Christie's from auctioning off Princess Margaret's possessions in the two-day sale organized by her children to pay off death duties on her estate. This time it was Tony who had been kept out of the loop, and he wrote in vain to the chairman of Christie's arguing that several of the items on offer were not his children's to sell.

Tony was now firmly settled in the Kensington residence which the Queen had bought for him at the time of his separation from Princess Margaret and where he was able to enjoy a life of enviable independence for over forty years. The Queen visited him in March 2006 so that Tony could take the official portraits for her eightieth birthday, thus sparing him an unnecessary trip to Buckingham Palace. His health had been weakened by the reappearance of his childhood polio, but there was no sense in which he was about to stop working. He travelled to Russia the following year on a gruelling trip that saw him cover 4,000 miles in less than a month. The resulting book of photographs (the twenty-third of Tony's career) was published by the Open Russia Foundation with a foreword by its founder Mikhail Khodorovsky, soon to embark on a ten-year prison sentence for tax fraud. There was less controversy surrounding the publication of his final monograph, *Snowdon: A Life in View*, which Tony produced together with his daughter Frances in 2014. To celebrate the occasion the National Portrait Gallery

The Queen and Prince Philip with David Linley (left) and Lady Sarah Chatto (right) after the memorial service for Lord Snowdon

mounted an exhibition of three dozen Snowdon portraits from the larger body of work that Tony had recently donated to the gallery. With many of his best-known images of royalty and celebrity on display, it was a fitting record of a life lived behind and in front of the camera.

Tony died on 13 January 2017, aged eighty-six. His funeral took place a week later at the remote Welsh church of St Baglan's overlooking the Menai Strait, where he was interred in the Armstrong-Jones family plot after a short service attended by his closest relatives. The memorial service held at St Margaret's, Westminster, on 7 April provided the occasion for a more public celebration of his life, with tributes from Welsh Paralympics champion Baroness Tanni Grey-Thompson and from Patrick Kinmonth of *Vogue*. The Queen, Prince Philip and other members of the Royal Family attended, as did Tony's second wife, Lucy, and many other figures from his private and public lives.

How good was Tony as a photographer? He is included as an important figure in histories of British photojournalism during the post-war era, and his contribution was formally recognized when he was awarded the Progress Medal, the highest honour of the Royal Photographic Society, in 1985. Yet his work was notably absent from the first ever historical review of British photography held at Tate Britain in 2007 – a show which featured over five hundred images from a broad range of artists.[27] Ironically, the advantages which came with Tony's entry into the Royal Family made it impossible to judge him on purely professional terms. As the art critic John Russell Taylor noted in his review of the National Portrait Gallery's retrospective in 2000, 'If he was known as simply Antony Armstrong-Jones, there appears little doubt that Lord Snowdon would have been taken much more seriously as a photographer.'[28]

As Tony's son David, now the Second Earl of Snowdon, said at his father's memorial service, he was 'a supremely talented amateur' in the old-fashioned sense. Tony's good fortune was that his marriage into the Royal Family allowed him to exercise his amateur enthusiasm on a grand scale in projects that would otherwise have been beyond his reach. In this respect he was different from the highest-ranked of his Messel forebears, his Great-Great-Uncle Alfred, whose apotheosis as court architect to the Kaiser was the culmination of a lifetime's fight against prejudice and exclusion. Tony's success as a photographer came through solid application. His status as 'the first royal rebel' granted him a charmed life.

The two Messel children of
Princess Margaret alongside
their aunt, Queen Elizabeth II,
at their mother's funeral

Epilogue

THE ADMISSION OF Tony Armstrong-Jones into the House of Windsor marked the culmination of the Messel family's remarkable journey from refugees to royalty. Yet the story does not end there. Tony's two children with Princess Margaret, David (now Second Earl of Snowdon) and Sarah (since her marriage, Lady Sarah Chatto), remain popular with the Royal Family and regularly join them for family occasions. Both have drawn on their Messel heritage by pursuing careers in the creative arts. David's furniture and design business, founded by him in 1985 under the trading name of Linley, provides a direct link with the training in cabinet-making followed by his three-times great-grandfather Simon Messel in Paris. The family's German-Jewish background is still a topic for occasional public interest, as when David's marriage to Serena Stanhope – whose maternal grandmother also had Jewish ancestry – was playfully referred to as the 'intriguing union of two lost Jews'.[1]

Sarah followed in the footsteps of her Great-Uncle Oliver Messel by training as a painter, first at the Camberwell School of Art and subsequently at the Royal Academy. Under her maiden name Sarah Armstrong-Jones she specializes in abstract landscape painting and is represented by the prestigious Redfern Gallery, which has mounted several solo exhibitions of her work over the past twenty-five years. Sarah and David's half-sister, Frances von Hoffmannsthal, collaborated with her father on the handsome retrospective of his career, *Snowdon: A Life in View*. Having worked for five years as assistant to the Italian photographer Paolo Roversi, Frances founded the cultural magazine *Luncheon* in 2016 as a vehicle for creative features on art and design. Tony's youngest child, Jasper Cable-Alexander, has followed in the family tradition of film-making, using a 16-millimetre camera for his music videos just as Rudolph Messel did for his socialist education pictures in the 1930s.

The scientific tradition embodied by the first Rudolph Messel was developed further by two of his sister Lina's sons. The elder of the two, Dr Richard Seligman, was a noted metallurgist who founded the Aluminium Plant and Vessel Company (later known as APV) supplying equipment to the brewing and dairy industries. His research led to the 'high-temperature short-time' process which is now the standard method of pasteurizing milk. Richard's younger brother Gerald joined him at APV but had long been a keen amateur skier and branched off to become a glaciologist, publishing his classic study *Snow Structure and Ski Fields* in 1936. Richard's son, Sir Peter Wendel Seligman, made his career at APV and was knighted in 1978 for services to the export trade. Peter's brother Madron Seligman also served as Managing Director of APV, as well as representing Great Britain in skiing at the 1952 Winter Olympics; a life-long friend of Prime Minister Edward Heath, he was elected a Conservative Member of the European Parliament for West Sussex in 1979, a position he held until 1994.

Other male members of the Seligman family made their way in the world of finance, with some cutting their teeth in their cousins' firm of L. Messel and Co. The eldest son of Lina and Isaac Seligman, Sir Charles Seligman, was senior partner in the firm of Seligman Brothers and from there developed a career as a diplomat and trade envoy. He served as honorary consul-general for Austria in London during the years running up to the start of the Second World War and took part in the British diplomatic mission to Japanese-occupied Manchuria in 1934. Sir Charles's brother Hubert Seligman was also a banker and devoted much of his time to Jewish and other charitable causes.

Paul de la Penha, elder son of Eugenie Messel and Eugene de la Penha, followed in his father's footsteps and became a stockbroker. His younger brother Alfred

The Lime Avenue
at Nymans

inherited the Messel passion for collecting, specializing in antiquities from the island of Cyprus, where he lived for much of his life. On his death in 1953 Alfred bequeathed his 450-piece collection to the Cypriot Department of Antiquities, although much was later sold to the Australian Institute of Archaeology. The University of Melbourne now displays items from the Penha Collection online in its Virtual Museum.

Even with all these links to the family's scientific, financial and artistic heritage, the most tangible connection to the Messel past is to be found in the field of horticulture and particularly through the garden at Nymans. The National Trust has not only honoured Ludwig Messel's original conception of the garden as a collection of rare and exotic plants but has succeeded in making Nymans a visually attractive visitor experience with seasonal interest all year round. The Trust has also put considerable effort into foregrounding the Messel family history at Nymans, with special exhibitions devoted to bringing out personal stories from the past. Recent displays have highlighted the role played by the family in the First World War; the contribution made by three generations of Messel women to the development of the garden; and an exploration of the Jewish heritage of the family as part of the annual celebration of European Days of Jewish Culture. The connection between the National Trust and the family is alive and well, and Ludwig Messel would be pleased to know that his descendants regularly gather at Nymans to share in plans for the garden's future.

The Messel name itself hangs by a thread. The second generation carrying the surname in Britain produced three boys: Linley, Oliver and Rudolph. Only Linley had children of his own, and of those four only one, Thomas, was a son. While his half-sister Victoria has kept the name of Messel in her professional life, Thomas is the only member of that generation to have passed the surname on to the next. His son Harold Linley Monnington Messel, known as Hal, is another to have inherited the family's artistic gene, making a career as a silversmith. While he has many cousins who retain an interest in their heritage, Hal is the last surviving descendant bearing the surname Messel in Britain.

In the USA the Messel family has produced considerably more boy children, and the name is more prevalent. The two surviving sons of the Louis Messel who emigrated to America in 1842 had a total of sixteen children between them. The younger of the two, George, stayed in Ohio and brought up his family in the town of Chillicothe, where the cemetery has a strong Messel presence. Yet this side of the family also had a preponderance of girl children, so that the Messel name has not survived into the current generation. The elder brother, William, moved across the state border into Indiana and raised his family in the town of Bicknell, Knox County; his descendants include several boy children, and Knox County is still home to many Messels today.

The success of the Messel family in Britain is a testament to their talents and to a context in which European migrants were treated with relative tolerance. The reception given to German-Jewish immigrants in Victorian Britain was a mixed one, with negative stereotypes openly paraded in literature, common parlance and the popular press. Yet in the considered assessment of historian Werner Mosse, himself a German-Jewish refugee from the Nazis, most Jews arriving from Germany in the nineteenth century were able to succeed in an environment where overt discrimination was rare.

> They had come to a freer society than the one they had left behind and one less saturated with anti-Jewish prejudice and intolerance towards the 'outsider'. They had emerged from what had been on the whole a narrow, claustrophobic and self-centred world into one with somewhat wider horizons. Even if they were not received warmly, they yet owed much to British pluralist society with its manifold opportunities.[2]

In September 2015 a dozen representatives of the British family journeyed back to the village of Messel, where we were welcomed by the mayor and by members of the local history museum. We visited Darmstadt to pay our respects at the family tombs in the Jewish cemetery and to see the buildings designed by Ludwig Messel's famous brother: the State Museum of Hesse and the elegant Alfred Messel House. Three years later a party of thirty-five enthusiasts from Messel paid a return visit to Nymans, revelling in the fact that their village's name is known among British gardeners through the many camellias, magnolias and rhododendrons called after Messel family members. The exodus that brought the Messels to Britain in the nineteenth century and the successful escape of our remaining cousins in the 1930s mean that there are no longer any family members living in Germany. Yet the connections binding the family to its historical roots are stronger today than they have ever been.

Acknowledgements

THIS IS A book about a family, and my initial thanks go to those family members who have helped me piece the story together. First and foremost, my mother Phoebe Hilary has put up with endless questioning and has borne all with great patience and good humour; I am truly grateful to her for this, as for so much else. My aunts Judith Hiller and Celia Carter and uncle Alistair Buchanan have been most generous in providing me with their recollections. Thomas and Pepe Messel have been unfailingly kind in offering me materials and contacts, and I am most grateful to Victoria Messel and Kate Allison for providing me with further information and introductions. I would like to register a special vote of thanks to my fourth cousin Michele Klein for reading the first chapters of the manuscript in draft and providing many new leads and also to Professor Abigail Green of Oxford University for bringing us together following her seminar on Jewish country houses in March 2018.

I would like to thank William, Seventh Earl of Rosse and Alison, Countess of Rosse for granting me access to the archive at Birr Castle and Lisa Shortall, the archivist at Birr, for helping me find my way round it. Special thanks are due to Marina Gibbes for first putting me in touch with Peter Owen Publishers and to Antonia Owen, Nick Kent and Benedict Richards for showing so much enthusiasm in the project. I am also grateful to Harro Bruck, Antony Wieler, Muriel and Ion Campbell, Michael and Veronica Gibbes, Polly and Jeremy Lewis, Tim Parker, Sophie Saunderson, Rachel Allen, Frances von Hoffmannsthal, Mary Lightbown, Edward and Barbara Gibbes, David Seligman, Patrick Parsons, Alicia Clements and Hal Messel for their help in making this a family enterprise.

I would like to express my most sincere thanks to Rebecca Graham, house manager of Nymans, for her constant encouragement and support. The National Trust has been very fortunate to have Rebecca in her post at Nymans for over twenty years, and without her help I would never have been able to see this project through to completion. I am also grateful to other staff and volunteers at Nymans, especially its general manager Zara Luxford and former curator Dr Alice Strickland, for showing such an interest in the Messel family. I owe a particular debt of gratitude to Shirley Nicholson; her published research into the

Messel and Sambourne families set the standard for all future accounts and her lively interest in all matters historical has challenged me to think more deeply about the meaning of the past. I am particularly grateful to Shirley for helping me find my way around the Sambourne Family Archive and for suggesting many sage improvements to my draft text.

In Germany I would like to thank above all Karl Wenchel, historian of the village of Messel, for being the inspiration behind this project when I first met him in July 2008. Both he and Jakob Lenhardt of the Messel Museum have been a source of great encouragement, as has the mayor of Messel, Andreas Larem. I would like to thank Udo Steinbeck for his warm welcome and assistance when we visited Darmstadt and Messel as a family group in 2015 and for his support with further documents since then. I am also grateful to the late Dr Theo Jülich and to Dr Wolfgang Glüber for giving us a personal tour of Alfred Messel's magnificent State Museum of Hesse. I would like to thank Jona Ostheimer, archivist of the town of Dieburg, for his generous help in allowing me into the Jewish cemetery there without the requisite notice and for his subsequent assistance. All translations from the German are my own, unless otherwise credited, and I would like to thank Barbara Gibbes for helping me make sense of one particularly impenetrable piece of old prose.

In the UK I would like to thank the staff of the West Sussex Record Office, London Metropolitan Archive, Imperial War Museum, British Library, Guildhall Library, German Historical Institute London, Wiener Library, Lindley Library, Quaker Library, Witt Library, London School of Economics archives and Wandsworth Libraries for their assistance. I would particularly like to thank Allan Hall of Battersea Library for managing to track down a loan copy of Rudolph Messel's 1934 novel *High Pressure*. I am also grateful to the staff of the British Film Institute for making possible a family screening of Rudolph Messel's anti-war film *Blow, Bugles, Blow* in December 2017, a unique opportunity to see his work at the cinema as he intended.

I would like to thank Dr Moira Goff, librarian of the Garrick Club, for granting me access to its candidates' pages and Alice Chadwyck-Healey for her efforts in trying to locate the same for the Arts Club. Dr Valerie Wilson and Mary Kitson of the Fan Circle International, Vida Milovanovic of the Linnean Society and Richard Seedhouse of the Victorian Society were most helpful, too. I am grateful to Sharon Todd and Jake Fox of the Society of Chemical Industry for allowing me access to papers relating to Dr Rudolph Messel; to Mark Dennis of the Library and Museum of Freemasonry for explaining the arcane meanings of Leonard Messel's Masonic regalia; and to Andrew Maloney of the Fitzwilliam Museum in Cambridge for granting me access to the Messel-Rosse fan collection while it was temporarily not on public display. My thanks go to Emma Howgill,

Gemma Brace, Jill Sullivan and all the staff of the University of Bristol Theatre Collection for providing me with access to their rich Oliver Messel archive; and to the curators of the Victoria and Albert Museum's Theatre and Performance Archives, especially Keith Lodwick, for helping me find my way around the parallel Oliver Messel archive in London. Thanks also to Dr John Ralph of the West Hoathly Local History Archive; to the Reverend Carl Smith, rector of St Mark's, Staplefield; to Jill Rolfe of the Danehill Parish Historical Society; to Barry Ray of Slaugham Archives; to Zara Moran of the National Gallery Research Centre; to Alexandra Aspinall at the Dorchester; to Dr Robin Darwall-Smith, archivist of University College, Oxford; to Sergio Angelini of the educational charity Learning on Screen; and to Dr Michael Jolles, author of *A Directory of Distinguished British Jews, 1830–1930*.

Finally, I wish to thank my wife Jan for her boundless generosity throughout the writing of this book. This included reading every word of the text in its draft form and improving it with numerous excellent suggestions, along with many other acts of kindness besides. I will always be deeply grateful.

Camellia 'Maud Messel', painted by Victoria Messel

Notes

Preface

1. BBC Radio 4 tribute, 6 June 1995.

2. Sarah Clelland, *The National Trust Book of Scones*, National Trust, Swindon, 2017, p. 92.

1 The Village of Messel

1. Michael Höllwarth, Manfred Raab, Siegfried Treichel, Bruno Vock and Karl Wenchel, *1200 Jahre Messel*, Gemeindevorstand der Gemeinde Messel, Messel, 2000, p. 32; Walter Bezzenberger, *Geschichte des Dorfes Messel*, P.L. Fink, Groß-Gerau, 1958, p. 7.

2. The early history of Messel is as nothing compared to its prehistory, and the Messel Pit outside the village is one of the most important fossil sites in the world.

3. See also the figures for Jewish burials from Messel in Eckhart Franz and Christa Wiesner, *Der jüdische Friedhof in Dieburg*, Kommission für die Geschichte der Juden in Hessen, Wiesbaden, 2009, p. 64.

4. Messel is one of the case studies in Toni Oelsner, 'Three Jewish Families in Modern Germany: A Study of the Process of Emancipation', *Jewish Social Studies*, 1942, Vol. 4, No. 3, pp. 241–68; Vol. 4, No. 4, pp. 349–98.

5. The 1763 Jewish Ordinance is reproduced in Arno Piechorowski, *Beiträge zur Geschichte der Juden in der Grafschaft Bentheim*, Verlag Heimatverein der Grafschaft Bentheim, Bad Bentheim, 1982, pp. 22–9.

6. For the German version, see Karl Wenchel, 'Die Geschichte der Messeler Juden', in Höllwarth, pp. 183–200.

7. Aharon and his sons are also referred to as SeGaL, the Hebrew acronym denoting membership of the ancient tribe of Levi. Gumpel's epitaph is recorded in Franz and Wiesner, p. 65.

8. Paul Arnsberg, *Die jüdischen Gemeinden in Hessen: Anfang, Untergang, Neubeginn*, Vol. 2, Societäts Verlag, Frankfurt, 1971, p. 74; Wenchel, p. 191.

2 Privileged Jews

1. Eckhart Franz, *Juden als Darmstädter Bürger*, Eduard Roether, Darmstadt, 1984, p. 347.

2. Klaus Schmidt, *Die Brandnacht: Dokumente von d. Zerstörung Darmstadts am 11. Sept 1944*, Reba, Darmstadt, 1964; Klaus Honold, *Darmstadt im Feuersturm: Die Zerstörung am 11. September 1944*, Wartberg, Gudensberg, 2004. In English, Max Hastings, *Bomber Command*, Michael Joseph, London, 1979, Chapter 13.

3. Described in full by Deborah Cadbury, *Queen Victoria's Matchmaking: The Royal Marriages That Shaped Europe*, Bloomsbury, London, 2017.

4. That is, the *Darmstädtisches Frag- und Anzeigeblatt*.

5. Franz, p. 345.

6. Selma Stern, *The Court Jew: A Contribution to the History of Absolutism in Europe*, Jewish Publication Society of America, Philadelphia, 1950.

7. Hannah Arendt, 'Privileged Jews', *Jewish Social Studies*, 1946, Vol. 8, No. 1, pp. 7–8.

8. Earlier etymologies, now dismissed as fanciful, speculated that 'Hep' might be an acronym for the mythical battle cry of the Crusaders, 'Hierosolyma est perdita': 'Jerusalem is lost'.

9. Ludwig Börne, 'Für die Juden', 1819, in his *Sämtliche Schriften*, Vol. 1, Joseph Melzer, Dreieich, 1977, p. 876.

10. A retrospective appraisal from the *Frankfurter Theater-Almanach für das Jahr 1845*, Heller and Rohm, Frankfurt, 1844, p. 39.

3 Founding a Dynasty

1. Clara Helfenbein Schmidt, 'Helfenbein Family – Personal Sketch', 1924, published online.

2. The school was renamed the Ludwig-Georgs-Gymnasium on its 250th anniversary in 1879.

3. The headstone appears in Eckhart Franz and Benno Szklanowski, *Haus des ewigen Lebens: Beit Hachajim. Der Jüdische Friedhof in Darmstadt: Grabstätten von 1714–1848*, Justus von Liebig, Darmstadt, 1988, p. 256.

4. In the original: 'Hier ruht SIMON MESSEL, geboren zu Darmstadt den 26 Dezember 1817, gestorben zu Vicosoprano den 11 September 1859. Als braver Gatte, guter Vater und treuer Freund konnte er mit ruhiger Zuversicht seine letzte Worte sprechen: Herr, in deine Hände befehle ich meinen Geist.'

5. The Bankhaus Aron Messel was renamed Bank Ferdinand Sander and remained so until it was acquired by Deutsche Bank in January 1914.

4 Architect to the Kaiser

1. Volker Viergutz, '"Das hätten wir in der Brüderstraße uns auch nicht träumen lassen." Anmerkungen zur Freundschaft von Ludwig Hoffmann und Alfred Messel', *Berlin in Geschichte und Gegenwart: Jahrbuch des Landesarchivs Berlin*, Gebr. Mann, Berlin, 2001, p. 77.

2. Included in Heinrich Albrecht, *Die Wohnungsnot in den Großstädten und die Mittel zu ihrer Abhülfe*, R. Oldenbourg, Munich, 1891, p. 84.

3. Alfred used the 'English square' design in his largest housing development, the Weisbachstraße project in the Friedrichshain district of Berlin. For more background, see Heinrich Albrecht and Alfred Messel, *Das Arbeiterwohnhaus*, Robert Oppenheim, Berlin, 1896.

4. '*Messelscher Pfeilertypus*': Alarich Rooch, 'Inszenierungsräume der Konsumkultur von der Jahrhundertwende bis 1930', in Werner Plumpe and Jörg Lesczenski (eds), *Bürgertum und Bürgerlichkeit zwischen Kaiserreich und Nationalsozialismus*, Philipp von Zabern, Mainz, 2009, p. 20.

5. Leo Colze, *Berliner Warenhäuser*, Fannei and Walz, Berlin, 1989 (originally 1908), p. 55.

6. Paul Göhre, *Das Warenhaus*, Vol. 12 of Martin Buber (ed.), *Die Gesellschaft: Sammlung sozialpsychologischer Monografien*, Rütten and Loening, Frankfurt, 1907, p. 8.

7. Hans Fallada, *Damals bei uns daheim*, Rowohlt, Stuttgart, 1941.

8. Fredric Bedoire, *The Jewish Contribution to Modern Architecture, 1830–1930*, KTAV, Jersey City, 2004, p. 250.

9. The Wertheim store was pulled down after the war. The architectural journal *The Builder* devoted an illustrated feature to it; 'An Eminent Berlin Architect', *The Builder*, 27 January 1906, pp. 81–4.

10. Deborah Barnstone, *Beyond the Bauhaus: Cultural Modernity in Breslau, 1918–33*, University of Michigan Press, Ann Arbor, 2016, p. 37.

11. Walter Curt Behrendt, *Alfred Messel*, Bruno Cassirer, Berlin, 1911, p. 116.

12. Wilhelm von Bode, *Mein Leben*, Vol. 2, Hermann Reckendorf, Berlin, 1930, p. 182.

13. The gift of the lions may have been made under pressure from Alfred; a letter survives from his widow Elsa, written shortly after his death, asking the two brothers in England to transfer the money needed to pay for the casting of the bronze: 10,000 marks from Ludwig and 15,000 from Rudolph.

14. Viergutz, pp. 99–100.

5 New Life in London

1. The correct date of Ludwig's arrival in England is given in his application for naturalization as a British subject four years later; National Archives HO/1/159/6350.

2. This culminated in the nationwide petition of 1880 calling for limits on Jewish rights and Jewish immigration, which was signed by a quarter of a million Germans and debated in the Prussian parliament over two days.

3. Gottfried Mehnert, 'Der Verein zur Abwehr des Antisemitismus in Marburg 1891/92', *Zeitschrift für hessische Geschichte und Landeskunde*, 2003, Vol. 108, pp. 215–30.

4. Colin Holmes, *Anti-Semitism in British Society, 1876–1939*, Edward Arnold, London, 1979, p. 105. The characterization 'low-key' comes from Anthony Julius, *Trials of the Diaspora: A History of Anti-Semitism in England*, Oxford University Press, Oxford, 2010, p. 349.

5. Todd Endelman, 'German-Jewish Settlement in Victorian England', in Werner Mosse (ed.), *Second Chance: Two Centuries of German-Speaking Jews in the United Kingdom*, Mohr, Tübingen, 1991, p. 44.

6. The Seligman family story is well told in Stephen Birmingham, *Our Crowd: The Great Jewish Families of New York*, Harper and Row, New York, 1967.

7. For Isaac Seligman's version, see his *Reminiscences*, Pynson, New York, 1926, pp. xviii–xix.

8. Lincoln House was pulled down in 1905, by which time the Seligmans had moved north of the river, eventually settling at 17 Kensington Palace Gardens.

9. Endelman, p. 47.

10. The total award was split between three beneficiaries, with three-quarters apparently going to the Cussans family; see the online database of the Centre for the Study of the Legacies of British Slave-Ownership at University College London.

11. Annie may have come into some of the Cussans money by a roundabout route. In 1834, almost forty years after the indiscretion which had led to her father's illegitimate birth, Annie's grandfather married a Georgina Losh at the chapel of the British Embassy in Paris. When the grandfather died in 1855 Georgina wrote Annie and her two sisters into her will in recognition of the fact that their father had

been 'the reputed natural Son of my late Husband'. When Georgina in turn died two years later she thus bequeathed an annual income to the three Cussans girls from shares held in trust until their twenty-first birthdays, when each would inherit the principal. The affidavit sworn by Annie's mother before the Divorce Court reveals that the family relied on this income to support itself in the years after the girls' father had deserted them. Details of the will are in Geoffrey Mead, *Cussans of Jamaica and England, Volume III*, typescript, 1972, held at the British Library.

12. From Matilda's 1866 petition to the Divorce Court: National Archives J 77/12/C199. Thomas was a better artist than husband: his paintings of south India survive in an album at the British Library (shelfmark WD484) and can be viewed online.

13. David Kynaston, *The City of London, Volume I: A World of Its Own, 1815–1890*, Chatto and Windus, London, 1994, p. 292.

14. Ranald Michie, *The London Stock Exchange: A History*, Oxford University Press, Oxford, 1999, p. 156; figures on the number of foreign-born members from *ibid.*, p. 144.

15. Victor Morgan and William Thomas, *The Stock Exchange: Its History and Functions*, Elek Books, London, 1962, p. 88.

16. Richard Grossman, 'Bloody Foreigners! Overseas Equity on the London Stock Exchange, 1870–1913', *Economic History Review*, 2015, Vol. 68, No. 2, p. 475.

17. David Kynaston, *The London Stock Exchange, 1870–1914: An Institutional History*, unpublished PhD thesis, London School of Economics and Political Science, 1983, p. 252.

18. David Kynaston, *The City of London, Volume II: Golden Years, 1890–1914*, Chatto and Windus, London, 1995, p. 310.

19. Letter of 4 July 1908 to Linley Sambourne; Sambourne Family Archive, ST/1/4/1002.

20. From Oliver's unpublished notes for an autobiography, now in the Oliver Messel Archive, University of Bristol Theatre Collection.

21. Duff Hart-Davis (ed.), *End of an Era: Letters and Journals of Sir Alan Lascelles, 1887–1920*, Hamish Hamilton, London, 1986, p. 153.

22. Frith's house was originally No. 10 Pembridge Villas; by the time the Messels arrived the street had been renumbered and he was living at No. 7.

6 Tyburnia

1. 'Unrivalled in its class in London or even Great Britain', according to the verdict in the *History of the County of Middlesex, Vol. 9: Paddington, Hampstead*, Victoria County History, London, 1989, pp. 204–12.

2. Vivian Lipman, 'The Rise of Jewish Suburbia', *Transactions of the Jewish Historical Society of England*, 1962, Vol. 21, p. 84. For more on Tyburnia, see the three articles by Gordon Toplis in *Country Life*: 15, 22 and 29 November 1973.

3. The number of synagogues within easy walking distance of Westbourne Terrace bears witness to Tyburnia's Jewish identity: Bayswater Synagogue (consecrated in 1863), the New West End Synagogue in St Petersburgh Place (1879) and Reform Judaism's flagship West London Synagogue in Upper Berkeley Street (1870).

4. Emma Harris, *Anglo-Jewry's Experience of Secondary Education from the 1830s until 1920*, unpublished PhD thesis, University College London, 2007, p. 76.

5. Todd Endelman, 'German Jews in Victorian England: A Study in Drift and Defection', in Jonathan Frankel and Steven Zipperstein (eds), *Assimilation and Community: The Jews in Nineteenth-Century Europe*, Cambridge University Press, Cambridge, 1992, pp. 57–87.

6. The *Jewish Chronicle* acclaimed it a 'good likeness, bold in execution': 8 May 1885, p. 10.

7. *The Times*, 4 February 1882, p. 8; there are at least forty instances of smaller gifts listed in the *Jewish Chronicle* from 1873 to 1911.

8. Henry Armstrong, *Essays on the Art and Principles of Chemistry, Including the First Messel Memorial Lecture*, Ernest Benn, London, 1927, p. 206.

9. From Rudolph's presidential address to the Society of Chemical Industry at its 1912 annual meeting in New York: *Journal of the Society of Chemical Industry*, 1912, Vol. 31, No. 18, pp. 854–7.

10. Rudolph was awarded the Militär-Sanitäts-Kreuz on 30 January 1871: *Verzeichnis der mit Großherzoglich hessischen Orden und Ehrenzeichen dekorirten Personen*, Chr. Fr. Will, Darmstadt, 1875, p. 87.

11. *The Times*, 26 June 1920, p. 19; his estate was valued at £174,537 16s. 9d.

12. For his 'brilliant' piano-playing: *Stratford Times*, 14 February 1877, p. 3; for the Napoleonic comedy *The Ladies' Battle*, which Rudolph put on at the Tate Institute in Silvertown: *Kentish Independent*, 29 November 1907, p. 5.

13. Aaron Watson, *The Savage Club: A Medley of History, Anecdote and Reminiscence*, Fisher Unwin, London, 1907, pp. 131–5.

7 Cultural Integration

1. *Illustrated London News*, 13 June 1896, p. 757.

2. Alfred Baldry, 'The Life and Work of Marcus Stone R.A.', *The Art Journal*, London, 1896, pp. 24–5.

3. Freya Spoor, *The Revival of Pastel in Late Nineteenth-Century Britain: The Transience of a Modern Medium*, unpublished PhD thesis, University of Edinburgh, 2017, Vol. 2, p. 59.

4. The Kauffman portrait is incorrectly listed in Messel family inventories as *Portrait of Mrs Osborne*.

5. August Mayer, *Velazquez: A Catalogue Raisonné of the Pictures and Drawings*, Faber and Faber, London, 1936, p. 93.

6. Despite her surname, the elder children's Nanny Meisenheimer was the English widow of a German baker, her maiden name being Eliza Noel.

7. Letter of 28 July 1893; Sambourne Family Archive, ST/2/2/78.

8. Rupert Hart-Davis, *Max Beerbohm: Letters to Reggie Turner*, Soho Square, London, 1964, p. 38.

9. *The Times*, 26 February 1953, p. 10.

10. *The Gentlewoman*, 13 June 1891, p. 821; Maud's drawings, signed with her initials, can be seen in *Punch*, 21 May 1892, p. 252; *ibid.*, 7 January 1893, p. 9; *ibid.*, 2 June 1894, p. 256; *ibid.*, 16 June 1894, p. 286; in *The Minster*, July 1895, pp. 98–107; *ibid.*, August 1895, pp. 162–73; *ibid.*, November 1895, pp. 558–70; and in the *Pall Mall Magazine*, September 1894, pp. 45–8.

11. Letter of July 1893; Sambourne Family Archive, ST/2/2/80.

12. Diary entry for 16 May 1897.

13. Diary entry for 6 May 1896.

14. In Chapter 21: 'Everybody Goes to Them'.

15. *Punch*, 24 April 1897, p. 194.

16. *Jewish Chronicle*, 20 October 1899, p. 12.

17. Letter of 21 May 1897 in Nymans archive, S/97/01; emphasis in original.

18. Leonee Ormond, *Linley Sambourne: Illustrator and Punch Cartoonist*, Paul Holberton, London, 2010, p. 212.

19. Diary entries for 2, 3 and 23 June 1897.

20. Letter of 28 June 1897; Sambourne Family Archive, ST/1/2/1380.

21. Linley Sambourne, diary entry for 13 July 1897.

22. Letter of 30 January 1898; Sambourne Family Archive, ST/1/2/426.

23. Letter of 2 May 1898 from Genoa; Sambourne Family Archive, ST/2/2/304. Maud's letters home make up one of the case studies in Helena Michie, *Victorian Honeymoons: Journeys to the Conjugal*, Cambridge University Press, Cambridge, 2006.

24. There are no grounds on which to speculate why Leonard was blackballed. He was already a member of the Arts Club, like his father, and of the Carlton Club, the spiritual home of Toryism, and of the Orleans, a minor club that operated out of Orleans House in Twickenham which was amalgamated into the Marlborough-Windham Club in 1945.

8 'Clear Out the Germans'

1. The wedding was originally planned for 13 August 1895 but was cancelled owing to the death of Ernest's mother and sister in the wreck of the SS *Catterthun* off New South Wales in the early hours of 8 August.

2. *South Bucks Standard*, 20 June 1902, p. 3.

3. Eric Parker, *Memory Looks Forward: An Autobiography*, Seeley, Service and Co., London, 1937, p. 43.

4. Marion Sambourne diary entry, 28 March 1882; Shirley Nicholson, *A Victorian Household: Based on the Diaries of Marion Sambourne*, Barrie and Jenkins, London, 1988, p. 71.

5. Beatrice Gibbes, *Travellers in Eternity*, Psychic Press, London, 1948, p. 177.

6. Examples include William Le Queux's novel *The Invasion of 1910*, serialized in the *Daily Mail*, and Guy du Maurier's drama *An Englishman's Home*, so successful that it ran in two West End theatres simultaneously; see James Hawes, *Englanders and Huns: How Five Decades of Enmity Led to the First World War*, Simon and Schuster, London, 2014, pp. 365–405.

7. German intelligence had set up its naval espionage department to target Britain in 1901. Christopher Andrew, *The Defence of the Realm: The Authorized History of MI5*, Allen Lane, London, 2009, pp. 10–52.

8. *Manchester Courier*, 12 May 1915, p. 1.

9. *Daily Mail*, 13 May 1915, pp. 5–6.

10. Panikos Panayi, '"The Hidden Hand": British Myths about German Control of Britain during the First World War', *Immigrants and Minorities*, 1988, Vol. 7, No. 3, p. 253.

11. *The Times*, 11 May 1915, p. 9.

12. *Ibid.*, 22 May 1915, p. 5.

13. For Ludwig's heart attack, see Marion Sambourne diary entry for 3 May 1913. He had long suffered from a heart condition; see Maud Messel's letters to her mother of 25 and 26 October 1899, Sambourne Family Archive, ST/2/2/387–8; in the latter Maud recounts the 'horrible dream' she had the night before in which Ludwig collapsed and died in her arms.

14. Armstrong, p. 204. The obituary of Rudolph in the *Journal of the Society of Chemical Industry* for 15 May 1920 notes that he suffered a stroke at this time which left him partially disabled; Vol. 39, No. 9, pp. 160–1R.

15. He is buried in the German military cemetery at Vauxbuin, Block 3, Grave 179.

16. Eric Hobsbawm, *Industry and Empire: From 1750 to the Present Day*, Penguin, Harmondsworth, 1969, p. 169.

9 Nymans

1. Richard James and Christopher Whittick, *Archaeological and Historic Landscape Survey: Nymans, Handcross, West Sussex*, Archaeology South-East, Portslade, 2008.

2. The 1863 prospectus is available at the British Library, Maps 137.b.9.(31).

3. The West Sussex Record Office in Chichester holds the deeds for the Nymans estate down the years; WSRO Add MSS 27105–27168.

4. Ludwig's thoughts as recollected by Anne, Countess of Rosse in *Nymans: The Home of Mrs Leonard Messel*, Country Life, London, 1966, p. 6.

5. The phrase is from Joe Mordaunt Crook, *The Rise of the Nouveaux Riches: Style and Status in Victorian and Edwardian Architecture*, John Murray, London, 1999, p. 26.

6. *The Times*, 2 August 1890, p. 15.

7. The occasion is recorded in the *Mid-Sussex Times*, 21 July 1891, p. 5.

8. *Ibid.*, 25 August 1891, p. 1.

9. *Ibid.*, 23 August 1892, p. 5.

10. *Ibid.*, 6 August 1901, p. 1. Ludwig took on honorary roles in the locality such as president of the Handcross Cricket Club and Handcross Brass Band, as well as vice-president of the Handcross Football Club and Handcross Athletic Sports: *ibid.*, 25 February 1908, p. 5; *ibid.*, 12 November 1907, p. 8; *ibid.*, 14 September 1909, p. 8; *ibid.*, 21 July 1908, p. 8.

11. *Ibid.*, 7 October 1902, p. 5.

12. *Ibid.*, 22 January 1895, p. 1.

13. *Sussex Agricultural Express*, 1 September 1893, p. 7; *Mid-Sussex Times*, 21 August 1894, p. 4.

14. *Mid-Sussex Times*, 8 October 1901, p. 5; *ibid.*, 11 March 1902, p. 5; *ibid.*, 22 September 1908, p. 1; *ibid.*, 17 August 1909, p. 8.

15. *Ibid.*, 21 June 1910, p. 1.

16. Leonard's performances are recorded in *Sussex Agricultural Express,* 25 November 1893, p. 6; *West Sussex County Times*, 25 November 1893, p. 8;

Mid-Sussex Times, 4 January 1898, p. 5. Other songs in his repertoire included 'My First Cigar', 'The Yaller Gal', 'I Love a Lovely Gal', 'My Sally', 'Brown of Camden Town', 'The Little Nipper', 'The Nipper's Lullaby', 'She Galloped Around the Arena' and 'The Noisy Johnny'.

17. *Mid-Sussex Times*, 5 January 1897, p. 5.

18. *Ibid.*, 16 May 1905, p. 8.

19. *Ibid.*, 6 June 1905, p. 5.

20. *Ibid.*, 22 October 1907, p. 8.

21. The licence for Ludwig's CGV, dated 25 April 1906, is in the Birr Castle archive; details of his Daimlers are in the Nymans archive: 80/2 (32).

22. His brother Rudolph Messel contributed a further £5: *Sussex Agricultural Express*, 14 July 1906, p. 12; *Mid-Sussex Times*, 17 July 1906, p. 5.

23. *Sussex Agricultural Express*, 21 December 1907, p. 6.

10 House and Garden

1. Alfred Messel, 'Anbau zum Landhaus Nymanns [*sic*] bei Crawley (England)', *Architektonische Rundschau*, 1896, Vol. 12, No. 3, Figures 17–18.

2. Clive Aslet, *The Edwardian Country House: A Social and Architectural History*, Frances Lincoln, London, 2012, p. 246.

3. Rudolph's judgement is contained in the unpublished notes for his autobiography; Oliver's comes from a personal communication recorded by his nephew Thomas Messel in his *Oliver Messel: In the Theatre of Design*, Rizzoli, New York, 2011, p. 18.

4. Letter of 29 December 1897; Sambourne Family Archive, ST/2/2/288. Maud's feelings about Nymans could vary with her mood: in a letter to her mother two years later she calls it 'this cold & unloved house'; Sambourne Family Archive, ST/2/2/393. Maud's brother Roy Sambourne regularly notes in his diaries for 1919 to 1921 how 'beastly cold' Nymans is, so Nonie may well have been justified in her complaint.

5. From Oliver's notes for an unpublished autobiography.

6. Nymans visitors' book, together with the diary entries of Linley and Marion Sambourne.

7. *Daily Mail*, 8 April 2017.

8. The West Sussex Record Office in Chichester holds an unpublished account of Comber's career written in 1932: WSRO Add Mss 30108. His obituary was carried in the *Gardeners' Chronicle*, 6 June 1953, p. 216.

9. Alfred Wilcox, 'Famous Gardeners at Home: No. 200 – Mr J. Comber, at The Gardens, Nymans, Crawley', *Garden Life*, 5 August 1905, p. 321.

10. An early photograph in a family album notes that the summer house was designed by the architect and Messel family friend Sir Ernest George.

11. See Ludwig Messel's description of the amateur gardener's progress as recounted by Eric Parker in *The Gardener's England*, Seeley Service, London, 1936, p. 127. 'He begins with plain flowers; he comes later to the rock garden, and thinks that he has gone far, but he has not gone as far as he thinks; for somewhere at the end of his journey, which perhaps he may never reach, there wait for him flowering shrubs.'

12. *Mid-Sussex Times*, 21 August 1900, p. 8; *ibid.*, 27 February 1900, p. 8.

13. *Ibid.*, 22 August 1905, p. 8; *West Sussex County Times*, 10 March 1906, p. 8.

14. Not 1888, as suggested elsewhere; see the minutes of the RHS council meeting of 10 May 1898.

15. Godfrey Loring, 'Notes from Colonel G. Loring on Early Plantings of *Eucryphia x nymansensis*', *Journal of the Kew Guild*, 1979, Vol. 9, No. 82, p. 698. Confusingly, *E. glutinosa* was formerly known as *E. pinnatifolia*.

16. *Mid-Sussex Times*, 8 May 1917, p. 2. Nonie Messel was head commissioner for the East Grinstead Division of the Girl Guides; *ibid.*, 11 September 1917, p. 6.

17. Details of Muriel's will were published in *The Times*, 12 April 1919, p. 15. On reading of the value of her estate Maud's brother Roy Sambourne noted in his diary, 'Muriel's will in paper, £90,000-odd, most to Ruth. These Messels are very rich indeed.'

18. Fred Whitsey, 'Arcadia for Plantsmen: Nymans, near Handcross, West Sussex', *Country Life*, 17 May 1984, p. 1362.

19. *Country Life*, 29 March 1919, p. 356.

20. *Kew Bulletin*, 1919, p. 240.

II For King and Country

1. Letter from October 1899; Sambourne Family Archive, ST/2/2/393.

2. Ottilie, now Mrs Ernest Loring, lived at Rusper Court, eight miles north-west of Nymans; Ruth and her husband Eric Parker built Feathercombe in the Surrey village of Hambledon, slightly further away than the others; Harold would buy Danehurst in the nearby village of Danehill in 1914; Hilda, by this time Mrs Arthur Gibbes, built her family home at Wickenden Manor ten miles east of Nymans between 1916 and 1920, after her father's death. The £8,500 advance given to Leonard is detailed in paragraph 63 of Ludwig Messel's will.

3. From Oliver's notes for an unpublished autobiography.

4. *Mid-Sussex Times*, 26 August 1902, p. 4; *ibid.*, 18 August 1903, p. 8; *ibid.*, 15 August 1905, p. 8; *ibid.*, 28 August 1906, p. 8; etc. By 1910 the young Master Oliver Messel was exhibiting 'plants raised from chestnuts' at the show, while his sister Anne was showing 'drumhead lettuce plants'; *ibid.*, 16 August 1910, p. 6.

5. *Ibid.*, 11 October 1904, p. 5.

6. *Ibid.*, 23 April 1907, p. 8; *ibid.*, 18 December 1906, p. 5; *ibid.*, 15 March 1910, p. 2; *ibid.*, 7 June 1910, p. 3; *Sussex Agricultural Express*, 28 October 1910, p. 6.

7. Leonard joined the 2nd (Volunteer) Battalion as a second lieutenant in December 1891 while he was still at Oxford. He was promoted to full lieutenant the following year and captain in 1900.

8. By this time the 2nd Volunteer Battalion had been incorporated into the newly formed Territorial Force to become the 4th Battalion of the Royal Sussex Regiment.

9. One copy of the book *Soldiers' Letters 1914–1920* is available for public consultation at the Imperial War Museum; IWM Documents 14633. Another is held at Nymans.

10. *Mid-Sussex Times*, 29 July 1924, p. 7.

11. J.A. Mangan, '*Manufactured' Masculinity: Making Imperial Manliness, Morality and Militarism*, Routledge, London, 2012, pp. 124–49.

12. *Mid-Sussex Times*, 13 January 1914, pp. 4 and 7.

13. Letter of 6 December 1898; Sambourne Family Archive, ST/2/2/344.

14. Charles Castle, *Oliver Messel: A Biography*, Thames and Hudson, London, 1986, p. 25.

15. From Oliver's notes for an unpublished autobiography.

16. Diary entry for 19 August 1911; for an early example see her diary entry for 18 September 1902.

17. Roy Sambourne unpublished diary, entry for 27 July 1926; for background see Shirley Nicholson, *An Edwardian Bachelor: Roy Sambourne, 1878–1946*, Victorian Society, London, 1999.

18. *Mid-Sussex Times*, 6 December 1904, p. 8; *ibid.*, 11 December 1906, p. 6; *ibid.*, 20 August 1907, p. 5; *ibid.*, 25 February 1908, p. 5.

19. *Sussex Agricultural Express*, 11 March 1905, p. 7.

20. *Mid-Sussex Times*, 24 November 1914, p. 7; *ibid.*, 26 October 1915, p. 5; *Sussex Agricultural Express*, 14 January 1916, p. 7. Maud's MBE is listed in the supplement to the *London Gazette* of 30 March 1920, p. 3848.

21. Michie, *London Stock Exchange*, p. 230.

22. L. Messel and Co. rose once again to become one of the foremost stockbroking firms after the Second

World War and was finally bought by Shearson Lehman Brothers in April 1986. On the eve of the firm's dissolution, the partners held a celebration to look back to its founding by Ludwig Messel in 1873.

23. Originally built in 1826 and set in its own rolling grounds, Danehurst was converted in the 1950s into a care home called St Raphael's, run by the Augustinian Order. They in turn put the estate up for sale in summer 2019.

24. *Mid-Sussex Times*, 2 November 1915, p. 5. Harold Messel also suffered from other anxieties. In an undated letter from the 1980s to my aunt Judith Hiller his niece Anne, Countess of Rosse recalls Harold having had the 'Messel stutter'.

25. I am most grateful to Shirley Nicholson for lending me her transcript of Roy Sambourne's unpublished diary, the primary source for the deterioration in Harold's mental health.

26. According to the unpublished notes for an autobiography that Harold's son Rudolph Messel wrote towards the end of his life, he and his sister Phoebe were on holiday in a seaside village outside Boulogne with their grandmother Jennie Gibson when they received a telegram informing them of their father's death.

27. Roy Sambourne records in his diary for 28 August 1920, 'To church, Danehill. Poor Harold's funeral. The Parkers, Cadogans, Arthur Gibbes, Maud, Lennie and children and several others present. Very sad as I have many happy memories of Harold. Johnny Cadogan drives me to Nymans, arrive shortly after 1. The Parkers also lunch. Considering everything we are quite cheerful.'

28. Published by the Psychic Press, the full title of the book is *Travellers in Eternity: Being Some Descriptions of Life After Death with Evidence from Scripts of Geraldine Cummins*. Bea had compiled a volume two years earlier entitled *They Survive* in which she describes twelve cases of automatic writing communicated through Cummins. The second case relates to Nigel Gibbes, elder son of Hilda Messel, who was wounded while fighting in Libya in November 1941 and who then died of further wounds when back on active service in May 1942.

29. At a talk given by Geraldine Cummins at the Ladies' Army and Navy Club on 8 November 1938 Eric Parker 'spoke of the many evidential messages he had received from his wife' through other mediums since her death five years earlier; *Psychic Science*, January 1939, Vol. 17, No. 4, p. 191.

30. From paragraph 43 of Ludwig Messel's will dated 27 July 1910, with a codicil of 20 April 1911. Ludwig's residuary estate was thus divided into eight parts, with each of his four daughters receiving one part and each of his two sons receiving two parts. The estate was valued at £589,706 6s. 9d.

12 Making History

1. *Mid-Sussex Times*, 11 July 1916, p. 8.

2. Mr Curius Crowe, the 'sanguine antiquary' cited in the article as the source of these historical attributions, is the *alter ego* Hussey adopted when writing letters to *Country Life* from his home at Scotney Castle.

3. Neil Bingham, 'Two Letters from Percy E. Newton to John Summerson', *Architectural History*, 1993, Vol. 36, p. 163.

4. In heraldic language the Messel arms are 'blazoned: Or, issuing from a mount in base a fir tree proper, in chief two barrulets azure'. The full coat of arms shows the escutcheon under a closed helmet topped with an eagle crest, a cross-reference to the Cussans arms of Leonard's mother Annie. The eagle clasps two reversed fylfots (swastikas) in its talons as symbols of good fortune, with a scroll bearing the family motto 'Dirigat Deus': 'God be my guide'. This is the version still in use by members of the Messel family today, although there is an apocryphal tradition of another motto having crept in over the years: 'What we have we hold'.

5. Royal Geographical Society archive: EE/9/3/28, 29, 37 and 41; the plants collected during the expedition are listed in Charles Howard-Bury, *Mount Everest: The Reconnaissance, 1921*, Edward Arnold and Co., London, 1922, pp. 346–50.

6. *Sussex Agricultural Express*, 13 February 1925, p. 6; *Gardeners' Chronicle*, 28 August 1926, p. 177; the Royal Horticultural Society confirms that Leonard won the Cory Cup for 1924 not 1926 as stated in other accounts. The name of the cultivar came about by accident, according to James Comber, as two seedlings had been prepared for the show, 'Nymans A' and 'Nymans B', but the second died during preparations so only the first was exhibited, and 'Nymans A' was converted phonetically into 'Nymansay' to make it look more like a name; J. Bausch, 'A Revision of the Eucryphiaceae', *Bulletin of Miscellaneous Information (Royal Botanic Gardens, Kew)*, 1938, No. 8, pp. 317–49.

7. Maud's father was remembered in the cultivar *Rhododendron* 'Linley Sambourne' which received the Award of Merit in 1927; the births of Leonard and Maud's first two grandchildren were commemorated in *Rhododendron* 'Susan' and *Rhododendron* 'Tony', both of which won the Award of Merit.

8. The Garden Club was a members' club for men and women founded by the writer Marion Cran which ran from 1924 to 1937. The Garden Society was restricted to a maximum of fifty members at the time Leonard was elected in 1925; Gerald Loder, *The Garden Society 1920*, revised edition, 1996.

9. *Mid-Sussex Times*, 27 May 1919, p. 2.

10. Available on the Slaugham Archives website; this second year saw Anne Messel play Maid Marian in the

pageant – a role she reprised in 1921; *Mid-Sussex Times*, 25 May 1920, p. 7; *ibid.*, 17 May 1921, p. 3.

11. *Sussex Agricultural Express*, 1 April 1927, p. 16; *ibid.*, 18 May 1928, p. 12.

12. Anne Rosse, 'The Eccentric Upbringing of a Collector's Daughter', *Bulletin of the Fan Circle International*, 1981, No. 17.

13. *Mid-Sussex Times*, 15 July 1919, p. 1; *ibid.*, 29 July 1919, p. 6.

14. *Ibid.*, 29 July 1919, p. 7.

15. *Ibid.*, 9 August 1921, p. 5.

16. *Bexhill-on-Sea Observer*, 3 April 1920, p. 4; also *Mid-Sussex Times*, 30 March 1920, p. 2.

17. *The Memoirs of Daphne Lucy Dengate*, unpublished manuscript, 1999. The interview recorded with Daphne at Handcross on 25 November 1992 is available at the British Library, NTPG41.

18. In addition to the domestic servants, James Comber still had seven gardeners helping him in the grounds.

19. As remembered by one who took part: Ethel Smith, *Little Ethel Smith: Her Story Told by Herself*, QueenSpark Books, Brighton, 1992.

20. *Mid-Sussex Times*, 2 January 1912, p. 6.

21. *Sussex Agricultural Express*, 5 January 1917, p. 8.

22. Interview with Philip Hatch recorded in 2011, British Library, C1367/21.

13 The Triumph of Hope

1. Hilda's other son Antony Gibbes served in the Royal Northumberland Fusiliers and survived, as did Ottilie's son Godfrey Messel Loring, a lieutenant-colonel in the Royal Army Ordnance Corps.

2. *The Times*, 20 February 1947, p. 4; the story was further embroidered in the *Manchester Guardian*, 20 February 1947, p. 4.

3. Contrary to later reports, the house at Nymans was insured. Leonard's solicitors sent him two cheques of £35,000 each in May 1947 as preliminary settlements from the Law Fire and Sun insurance companies, with further sums to follow.

4. *West Sussex Gazette*, 15 November 1951, p. 3; *ibid.*, 3 April 1952, p. 2; *West Sussex County Times*, 19 March 1954, p. 9.

5. Anne Rosse, 'Nymans Gardens', *Journal of the Royal Horticultural Society*, 1954, Vol. 79, p. 178.

6. Paul Atterbury, 'Nymans Land', *The Connoisseur*, June 1981, Vol. 207, No. 832, p. 101.

7. Nice himself was awarded the British Empire Medal in the New Year's Honours for 1974.

8. *West Sussex Gazette*, 1 April 1954, p. 6; Sackville-West wrote up the event in the *Observer*, 18 April 1954, p. 9.

9. Shirley Nicholson, *Nymans: The Story of a Sussex Garden*, Alan Sutton, Stroud, 1992.

10. *The Times*, 9 March 1960, p. 15.

11. *Ibid.*, 23 July 1925, p. 17; *The Sketch*, 29 July 1925, p. 151.

12. *The Sphere*, 12 April 1930, p. 61.

13. He was famously dubbed the 'Adonis of the Peerage' by one Australian newspaper.

14. In his diaries Anne's uncle Roy Sambourne deplores what he sees as her increasingly snobbish behaviour but lays the blame on her brother Oliver. When Anne tells him of her new liaison with Michael Rosse, Roy is mortified – as revealed by his diary entry for 28 December 1932. 'I am disgusted with Anne & grieve for her Mother and Father. Is she going straight to the devil?'

15. John Sales, *Shades of Green: My Life as the National Trust's Head of Gardens*, Unicorn, London, 2018; Chapter 5 is devoted to Nymans.

16. In the second codicil to his will, dated 19 February 1949, through which Leonard also established Oliver's right to occupy the property of Old House on the Nymans estate during his lifetime.

17. Interview broadcast by BBC Radio Sussex, 16 May 1988; British Library NTPG15.

18. James Lees-Milne, *Deep Romantic Chasm: Diaries 1979–1981*, John Murray, London, 2000, p. 42.

19. 'Technicolour and Technology', Part 7 of the Thames Television series *The English Garden*, broadcast on 20 May 1980.

14 Serious Collecting

1. Leonard recorded that he paid £220 to Bernard Quaritch in October 1937 for the ten volumes of the *Flora Graeca* compiled by John Sibthorp and Ferdinand Bauer and published from 1806 to 1840.

2. Eleanour Sinclair Rohde, 'The Nymans Garden Library', *Journal of the Royal Horticultural Society*, 1933, Vol. 58, pp. 329–43. When presenting him with the Victoria Medal of Honour at the Royal Horticultural Society's annual general meeting in February 1946 Lord Aberconway remarked that, after the society's own library, Leonard had put together 'the finest collection of horticultural books in the world'.

3. Russell Belk, 'Collectors and Collecting', in Susan Pearce (ed.), *Interpreting Objects and Collections*, Routledge, London, 1994, p. 320; emphasis in original.

4. Anne Rosse, 'Eccentric Upbringing'. Unless otherwise indicated this short memoir is the source of Anne's other quotes in this chapter.

5. Letter of 9 May 1898; Sambourne Family Archive, ST/1/2/1223.

6. Trevor Keeble, '"Everything Whispers of Wealth and Luxury": Observation, Emulation and Display in the Well-to-do Late-Victorian Home', in Elizabeth Darling and Lesley Whitworth (eds), *Women and the Making of Built Space in England, 1870–1950*, Routledge, London, 2007, pp. 69–86.

7. James Laver, *Vulgar Society: The Romantic Career of James Tissot, 1836–1902*, Constable, London, 1936, p. 43.

8. *Aberdeen Daily Journal*, 26 April 1905, p. 5; *Illustrated London News*, 16 February 1907, p. 260. A photograph of the Brough portrait exists in the Sambourne Family Archive at Leighton House.

9. The miniature is No. 1133 in the Royal Academy exhibition catalogue for 1910.

10. Oliver interviewed in *Time and Tide*, 1–8 November 1962.

11. The double portrait of Anne and Oliver is reproduced in Albert Sewter, *Glyn Philpot: 1884–1937*, Batsford, London, 1951, Plate 25. The reproduction of the solo portrait of Linley, also lost in the fire, in Robin Gibson's monograph on Philpot is incorrectly labelled as a portrait of Oliver; Robin Gibson, *Glyn Philpot, 1884–1937: Edwardian Aesthete to Thirties Modernist*, National Portrait Gallery, London, 1984, p. 137.

12. Simon Toll, *Herbert Draper, 1863–1920: A Life Study*, Antique Collectors' Club, Woodbridge, 2003, p. 139, which includes an image of the drawing. Toll suggests Anne was six when sitting for the portrait. As shown by the Latin inscription on the drawing and confirmed by the diary of Marion Sambourne, the sittings took place in 1913 when Anne was eleven.

13. Amy de la Haye, Lou Taylor and Eleanor Thompson, *A Family of Fashion – The Messels: Six Generations of Dress*, Philip Wilson, London, 2005, p. 74.

14. Lou Taylor, 'The Wardrobe of Mrs Leonard Messel, 1895–1920', in Christopher Breward, Becky Conekin and Caroline Cox (eds), *The Englishness of English Dress*, Berg, Oxford, 2002, especially pp. 121–6.

15. Anne Rosse, 'Charles James: The Couturier', in E.A. Coleman (ed.), *The Genius of Charles James*, Holt, Rinehart and Winston, New York, 1982, p. 111.

16. Robert O'Byrne, 'Couture for a Countess: Lady Rosse's Wardrobe', *Irish Arts Review Yearbook*, 1996, Vol. 12, p. 157.

17. The Messel Standing Feather Fan is depicted in the review of Woolliscroft Rhead's book carried by the *Illustrated London News*, 1 January 1910, p. 18; two further fans from Leonard's collection are shown in the review published in *The Sphere*, 8 January 1910, p. viii.

18. *Daily Graphic*, 27 August 1910; cited in Hirokichi Mutsu, *The British Press and the Japan–British Exhibition of 1910*, Routledge, London, 2001, p. 154.

19. *Connaissance des Arts*, April 1963, p. 94.

20. *Financial Times*, 31 October 1985, p. 27.

15 Preserving the Past

1. Marcus Binney, 'A Grand Time Had by Hall', *The Times*, 23 April 2004, p. 6 (S1).

2. Mark Girouard, 'Fifty Not Out', *The Victorian*, 2008, No. 27, p. 4.

3. Michael served as chairman of the Georgian Group from 1947 to 1968 and as its president thereafter.

4. Timothy Brittain-Catlin, 'The Bishop's House in Birmingham', in Rosemary Hill and Michael Hall (eds), *Studies in Victorian Architecture and Design, Volume 1: The 1840s*, Victorian Society, London, 2008, pp. 96–105.

5. Lord Briggs, Victorian Society fiftieth anniversary lecture, delivered at the Royal Institute of British Architects, 12 May 2008.

6. Peter Clarke, *Marching Songs for Victorian Walkers*, Victorian Society, London, 1983, pp. 9–10.

7. *The Times*, 7 November 1957, p. 6.

8. Girouard, p. 4. Viscount Esher was elected first chair of the Victorian Society, with Anne and Betjeman as vice-chairs.

9. The National Land Fund provided a full grant of £150,000 for the acquisition of 18 Stafford Terrace on the condition that the Greater London Council put in £75,000 to buy the original contents. Nick Chapple, *A History of the National Heritage Collection, Vol. 8, 1970–1983*, English Heritage, London, 2012, p. 41.

10. The London Conservation Award medallion presented to Anne is preserved at 18 Stafford Terrace.

11. From John Cornforth's address at Anne's funeral, in the Messel family archive at Nymans.

12. From his obituary of Anne in the *Independent*, 8 July 1992.

13. James Lees-Milne, *Ceaseless Turmoil: Diaries 1988–1992*, John Murray, London, 2004, pp. 309–10.

16 Bright Young Things

1. Marion Sambourne diary entry, 13 January 1904.

2. This and other reminiscences included here are taken from Oliver's notes for an unpublished autobiography, now in the Oliver Messel Archive, University of Bristol Theatre Collection.

3. Castle, p. 20.

4. Robert Colls, *George Orwell: English Rebel*, Oxford University Press, Oxford, 2013, p. 102.

5. Barbara Cartland, *We Danced All Night*, Hutchinson, London, 1970, p. 162.

6. *The Era*, 26 June 1929, p. 9.

7. Oliver Messel Archive, University of Bristol Theatre Collection, OHM/4/1/1/10.

8. The exhibition was reviewed in *The Sphere*, 1 August 1925, p. 139, and photographs from it carried in *The Sketch*, 5 August 1925, p. 230.

9. Georges Braque was the original designer when the ballet premièred in Monte Carlo, but his headdresses were out of keeping, and Diaghilev ordered revisions as the production transferred to the London stage.

10. *The Sphere*, 3 April 1926, p. 14.

11. *The Bystander*, 15 September 1926, p. 615.

12. *Ibid.*, 4 July 1928, p. 14.

13. From Oliver's notes for an unpublished autobiography.

14. *The Sketch*, 4 July 1928, p. xviii.

15. Siân Evans, *Queen Bees: Six Brilliant and Extraordinary Society Hostesses Between the Wars*, Two Roads, London, 2016, pp. 183–4.

16. Sybil Rosenfeld, *A Short History of Scene Design in Great Britain*, Basil Blackwell, Oxford, 1973, p. 166.

17. *Illustrated London News*, 17 October 1936, p. 45.

18. *Vogue* (US edition), 15 January 1937, p. 69.

19. *Country Life*, 24 July 1937, p. 95.

20. From Sir Ralph Richardson's introduction to the Folio Society's 1957 edition of *A Midsummer Night's Dream*.

21. Oliver is photographed in costume in *The Sketch*, 19 July 1939, p. 23.

22. Carol King and Richard Havers, *Peter Glenville: The Elusive Director Who Charmed Hollywood and Triumphed on Broadway*, Peter Glenville Foundation, Los Angeles, 2010, p. 73.

23. Adrian Clark, *Queer Saint: The Cultured Life of Peter Watson*, Metro, London, 2015, p. 81.

24. Oliver Messel as Olive Mason, Cecil Beaton as Cecily Seymour and so on.

25. Beverley Nichols, *The Sweet and Twenties*, Weidenfeld and Nicolson, London, 1958, p. 162.

26. *Why Shakespeare?*, BBC World Service, 30 December 1947; transcript in the Oliver Messel Archive, University of Bristol Theatre Collection, OHM/4/1/2/5.

27. *Variety*, 26 August 1936, p. 20.

28. Oliver Messel Archive, University of Bristol Theatre Collection, OHM/1/9/1/2. The Assistant Director of Tank Supply wrote to Oliver on 10 August 1940 thanking him for his suggestion. 'I am returning to you your attractive sketches with some reluctance, as I should like to have kept them to decorate our office!'

29. Julian Trevelyan, *Indigo Days*, MacGibbon and Kee, London, 1957, p. 122. The fascinating article by David Hunt and Christopher Webster, 'The Taunton Stop Line and Its Camouflage: The Work of Oliver Messel and Others in Wartime Somerset', *The Antiquaries Journal*, 2020, Vol. 100, pp. 408–31, appeared after this book had entered production.

30. Harold Acton, *More Memoirs of an Aesthete*, Methuen, London, 1970, p. 94.

31. *The Spectator* noted that Oliver's name was given equal billing with that of Cocteau himself but did not quibble given that 'the most satisfying memory of this performance is the décor'; 12 September 1940, p. 11.

32. *The Tatler*, 28 January 1942, p. 114; see also *The Sketch*, 28 January 1942, p. 57.

33. Oliver Messel Archive, University of Bristol Theatre Collection, OHM/1/4/2/2.

34. Castle, p. 119.

35. The river was diverted into vast tanks to accommodate Caesar's galleys, while the studio hired its own private police force to protect the city overnight; *Illustrated London News*, 15 December 1945, p. 665.

36. Marjorie Deans, *Meeting at the Sphinx: Gabriel Pascal's Production of Bernard Shaw's Caesar and Cleopatra*, MacDonald and Co., London, 1946, p. 108.

37. James Agate in *The Tatler*, 26 December 1945, p. 388; C.A. Lejeune in the *Observer*, 23 December 1945, included in the anthology of her film reviews, *Chestnuts in Her Lap*, Phoenix House, London, 1947, pp. 166–7.

38. *The People*, 9 December 1945, p. 6.

39. *Daily Herald*, 20 December 1945, p. 4.

40. Ninette de Valois, *Come Dance With Me*, Hamish Hamilton, London, 1957, pp. 167–8.

41. Margot Fonteyn, *Margot Fonteyn*, W.H. Allen, London, 1975, p. 120.

17 Fame and Fortune

1. *The Times*, 24 August 1950, p. 6.

2. *Vogue* (US edition), 15 October 1951, pp. 94–9, 170.

3. *Country Life*, 17 March 1950, p. 729.

4. *Vogue* (US edition), 1 December 1950, p. 158.

5. Dorchester Hotel press release, in the Victoria and Albert Museum's Oliver Messel archive, THM/321/60/4.

6. *Country Life*, 25 April 2002, pp. 108–13.

7. Jeremy Musson, 'The Magic of Messel and the Theatre of the Interior', in Thomas Messel, pp. 86–141.

8. Raymond Bennett, 'Setting for a Stage Designer', *Housewife*, October 1958, Vol. 20, No. 10, pp. 46–9, which includes a photograph of two of the male staff sporting the livery.

9. Castle, p. 8.

10. Vagn Riis-Hansen, 'Marvellous Food at Messel's', *Vogue* (US edition), 1 December 1963, Vol. 142, No. 10, p. 136.

11. Oliver Messel Archive, University of Bristol Theatre Collection, OHM/4/2/8/1.

12. Comic actor Johnny Dallas in *The Stage*, 22 August 2002, p. 9.

13. John Gates, *British Artists in Crystal*, Steuben Glass, New York, 1954, Plate 12. The goblet is now in the Cleveland Museum of Art.

14. Ronald Crichton, 'A Glyndebourne Retrospect', *Musical Times*, 1984, Vol. 125, No. 1695, pp. 262–5.

15. 'A Master of Décor Speaks of His Art', *The Tatler*, 29 August 1956, pp. 380–81.

16. Porter and Newton both cited in Spike Hughes, *Glyndebourne: A History of the Festival Opera*, Methuen, London, 1965, pp. 202–8.

17. John Jolliffe, *Glyndebourne: An Operatic Miracle*, John Murray, London, 1999, p. 63.

18. Cartland, p. 162.

19. Arthur Boys, 'Oliver Messel – English Designer', in Duncan Melvin (ed.), *Souvenirs de Ballet*, Mayfair, London, 1949, p. 28.

20. *Illustrated London News*, 8 January 1966, p. 30.

21. *The Tatler*, 22 October 1966, p. 22.

22. Polly Devlin, 'Maddox: House of Messel', *Vogue* (US edition), 1 March 1969, pp. 195–6.

23. In Thomas Messel, p. 224.

24. Castle, p. 250.

25. Sofka Zinovieff, *The Mad Boy, Lord Berners, My Grandmother and Me*, Jonathan Cape, London, 2014, p. 124.

26. Neil Parsons, 'The Impact of Seretse Khama on British Public Opinion, 1948–56 and 1978', in David Killingray (ed.), *Africans in Britain*, Routledge, London, 1994, p. 205.

27. Edward Mutesa, *Desecration of My Kingdom*, Constable, London, 1967, p. 99.

28. As stated in Oliver's letter to Sir Thomas Lloyd of the Colonial Office, 7 January 1954, now in the Oliver Messel Archive, University of Bristol Theatre Collection, OHM/4/5/5/49.

29. When Mutesa II finally flew back to regain his kingdom in October 1955 he was accompanied by Oliver, Vagn and various politicians, lawyers and campaigners who had helped him during his exile. Oliver took time out to decorate the formal rooms of the Kabaka's palace 'in elegant blues and pinks'. Mutesa, p. 142, where Messel is corrupted to Musd.

30. Oliver Messel Archive, University of Bristol Theatre Collection, OHM/1/2/4/4/6–9.

31. Roger Pinkham, *Oliver Messel*, Victoria and Albert Museum, London, 1983, p. 171.

32. *New York Post*, 16 June 1976, p. 3.

33. Castle, p. 255.

34. Roy Strong, *The Roy Strong Diaries, 1967–1987*, Weidenfeld and Nicolson, London, 1997, p. 229.

35. *The Stage*, 20 July 1978, p. 23.

36. *The Times*, 15 July 1978, p. 14.

37. 'Messel on Stage', in Thomas Messel, pp. 54–83.

18   Cinema and Socialism

1. This and other reminiscences are taken from Rudolph Messel's unpublished notes for an autobiography, my transcript of which is in the Messel family archive at Nymans.

2. This and the other descriptions of Rudolph in this paragraph are taken from Oliver's notes for an unpublished autobiography, now in the Oliver Messel Archive, University of Bristol Theatre Collection.

3. The description comes from a version of the club rule book preserved in the archives of University College, Oxford. The Hypocrites' name stemmed from the club's Pindaric motto, ἄριστον μὲν ὕδωρ: 'Water is best'.

4. Evelyn Waugh, *A Little Learning: The First Volume of an Autobiography*, Chapman and Hall, London, 1964, p. 179.

5. *Isis*, 14 May 1924; cited, with many more details on the Hypocrites, in Humphrey Carpenter, *The Brideshead Generation: Evelyn Waugh and His Friends*, Weidenfeld and Nicolson, London, 1989, p. 78.

6. Harold Acton, *Memoirs of an Aesthete*, Methuen, London, 1948, p. 124.

7. Paula Byrne, *Mad World: Evelyn Waugh and the Secrets of Brideshead*, Harper Press, London, 2009, p. 55.

8. Entry for 14 November 1963, in Michael Davie (ed.), *The Diaries of Evelyn Waugh*, Weidenfeld and Nicolson, London, 1976, p. 792.

9. *Movie Makers*, March 1930, Vol. 5, No. 3, p. 181.

10. *The Bioscope*, 21 July 1927, p. 32.

11. The judgement 'eccentric' is from Richard Koszarski, *Von: The Life and Films of Erich Von Stroheim*, Limelight, New York, 2001, p. 172. *The Northern Whig and Belfast Post* called the book 'one of the wittiest, most acute, and trenchant volumes that have yet appeared upon this world-wide and world-shaping force'; 20 October 1928, p. 11.

12. Rudolph Messel, *This Film Business*, Ernest Benn, London, 1928, p. 295.

13. Terence Greenidge, *Degenerate Oxford? A Critical Study of Modern University Life*, Chapman and Hall, London, 1930, pp. 179–80.

14. Rachelle Saltzman, *A Lark for the Sake of Their Country: The 1926 General Strike Volunteers in Folklore and Memory*, Manchester University Press, Manchester, 2012.

15. Interview with Rudolph Messel, *Western Morning News*, 27 March 1929, p. 11.

16. Rudolph's phrase in the unpublished notes for his autobiography.

17. *Western Morning News*, 27 May 1929, p. 4.

18. *Devon and Exeter Gazette*, 1 June 1929, p. 5.

19. *Socialist Review*, summer 1932, Vol. 4, No. 2, p. 92.

20. *Ibid.*, June 1933, Vol. 5, No. 3, p. 144.

21. *New Clarion*, 3 December 1932, pp. 613–19.

22. *Ibid.*, 25 February 1933, p. 227.

23. Rudolph Messel, *High Pressure*, Fortune Press, London, 1934, p. 241.

24. *Ibid.*, p. 279; 'Union of Socialist Soviet Republics' (*sic*).

25. *Birmingham Gazette*, 30 May 1934, p. 10; *Dundee Courier*, 31 July 1934, p. 10; *Western Morning News*, 4 June 1934, p. 2.

26. *Daily Herald*, 19 May 1934, p. 10.

19 A Pacifist at War

1. Rudolph Messel, *This Film Business*, p. 85.

2. *Socialist Review*, September 1933, Vol. 5, No. 6, p. 357.

3. Trevor Ryan, *Labour and the Media in Britain, 1929–1939*, unpublished PhD thesis, University of Leeds, 1986, p. 400.

4. *Cinema Quarterly*, autumn 1933, Vol. 2, No. 1, p. 67.

5. John Grierson, 'Labour's First Film', *The New Clarion*, 12 August 1933, p. 158.

6. *Kine Weekly*, 4 October 1934, p. 21; cited in Bert Hogenkamp, *Deadly Parallels: Film and the Left in Britain, 1929–1939*, Lawrence and Wishart, London, 1986, p. 100.

7. *The New Leader*, 2 September 1938, p. 7.

8. Subsequently dubbed the Messel Expedition; see David Talbot Rice, 'Excavations at Bodrum Camii 1930: The Messel Expedition', *Byzantion*, 1930, Vol. 8, No. 1, pp. 151–74.

9. As the promotional slogan put it, 'A sixpenny monograph published on the 15th of every month'.

10. John and Mary Postgate, *A Stomach for Dissent: The Life of Raymond Postgate, 1896–1971*, Keele University Press, Keele, 1994, p. 200.

11. George Lansbury, *My Quest for Peace*, Michael Joseph, London, 1938, p. 255.

12. Rudolph Messel, *Refuge in the Andes*, John Lane, London, 1939, p. 175.

13. The letters are in the George Lansbury archive at the London School of Economics; Section 1, items 24–9.

14. The War Resisters' International also succeeded in securing the safe passage of Jewish and other refugees to New Zealand, Australia, Paraguay, Palestine, Cuba, Mexico, Chile, Ireland and the USA.

15. Frederic Raphael, *Going Up: To Cambridge and Beyond*, Robson Press, London, 2015, p. 188.

16. *The Times*, 8 May 1958, p. 12.

17. Rudolph Messel, 'Starting Again', War Resisters' International, Enfield, 1938.

18. Letter from Harold Acton, 18 February 1988, in the Nymans archive, 80/2 (23).

19. Waugh, *A Little Learning*, p. 181.

20 Royal Wedding

1. James Lees-Milne, *Ancient as the Hills: Diaries, 1973–1974*, John Murray, London, 1974, pp. 207–8.

2. Tony Atkinson, *A Prescribed Life*, Affirm Press, Melbourne, 2016, Chapter 3.

3. Antony Armstrong-Jones, *Snowdon: A Life in View*, Rizzoli, New York, 2014, p. 49.

4. Snowdon, *Personal View*, Weidenfeld and Nicolson, London, 1979, p. 9.

5. Sarah Bradford, *Elizabeth: A Biography of Her Majesty the Queen*, Heinemann, London, 1996, p. 270.

6. *The Tatler*, 19 September 1951, p. 551.

7. *Ibid.*, 26 September 1951, p. 611; *ibid.*, 10 October 1951, p. 63.

8. *The Sketch*, 13 July 1955, pp. 24–5.

9. *Daily Mail*, 14 November 1956, p. 14.

10. National Portrait Gallery reference NPG P1641, released on 10 October 1957.

11. Martin Harrison, interviewed in the BBC documentary *Fame, Fashion and Photography: The Real Blow-Up*, broadcast in August 2002.

12. *The Photographic Journal*, September 1957, Vol. 97, No. 8, pp. 150–55.

13. Martin Harrison, *Young Meteors: British Photojournalism 1957–1965*, Jonathan Cape, London, 1998, p. 56.

14. Sacheverell Sitwell and Tony Armstrong-Jones, *Malta*, Batsford, London, 1958, p. 87.

15. Three years later Tony would fight a losing battle to save the houses when they were demolished to make room for a public park and promenade.

16. Alistair Horne, *Macmillan, 1957–1986: Volume II of the Official Biography*, Macmillan, London, 1989, p. 170.

17. *Daily Mail*, 27 February 1960, p. 1.

18. William Glenton, *Tony's Room: The Secret Love Story of Princess Margaret*, Pocket Books, New York, 1965, p. 48.

19. Sally Bedell Smith, *Elizabeth the Queen: The Woman Behind the Throne*, Penguin, London, 2012, p. 151.

20. Letter of 28 April 1960 to Ann Fleming, in Mark Amory (ed.), *The Letters of Evelyn Waugh*, Weidenfeld and Nicolson, London, 1980, p. 537.

21. Zachary Leader, *The Letters of Kingsley Amis*, HarperCollins, London, 2001, p. 572; the previous incident, when Tony had abandoned Amis and his wife in a country pub, rankled so much that Amis gave it a whole chapter in his *Memoirs*, Hutchinson, London, 1991.

22. Hugo Vickers, *Cecil Beaton: The Authorized Biography*, Phoenix Press, London, 2002, p. 436.

23. Hugo Vickers, *Elizabeth, The Queen Mother*, Arrow, London, 2005, p. 369. Tony's mother Anne was happy to reciprocate, referring to Princess Margaret as 'my *darling* daughter-in-law'; Nicky Haslam, *Redeeming Features: A Memoir*, Vintage, London, 2010, p. 83; emphasis in original.

24. Noël Coward, *The Noël Coward Diaries*, Orion, London, 2000, pp. 431, 437.

25. *New Statesman*, 14 May 1960, p. 703.

26. *Evening Standard*, 6 May 1960, p. 1.

27. *Birmingham Post*, 4 May 1960, p. 1.

28. Unpublished passages from Harold Nicolson's diary, cited in Robert Lacey, *Monarch: The Life and Reign of Elizabeth II*, Free Press, New York, 2003, p. 216.

29. Theo Aronson, *Princess Margaret: A Biography*, Michael O'Mara, London, 1997, p. 194; Noel Botham, *Margaret: The Last Real Princess*, Blake, London, 2002, p. 195.

30. *Daily Mirror*, 21 June 1960, p. 14. The culprits turned out to be three former public schoolboys out for a laugh; *Daily Mirror*, 13 August 1960, p. 7.

31. Cronin's revelations were published in *The People* every Sunday from 18 September to 30 October 1960. The tale took another twist forty years later when Cronin was supposedly unmasked as a Soviet spy; Jason Lewis and Kim Willsher, 'The KGB's Spy at the Palace', *Mail on Sunday*, 20 February 2000.

32. Lees-Milne, *Deep Romantic Chasm*, p. 40.

33. *The People*, 8 October 1961, p. 12.

21 **Disability Campaigner**

1. Tony's address is reported in the *Journal of the Royal Institute of British Architects*, August 1961, Vol. 68, No. 10, pp. 378–80.

2. Snowdon, *Personal View*, p. 16.

3. David Yeomans, 'The Design of the Snowdon Aviary and the Nature of Collaboration', *Architectural History*, 2018, Vol. 61, pp. 235–57.

4. 'Top Birds for Luxury Aviary', *British Pathé*, 30 May 1965.

5. Hugo Vickers, *Beaton in the Sixties: The Cecil Beaton Diaries as They Were Written*, Weidenfeld and Nicolson, London, 2003, p. 44.

6. Huw Edwards presenting the *Timewatch* episode 'The Prince and the Plotter' on BBC2, 4 July 2009; reported in the *Daily Telegraph* of the same day.

7. For a full account see John Ellis, *Investiture: Royal Ceremony and National Identity in Wales, 1911–1969*, University of Wales Press, Cardiff, 2008.

8. Michael Rand interviewed in the *Royal Photographic Society Journal*, September 2006, Vol. 146, No. 7, pp. 306–9.

9. 'The Old', *Sunday Times Magazine*, 25 October 1964; 'Some of Our Children', *ibid.*, 29 August 1965; 'Loneliness', *ibid.*, 18 December 1966; 'Mental Hospitals', *ibid.*, 29 September 1968; 'Children Under Stress', *ibid.*, 10 May 1970; and 'Unlocking the Doors', *ibid.*, 13 March 1977.

10. Robin Muir, *In Camera: Snowdon*, Pallant House Gallery, Chichester, 2007, p. 14.

11. Harrison, p. 144.

12. *Birmingham Post*, 6 April 1968, p. 8; *Daily Mirror*, 5 April 1968, p. 20.

13. *The Stage*, 16 May 1968, p. 11; *ibid.*, 4 July 1968, p. 9; *ibid.*, 12 September 1968, p. 11; *ibid.*, 29 May 1969, p. 9.

14. *Birmingham Post*, 13 December 1971, p. 6.

15. Science Museum reference no. 2004–8; see also 'Lord Snowdon's Chairmobile', *British Journal of Occupational Therapy*, 1972, Vol. 35, No. 6, pp. 404–6.

16. *Hansard*, HL Deb, 10 April 1974, Vol. 350, C1246.

17. Armstrong-Jones, *Snowdon*, p. 246.

18. The charity was given a further boost through corporate sponsorship when Tony was invited to start the London Marathon three years in a row.

19. The *Jewish Chronicle* noted that Tony had spoken proudly of his Jewish heritage on other occasions and concluded charitably that this particular outburst against his wife had been 'a bit unnecessary'; *Jewish Chronicle*, 20 June 2008, p. 19.

20. The handsome property at 22 Launceston Place can be viewed as furnished and lived in by Tony in the January 2009 issue of *The World of Interiors*, pp. 142–51. It was not registered in his name but held in trust for the two children of the royal marriage and sold after Tony's death for one hundred times its 1976 price.

21. *Aberdeen Evening Express*, 29 January 1975, p. 9.

22. Willie Hamilton, *My Queen and I*, Quartet Books, London, 1975, pp. 182–3.

23. *Sunday Telegraph*, 1 June 2008, p. 17.

24. Lees-Milne, *Deep Romantic Chasm*, p. 96.

25. Roy Strong, *Scenes and Apparitions: Diaries 1988–2003*, Weidenfeld and Nicolson, London, 2016, p. 335.

26. The sale of the Old House lease went through in May 2002 for £1.5 million, while the contents fetched a further £180,000 at Sotheby's 'Interior Decorator' sale on 30 September; *The Argus*, 30 September 2002.

27. Tony's omission from the Tate show was remarked on by one critic who felt that at least the pioneering album *London* should have been included; Guy Lane, 'A Photographic Encounter with Britain', *The Art Book*, 2008, Vol. 15, No. 1, pp. 64–6.

28. *The Times*, 22 April 2000, Metro section, p. 42.

Epilogue

1. Emma Klein, *Lost Jews: The Struggle for Identity Today*, Palgrave Macmillan, London, 1996, p. 39.

2. Werner Mosse, 'To Give and to Take: A Balance Sheet', in Mosse (ed.), *Second Chance*, pp. 611–22.

Select Bibliography

Much of the material for this book comes from unpublished papers and letters in the Messel family archives held at Nymans, Birr Castle and elsewhere. At the same time, I have drawn on a wide range of other primary sources and published studies to provide further information for each chapter. References are provided in the notes, while those works listed below are the most directly relevant for further reading. The diaries of Marion and Linley Sambourne, transcribed by Shirley Nicholson and offering such a rich source of information from the 1880s to the First World War, are freely available to read on the website of the Royal Borough of Kensington and Chelsea, while their family letters are held in the Sambourne Family Archive, catalogued online. The Oliver Messel archive is divided between the Victoria and Albert Museum in London and the University of Bristol Theatre Collection; again, catalogues for both collections are available online.

Albrecht, Heinrich and Alfred Messel, *Das Arbeiterwohnhaus*, Robert Oppenheim, Berlin, 1896

Armstrong, Nancy, *Fans from the Fitzwilliam: A Selection from the Messel-Rosse Collection*, Fitzwilliam Museum, Cambridge, 1985

Armstrong-Jones, Antony, *Snowdon: A Life in View*, Rizzoli, New York, 2014

Armstrong-Jones, Tony, *London*, Weidenfeld and Nicolson, London, 1958

Aronsfeld, Caesar, 'German Jews in Victorian England', *Leo Baeck Institute Yearbook*, 1962, Vol. 7, pp. 312–29

Aronson, Theo, *Princess Margaret: A Biography*, Michael O'Mara Books, London, 1997

Aslet, Clive, 'Enchanted World of Lord Snowdon's Not-So-Old House', *Country Life*, 9 May 2002, pp. 96–9

Atterbury, Paul, 'Nymans Land', *The Connoisseur*, June 1981, Vol. 207, No. 832, pp. 100–3

Barkai, Avraham, 'German-Jewish Migrations in the Nineteenth Century, 1830–1910', *Leo Baeck Institute Yearbook*, 1985, Vol. 30, pp. 301–18

Bezzenberger, Walter, *Geschichte des Dorfes Messel*, P.L. Fink, Groß-Gerau, 1958

Blauert, Elke (ed.), *Alfred Messel 1853–1909: Visionär der Großstadt*, Minerva, Berlin, 2009

Brown, Craig, *Ma'am Darling: 99 Glimpses of Princess Margaret*, Fourth Estate, London, 2017

Campbell, Katie, *British Gardens in Time: The Greatest Gardens and the People Who Shaped Them*, Frances Lincoln, London, 2014

Castle, Charles, *Oliver Messel: A Biography*, Thames and Hudson, London, 1986

Cathcart, Helen, *Lord Snowdon*, W.H. Allen, London, 1968

Chapman, Stanley, 'Merchants and Bankers from Germany in Britain', in Werner Mosse (ed.), *Second Chance: Two Centuries of German-Speaking Jews in the United Kingdom*, Mohr, Tübingen, 1991, pp. 335–46

Comber, James, 'Eucryphia Nymansay', *Gardeners' Chronicle*, 6 September 1924, Vol. 76, No. 1967, p. 161

Cornforth, John, 'Nymans, Sussex: A Property of the National Trust', *Country Life*, 5 June 1997, pp. 60–65

de Courcy, Anne, *Snowdon: The Biography*, Weidenfeld and Nicolson, London, 2008

de la Haye, Amy, Lou Taylor and Eleanor Thompson, *A Family of Fashion – The Messels: Six Generations of Dress*, Philip Wilson, London, 2005

Dempster, Nigel, *H.R.H. The Princess Margaret: A Life Unfulfilled*, Quartet, London, 1981

Eisenschmidt, Alexander, 'Metropolitan Architecture: Karl Scheffler and Alfred Messel's Search for a New Urbanity', *Grey Room*, 2014, No. 56, pp. 90–115

Endelman, Todd, 'German Jews in Victorian England: A Study in Drift and Defection', in Jonathan Frankel and Steven Zipperstein (eds), *Assimilation and Community: The Jews in Nineteenth-Century Europe*, Cambridge University Press, Cambridge, 1992, pp. 57–87

Franz, Eckhart, *Juden als Darmstädter Bürger*, Eduard Roether, Darmstadt, 1984

Franz, Eckhart, '"Schutzjuden und Judenbürger": Die jüdische Geschichte des Kreisgebiets vom Mittelalter bis ins 19. Jahrhundert', in Thomas Lange (ed.), 'L'chajim':

Die Geschichte der Juden im Landkreis Darmstadt-Dieburg, Landkreis Darmstadt-Dieburg, Reinheim, 1997, pp. 5–26

Gärtner, Artur, Robert Habel and Hans-Dieter Nägelke, *Alfred Messel: Ein Führer zu seinen Bauten*, Ludwig, Kiel, 2010

Gaunt, William, 'Masks by Oliver Messel', *The Studio*, 1928, Vol. 96, No. 427, pp. 249–55

Gibbes, Beatrice, *Travellers in Eternity*, Psychic Press, London, 1948

Girouard, Mark, 'Fifty Not Out', *The Victorian*, 2008, No. 27, pp. 4–5

Glenton, William, *Tony's Room: The Secret Love Story of Princess Margaret*, Pocket Books, New York, 1965

Habel, Robert, *Alfred Messels Wertheimbauten in Berlin: Der Beginn der modernen Architektur in Deutschland*, Gebr. Mann, Berlin, 2009

Heald, Tim, *Princess Margaret: A Life Unravelled*, Weidenfeld and Nicolson, London, 2007

Hoey, Brian, *Snowdon: Public Figure, Private Man*, History Press, Stroud, 2005

Hughes, Therle, 'Fantasy in Plume and Parchment: European Fans from the Leonard Messel Collection', *Country Life*, 8 June 1972, pp. 1455–8

Hughes, Therle, 'Storm Dragons and Plum Blossom: Oriental Fans in the Leonard Messel Collection', *Country Life*, 15 June 1972, pp. 1539–42

Hunt, David and Chris Webster, 'The Taunton Stop Line and its Camouflage: The Work of Oliver Messel and Others in Wartime Somerset', *The Antiquaries Journal*, 2020, Vol. 100, pp. 408–31

Hussey, Christopher, 'Nymans', *Country Life*, 10 September 1932, pp. 292–7; 17 September 1932, pp. 320–25

James, Kathleen, 'From Messel to Mendelsohn: German Department Store Architecture in Defence of Urban and Economic Change', in Geoffrey Crossick and Serge Jaumain (eds), *Cathedrals of Consumption: The European Department Store, 1850–1939*, Ashgate, Aldershot, 1999, pp. 252–78

Jülich, Theo, *Alfred Messel und sein Darmstädter Landesmuseum: Geschichte und Architektur*, Schnell and Steiner, Regensburg, 2014

Katz, Jacob, *Die Hep-Hep Verfolgungen des Jahres 1819*, Metropol, Berlin, 1994

Küster, Martin, '". . . mit etwas Liebe und künstlerischem Können". Der Architekt Alfred Messel und seine Berliner Arbeiterwohnhäuser', *Berlinische Monatschrift*, 1998, No. 11, pp. 4–15

Messel, Alfred, 'Arbeiter-Wohnungen in Berlin', *Deutsche Bauzeitung*, 1891, No. 30, pp. 181–2

Messel, Leonard, 'Nymans', *Journal of the Royal Horticultural Society*, 1940, Vol. 65, pp. 203–10

Messel, Mrs Harold, 'The Higher Side of the Guide Movement', in Olave Baden-Powell (ed.), *Training Girls as Guides: Hints for Commissioners and All Who Are Interested in the Welfare and Training of Girls*, C. Arthur Pearson, London, 1917, pp. 62–70

Messel, Muriel, *A Garden Flora: Trees and Flowers Grown in the Garden at Nymans by L. Messel, 1890–1915*, Country Life, London, 1918

Messel, Oliver, *Stage Designs and Costumes*, Bodley Head, London, 1933

Messel, Rudolph, *This Film Business*, Ernest Benn, London, 1928

Messel, Rudolph, 'Socialism Five Hundred Years Ago', *Socialist Review*, 1932, Vol. 4, No. 2, pp. 90–92

Messel, Rudolph, 'The Film in Russia', in Margaret I. Cole (ed.), *Twelve Studies in Soviet Russia*, Victor Gollancz, London, 1933, pp. 265–76

Messel, Rudolph, *High Pressure*, Fortune Press, London, 1934

Messel, Rudolph, *Refuge in the Andes*, John Lane, London, 1939

Messel, Thomas, *Oliver Messel: In the Theatre of Design*, Rizzoli, New York, 2011

Muir, Robin, *In Camera: Snowdon*, Pallant House Gallery, Chichester, 2007

Nicholson, Shirley, *A Victorian Household: Based on the Diaries of Marion Sambourne*, Barrie and Jenkins, London, 1988

Nicholson, Shirley, *Nymans: The Story of a Sussex Garden*, Alan Sutton, Stroud, 1992

Nicholson, Shirley, *An Edwardian Bachelor: Roy Sambourne, 1878–1946*, Victorian Society, London, 1999

O'Byrne, Robert, 'Couture for a Countess: Lady Rosse's Wardrobe', *Irish Arts Review Yearbook*, 1996, Vol. 12, pp. 156–63

Oelsner, Toni, 'Three Jewish Families in Modern Germany: A Study of the Process of Emancipation', *Jewish Social Studies*, 1942, Vol. 4, No. 3, pp. 241–68; Vol. 4, No. 4, pp. 349–98

Ormond, Leonee, *Linley Sambourne: Illustrator and Punch Cartoonist*, Paul Holberton, London, 2010

Panayi, Panikos, *The Enemy in Our Midst: Germans in Britain During the First World War*, Bloomsbury, London, 1991

Panayi, Panikos, 'Anti-German Riots in Britain during the First World War', in Panikos Panayi (ed.), *Racial Violence in Britain, 1840–1950*, University of Leicester Press, Leicester, 1993, pp. 65–91

Pinkham, Roger, *Oliver Messel*, Victoria and Albert Museum, London, 1983

Postgate, John, 'Raymond Postgate and the Socialist Film Council', *Sight and Sound*, 1990, Vol. 60, No. 1, pp. 19–21

Prasad, Devi, *War Is a Crime Against Humanity: The Story of War Resisters' International*, War Resisters' International, London, 2005

Robertson, Bryan, John Russell and Lord Snowdon, *Private View: The Lively World of British Art*, Nelson, London, 1965

Rohde, Eleanour Sinclair, 'The Nymans Garden Library', *Journal of the Royal Horticultural Society*, 1933, Vol. 58, pp. 329–43

Rohrbacher, Stefan, 'The "Hep-Hep" Riots of 1819: Anti-Jewish Ideology, Agitation, and Violence', in Christhard Hoffmann, Werner Bergmann and Helmut Smith (eds), *Exclusionary Violence: Antisemitic Riots in Modern German History*, University of Michigan Press, Ann Arbor, 2002, pp. 23–42

Rosse, Anne, 'Nymans Gardens', *Journal of the Royal Horticultural Society*, 1954, Vol. 79, pp. 174–9

Rosse, Anne, *Nymans: The Home of Mrs Leonard Messel*, Country Life, London, 1966

Rosse, Anne, 'The Eccentric Upbringing of a Collector's Daughter', *Bulletin of the Fan Circle International*, 1981, No. 17

Rosse, Michael, 'The Gardens at Nymans', *Journal of the Royal Horticultural Society*, 1971, Vol. 96, pp. 482–91

Savonius, Moira, 'The Gardens at Nymans', *Gardeners' Chronicle*, 31 August 1963, pp. 154–5

Shiner, Helen, 'Embodying the Spirit of the Metropolis: The Warenhaus Wertheim, Berlin, 1896–1904', in Iain Whyte (ed.), *Modernism and the Spirit of the City*, Routledge, London, 2003, pp. 97–118

Sierschynski, Petia, 'The *Warenhaus* in the Competition of the Nations: Alfred Messel's Wertheim and Wilhelmine Imperial Ambitions (1898–1905)', in Godela Weiss-Sussex and Ulrike Zitzlsperger (eds), *Das Berliner Warenhaus: Geschichte und Diskurs / The Berlin Department Store: History and Discourse*, Peter Lang, Frankfurt, 2013, pp. 199–222

Sinclair, David, *Snowdon: A Man for Our Times*, Proteus, London, 1982

Snowdon, *Personal View*, Weidenfeld and Nicolson, London, 1979

Stamp, Gavin, *Saving a Century: The Victorian Society, 1958–2008*, Victorian Society, London, 2008

Strong, Roy, 'The Rule of Taste: Design at Glyndebourne, 1935–84', *Musical Times*, 1984, Vol. 125, No. 1695, pp. 258–62

Taylor, George, 'Nymans: The Gardens', *Country Life*, 24 September 1932, pp. 346–52

Taylor, Lou, 'The Wardrobe of Mrs Leonard Messel, 1895–1920', in Christopher Breward, Becky Conekin and Caroline Cox (eds), *The Englishness of English Dress*, Berg, Oxford, 2002, pp. 113–32

Tracey, Frances, 'The Decorative Work of Oliver Messel', *Decoration*, January 1937, No. 21, pp. 10–15

Viergutz, Volker, '"Das hätten wir in der Brüderstraße uns auch nicht träumen lassen." Anmerkungen zur Freundschaft von Ludwig Hoffmann und Alfred Messel', *Berlin in Geschichte und Gegenwart: Jahrbuch des Landesarchivs Berlin*, Gebr. Mann, Berlin, 2001, pp. 73–124

Warwick, Christopher, *Princess Margaret: A Life of Contrasts*, André Deutsch, London, 2018

Wenchel, Karl, 'Die Geschichte der Messeler Juden', in Michael Höllwarth, Manfred Raab, Siegfried Treichel, Bruno Vock and Karl Wenchel (eds), *1200 Jahre Messel*, Gemeindevorstand der Gemeinde Messel, Messel, 2000, pp. 183–200

Whitsey, Fred, 'Arcadia for Plantsmen: Nymans, Near Handcross, West Sussex', *Country Life*, 17 May 1984, pp. 1362–5

Wilcox, Alfred, 'Famous Gardeners at Home: No. 200 – Mr J. Comber, at the Gardens, Nymans, Crawley', *Garden Life*, 5 August 1905, pp. 321–3

Woolliscroft Rhead, George, 'Lt.-Col. L.C.R. Messel's Collection of Fans, Part I – Japanese', *The Connoisseur*, September 1919, Vol. 55, No. 217, pp. 19–30

Woolliscroft Rhead, George, 'Lt.-Col. L.C.R. Messel's Collection of Fans, Part II – European Fans of the Eighteenth Century', *The Connoisseur*, October 1920, Vol. 58, No. 230, pp. 75–82

Picture Credits

Alamy Stock Photos: pp. 79, 162, 202, 205, 207, 211, 216, 220

Author's photographs: pp. 12, 31, 33, 43 (bottom)

Bildarchiv Foto Marburg: pp. 36, 39

Country Life Picture Library/Alfred E. Henson: p. 113

Dagmar von Taube, for *Welt am Sonntag*: p. 174 (both images)

Desmond O'Neill Features: p. 147

The Dorchester Hotel: pp. 164, 167

Fitzwilliam Museum, Cambridge: pp. 132, 140

Fustic House, Barbados: p. 173

Getty Images: p. 219

Harvard Theatre Collection, Houghton Library, Harvard University (Angus McBean photograph, MS Thr 581): p. 150

Heidelberg University Library: p. 90

Hessische Hausstiftung: p. 30

Hessisches Landesmuseum: p. 22

Illustrated London News Ltd/Mary Evans Picture Library: p. 157

John Frost Newspapers/Mary Evans Picture Library: p. 72

London Borough of Lambeth, Archives Department: p. 49

Magnum Photos: p. 145

Museum of London: p. 56

National Portrait Gallery, London: p. 142

National Trust Images: front cover (Andrew Butler), pp. 8 (Andreas von Einsiedel), 82 (David Sellman), 97 (Andrew Butler), 110 (James Dobson), 129 (Nick Meers), 229 (Stephen Robson), back cover (Chris Lacey)

Nymans Archive, National Trust: pp. 28, 32, 46, 48 (top), 50, 52, 58, 61, 67, 69, 71, 74, 75, 81, 87, 94, 98, 100, 102, 105, 106 (both images), 114, 117, 120, 125, 127, 136, 137, 139, 152, 153, 180, 182, 186, 190, 193

Oliver Messel Archive, University of Bristol Theatre Collection: pp. 160, 168, 176

PA Images: pp. 213, 215, 224, 226

PantherMedia: pp. 15 (Steffen Spitzner), 42 (Daniel Kühne)

Pixabay: p. 45

Princeton University Art Museum, Museum Purchase, Surdna Fund and Fowler McCormick (Class of 1921) Fund: p. 64

Private collection: pp. 25, 38 (bottom), 48 (bottom), 54, 62, 76 (both images), 84, 185, 196, 200

Ramsey and Muspratt, Cambridge: p. 198

Royal Borough of Kensington and Chelsea, 18 Stafford Terrace: p. 148

Slaugham Archives: pp. 115, 122

Stiftung Stadtmuseum Berlin: p. 34

Su Reed: p. 118

Technical University of Berlin, University Library Digital Collection: pp. 38 (top), 40, 43 (top)

Technical University of Darmstadt, Digital Collection: p. 20

Tony Hisgett: p. 217

TopFoto: p. 187

Trunk Archive: p. 208

United States Holocaust Memorial Museum Collection, Gift of the Katz Family: p. 26

Victoria and Albert Museum, London: pp. 154, 159, 170, 171, 178

Victoria Messel: pp. 131, 233

Wellcome Collection: p. 134

Wikimedia Commons: p. 18

Index

The Later Messel Family Tree

Those born a Messel in orange text

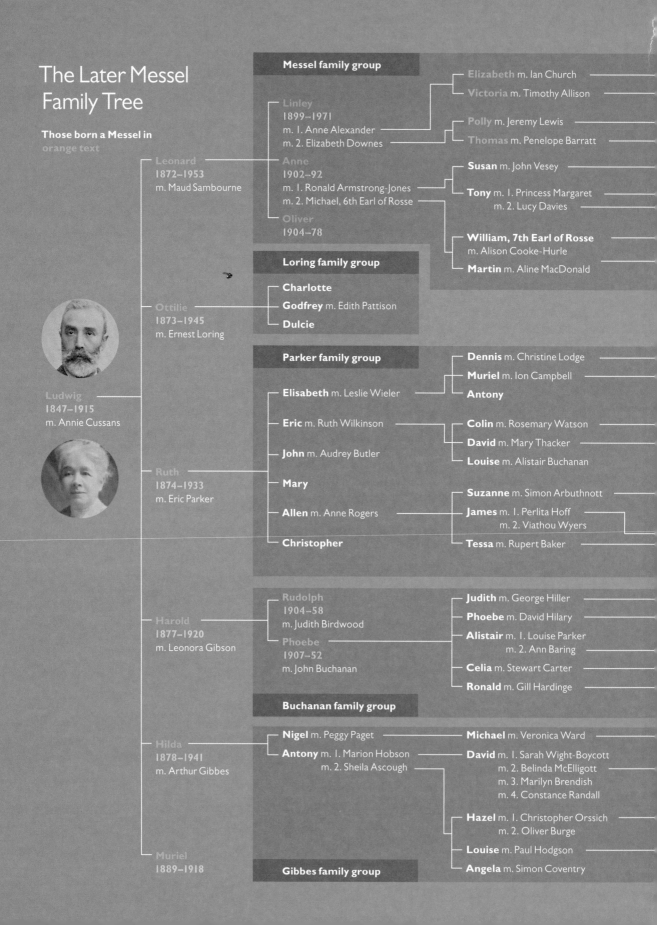

Ludwig
1847–1915
m. Annie Cussans

Leonard
1872–1953
m. Maud Sambourne

Messel family group

Linley
1899–1971
m. 1. Anne Alexander
m. 2. Elizabeth Downes

- Elizabeth m. Ian Church
- Victoria m. Timothy Allison
- Polly m. Jeremy Lewis
- Thomas m. Penelope Barratt

Anne
1902–92
m. 1. Ronald Armstrong-Jones
m. 2. Michael, 6th Earl of Rosse

- **Susan** m. John Vesey
- **Tony** m. 1. Princess Margaret
  m. 2. Lucy Davies
- **William, 7th Earl of Rosse** m. Alison Cooke-Hurle
- **Martin** m. Aline MacDonald

Oliver
1904–78

Loring family group

Ottilie
1873–1945
m. Ernest Loring

- **Charlotte**
- **Godfrey** m. Edith Pattison
- **Dulcie**

Parker family group

Ruth
1874–1933
m. Eric Parker

Elisabeth m. Leslie Wieler
- **Dennis** m. Christine Lodge
- **Muriel** m. Ion Campbell
- **Antony**

Eric m. Ruth Wilkinson
- **Colin** m. Rosemary Watson
- **David** m. Mary Thacker
- **Louise** m. Alistair Buchanan

John m. Audrey Butler

Mary

Allen m. Anne Rogers
- **Suzanne** m. Simon Arbuthnott
- **James** m. 1. Perlita Hoff
  m. 2. Viathou Wyers
- **Tessa** m. Rupert Baker

Christopher

Harold
1877–1920
m. Leonora Gibson

Rudolph
1904–58
m. Judith Birdwood

Phoebe
1907–52
m. John Buchanan

- **Judith** m. George Hiller
- **Phoebe** m. David Hilary
- **Alistair** m. 1. Louise Parker
  m. 2. Ann Baring
- **Celia** m. Stewart Carter
- **Ronald** m. Gill Hardinge

Buchanan family group

Hilda
1878–1941
m. Arthur Gibbes

Nigel m. Peggy Paget
Antony m. 1. Marion Hobson
m. 2. Sheila Ascough

- **Michael** m. Veronica Ward
- **David** m. 1. Sarah Wight-Boycott
  m. 2. Belinda McElligott
  m. 3. Marilyn Brendish
  m. 4. Constance Randall
- **Hazel** m. 1. Christopher Orssich
  m. 2. Oliver Burge
- **Louise** m. Paul Hodgson
- **Angela** m. Simon Coventry

Muriel
1889–1918

Gibbes family group